Brain-
Compatible
Learning
for the **BLOCK**

Second Edition

Brain-Compatible Learning
for the **BLOCK**

Second Edition

R. Bruce Williams

Steven E. Dunn

CORWIN PRESS
A SAGE Company
Thousand Oaks, CA 91320

For information:

 Corwin Press
A SAGE Company
2455 Teller Road
Thousand Oaks, California 91320
www.corwinpress.com

SAGE Ltd.
1 Oliver's Yard
55 City Road
London, EC1Y 1SP
United Kingdom

SAGE India Pvt. Ltd.
B 1/I 1 Mohan Cooperative
Industrial Area
Mathura Road, New Delhi 110 044
India

SAGE Asia-Pacific Pte. Ltd.
33 Pekin Street #02-01
Far East Square
Singapore 048763

Printed in the United States of America

Library of Congress Cataloging-in-Publication Data

Williams, R. Bruce.
Brain-compatible learning for the block / R. Bruce Williams and Steven E. Dunn. — 2nd ed.
   p. cm.
Includes bibliographical references and index.
ISBN 978-1-4129-5183-8 (cloth)
ISBN 978-1-4129-5184-5 (paper)
   1. Block scheduling (Education) 2. Learning. I. Dunn, Steven E. II. Title.

LB3032.2.W55 2008
371.2'42—dc22

2007040299

This book is printed on acid-free paper.

07 08 09 10 11 10 9 8 7 6 5 4 3 2 1

Acquisitions Editor: Cathy Hernandez
Editorial Assistants: Megan Bedell
Production Editor: Appingo Publishing Services
Cover Designer: Monique Hahn
Graphic Designer: Lisa Miller

Contents

List of Tables and Figures vii

Preface xi

Acknowledgments xiii

About the Authors xv

Introduction xvii

Chapter 1—Physiology and Philosophy 1

The Brain's Structure and Functions 1

Brain Compatibility and Multifaceted Learning 23

Brain-Compatible Learning Climate 30

Sample Four-Phase Lesson Plan—What's on Your Mind? 33

Reflective Questions 42

Chapter 2—Four-Phase Lesson and Unit Design 43

Inquiring—Gathering—Processing-—Applying 43

Four Phases Assist in Schemata Formation 52

Essential Questions 55

Attend—Experience—Reflect 58

Internal Structure 59

Integrated Assessment 60

Compare/Contrast Four-Phase Lesson
   With Traditional Lessons 60

Benefits of Four-Phase Lesson Design 60

Planning a Unit and a Lesson 62

Reflective Questions 70

Chapter 3—Extended Time Formats Including Block Scheduling 71

Adequate Time 71

Alternative Scheduling Formats 81

Sample Four-Phase Lesson Plan—Can Prejudice Kill
   a Mockingbird? 85

Reflective Questions 93

Chapter 4—Content and Curriculum 95

To Cover or To Catalyze Learning? 95

Prioritizing Curriculum in Extended Time Formats 97

Brain-Compatible Curriculum 107

Sample Four-Phase Lesson Plan—Circles That Cycle 110

Reflective Questions 119

**Chapter 5—Instruction: The Art and Science of
Teaching in Extended Time Formats**   **121**

    Opportunity for Growth and Change   121

    Energizing Educational Principles   122

    Brain-Compatible Instructional Strategies   126

    Professional Learning Communities:

        Pathway to a New Paradigm   156

    Sample Four-Phase Lesson Plan—Gender, Age, and

        Pyramids—Only Your Sarcophagus Knows for Sure!   158

    Reflective Questions   167

**Chapter 6—Assessment: Measuring Achievement
and Growth in Extended Time Formats**   **169**

    The Right Stuff   169

    Caught in the Act of Learning: Authentic Assessment   171

    Assessment for Learning   176

    No Child Left Behind (NCLB)   177

    Testing Matters   178

    Assessment in Four-Phase Lesson and Unit Design   181

    Sample Four-Phase Lesson Plan—Science Schmience or

        Who Framed Sir Isaac Newton?   182

    Reflective Questions   190

References   191

Index   195

List of Tables and Figures

Chapter 1

Figure 1.1   Hemispheres of the Brain
Figure 1.2   Brain Cells
Table 1.1   Descriptions of Brain Cell Parts
Table 1.2   Description of Three Sections of the Brain
Figure 1.3   Parts of the Exterior Brain
Table 1.3   Description of the Parts of the Exterior Brain
Figure 1.4   Parts of the Inner Brain
Table 1.4   Description of the Parts of the Inner Brain
Table 1.5   Description of Nondeclarative Memory
Table 1.6   Description of Declarative Memory
Table 1.7   Memory Paths With Instructional Strategies
Table 1.8   Three Major Elements of the Environment
Table 1.9   Differences Between Male and Female Brains
Table 1.10   Reflections on Differences Between Male
              and Female Brains
Figure 1.5   Brain Compatibility in Focus
Figure 1.6   Student Tic-Tac-Toe
Figure 1.7   K-W-L Chart
Table 1.11   Group Presentation Rubric

Chapter 2

Figure 2.1   The Processing Model and the Four-Phase
              Lesson Design
Figure 2.2   Natural Learning Progression
Figure 2.3   Lesson Plan
Figure 2.4   Four Phases for Lesson and Unit Planning
Table 2.1   Schemata Development Guidelines
Table 2.2   Guidelines for Using the Four Phases
Table 2.3   Guidelines for the Inquire Phase
Table 2.4   Guidelines for the Gather Phase
Table 2.5   Guidelines for the Process Phase
Table 2.6   Guidelines for the Apply Phase

Table 2.7   Comparing and Contrasting a Four-Phase Lesson
                   With a Traditional Lesson
Figure 2.5   Unit Plan
Figure 2.6   Emphasis at Each Phase of the Unit
Figure 2.7   Unit Plan

Chapter 3
Figure 3.1   Five Elements of Brain-Compatible Learning
Figure 3.2   Expanding on the Five Elements of
                   Brain-Compatible Learning
Figure 3.3   Block 8 Schedule
Figure 3.4   4 X 4 Schedule
Figure 3.5   The Copernican Schedule
Figure 3.6   Prejudice Is Like a Ghost Because . . .
Figure 3.7   Analogy Chart
Figure 3.8   Rubric for a Venn Diagram

Chapter 4
Figure 4.1   Prioritizing Curriculum in Extended Time Formats
Figure 4.2   Selective Abandonment Criteria
Figure 4.3   Circles Make the World Go 'Round
Figure 4.4   Curriculum Mapping
Figure 4.5   Toward an Integrated Curriculum
Figure 4.6   Observation Log
Figure 4.7   Student Observation Log
Figure 4.8   Circle Scavenger Hunt Log
Figure 4.9   Student Self-Assessment

Chapter 5
Figure 5.1   Educational Principles Centered Around Brain-
                   Compatible Instructional Strategies
Figure 5.2   Pulsed Learning
Figure 5.3   Brain-Compatible Methods of Content Presentation
Figure 5.4   BUILD Cooperative Learning Fundamentals
Figure 5.5   Gardner's Eight Intelligences
Table 5.1   Multiple Intelligences With Four-Phase
                   Lesson Design
Figure 5.6   Mind Reader
Figure 5.7   Group Knots
Figure 5.8   Machines
Table 5.2   Instructional Strategies—Best Practices
Table 5.3   P-A-C Thinking Skills and Learning and Assessment
Table 5.4   P-A-C Thinking Skills and Content Disciplines
Table 5.5   P-A-C Thinking Skills Applied to Elementary, Middle,
                   and High Schools
Table 5.6   P-A-C Thinking Skills and Four Phases
Figure 5.9   The Three-Story Intellect
Figure 5.10   Graphic Organizers

Figure 5.11   Staff Development in a Semester System
Figure 5.12   Staff Development in a Trimester System
Figure 5.13   Population Pyramid
Figure 5.14   Portfolio Evaluation Rubric
Figure 5.15   Four-Level Homework Evaluation Rubric

Chapter 6
Figure 6.1   Standardized Tests Versus
                       Brain-Compatible Assessment
Figure 6.2   Forms of Assessment
Figure 6.3   Rubric Template
Figure 6.4   Evaluation Tools Modeled
Figure 6.5   Mock Question Criteria

Preface

This book results from a great deal of experience working with teachers at just about every stage of implementing instruction in the block and other expanded time formats. We believe it will be of great practical assistance in increasing student achievement in classrooms with any extended time format.

For the last several years, we have had numerous opportunities to work with teachers who are making the shift from a traditional time format to 80- to 100-minute extended time blocks.

Most of the teachers that we have had the pleasure to meet are competent, skilled professionals, with solid experience in the classroom. The prospect of working with students in extended time blocks has both inspired and terrified them. Changes in their usual classroom presentations and their tried-and-true lesson plans, developed and refined over many years, have presented the teachers with a myriad of substantial challenges. We decided to produce a book that would help these teachers—and in the process, help students—make their way in the world of varying time blocks.

Teachers using some form of extended time block tell us that good teachers will really shine in this situation. In a way, these extended formats are what the skilled teacher has been waiting for. Good teachers have always been those who are flexible, resourceful, and creative—all qualities and attributes that will serve them well in an extended period. On the other hand, underskilled, lecture-dependant teachers are destined to experience great difficulty when confronted with more than forty to forty-five minutes. Often such teachers merely take two old lessons and paste them together to make one lesson. Or, teachers may present the usual forty-five- to fifty-minute lesson and have students do homework for the remainder of class time. Neither of these approaches makes effective use of the gift of more student contact time.

We believe that extended time formats offer the best environment in which to fully utilize brain-compatible instructional techniques and approaches. Yet merely lengthening the time of each period will not make much difference. In fact, it may put obstacles in student achievement. The lengthened class time is advantageous only when teachers employ additional and varied instructional strategies so that curriculum content can move from disaggregated facts to meaningful information and relevant concepts. We have presented here several options and ideas, which have been informed by recent neuro scientific research, for creating lesson plans and units that make the most of these extended time formats.

It is only when the content of the curriculum shifts to relevancy and application from memorization and recitation that the substance of the content can have a lasting hold on the student. We believe that the material in this book can enable teachers to teach more for the long-term success in real life than for the short-term purposes of tests and quizzes.

One of the reasons that we have been so excited by the continuing opportunity to work with so many teachers all over North America is that the advent of extended time formats has brought to the fore questions about instruction for the first time in decades. As a result, there is a rare and valuable open dialogue as teachers wrestle with how to use extended time formats most effectively.

We see this book as a real handbook, a practical toolbox for the teacher instructing in block scheduling or other alternative extended time format, and we hope that teachers and administrators will use it as such. We send you out on this journey of exploration to discover not only what increases your effectiveness as a teacher, but also what enhances the learning and achievement of your students.

Acknowledgments

I wish to show my appreciation to all the teachers who have worked with me these past few years as they have made the transition to various kinds of extended time formats. Their stories of successes inspired me to write this book. Their stories of difficulties convinced me of the need for this book. Most of all, I have been struck by the openness and courage these teachers embodied as they left the comfort of tried- and true-lesson plans in the tried-and-true traditional schedules and journeyed forth into the uncharted territory of using new instructional strategies in differing time formats.

I thank my friend and coauthor, Steve Dunn, for joining me on this wild ride of writing a book together and then creating a second edition. I have appreciated the fresh instructional tools and insights he has brought to this book.

I also name Richard, Jim, and John as some of the many others who have encouraged me along.

—R.B.W.

I want to thank the thousands of students, past and present, who taught me during the more than twenty-five years I have been teaching in the classroom. The variety of ways they learned made it clear to me that learning is as unique as each individual. I also want to thank the many inspiring educators with whom I have worked as a consultant over the past twenty years. Their demand for excellence motivated me to expand my learning and to try to be a better educator. I am continually awed by their love of learning, their dedication to their students, and their creativity in the teaching process.

I especially want to thank the faculty at Logan High School in Logan, Utah, who gave me invaluable insights into the learning process and practical lesson design for this book, especially Kathleen Cottle, Cathy Johnson, and Tim Cybulski. I am forever in the debt of the many outstanding teachers who devoted countless hours of their time to my four children. I want to thank my children, Meg, Bess, Joseph, and Daniel. I value the many ways they challenge me and support me. I love them and I'm proud to be their dad. And finally, I also want to thank my coauthor, Bruce Williams, for his friendship and for modeling how effective our lesson design can be.

—S.E.D.

Publisher's Acknowledgments

Corwin Press gratefully acknowledges the contributions of the following reviewers:

Melissa Awenowicz, Coordinator of Field Placements and
Clinical Instructor of English Education
University of Pittsburgh, PA

Cindy Bell, Seventh-Grade Teacher
Still Middle School, Aurora, IL

Kim Brown, Fourth-Grade Teacher
Scotland Accelerated Academy, Laurel Hill, NC

Nancy Elliott, Middle School Science Teacher
Chillicothe Middle School, Chillicothe, MO

Mark Johnson, Fifth-Grade Teacher
Windy Hills Elementary School, Kearney, NE

Anne Smith, Education Research Analyst
Office of Special Education Programs
U.S. Department of Education, Washington, DC

Randy Thompson, President
MaKITSO Educational Consulting, Antioch, TN

About the Authors

 **R. Bruce Williams** has over thirty-five years of international consulting experience and is noted for his expert group facilitation and his skills in planning and team-building methodologies. He has authored *More Than 50 Ways to Build Team Consensus*, *Twelve Roles of Facilitators for School Change*, and *36 Tools for Building Spirit in Learning Communities* published by Corwin Press. He is also the coauthor of *Valuing Diversity in the School System* and *Brain-Compatible Learning for the Block*, again, published by Corwin Press. Recently released are his books *Cooperative Learning: A Standard for High Achievement*, *Multiple Intelligences for Differentiated Learning*, and *Higher Order Thinking Skills: Challenging All Students to Achieve*, also published by Corwin Press. His specialty is facilitating participative, interactive group workshops, whether these are focused on strategic planning and consensus building or instructional methodologies for the classroom. Recently, his workshops on brain-compatible learning and school change facilitation have been popular. In addition, he frequently presents in the areas of cooperative learning, higher order thinking skills, and authentic assessment.

Bruce brings exceptional skills at dealing with diverse populations aided by his seven years of experience in Japan and Korea teaching English as a second language. His thirty-six years of experience in adult training have enabled him to be an invaluable resource in facilitating school change.

In addition to conference workshops in 2002 in Australia and New Zealand, he has been invited three times in the last two years to present workshops for teachers in Singapore. In April of 2004, Bruce was the keynote speaker for 400 principals and teachers in Beijing, People's Republic of China.

 **Steven E. Dunn**, EdD, currently resides in Wichita, Kansas with his twin sons. His two daughters live and work in Chicago, Illinois. Dr. Dunn joined the School of Education faculty at Newman University in the fall of 2002. Before joining the Newman faculty, Dr. Dunn worked as an independent consultant beginning in 1992. His mission as a consultant was to provide professional development in effective instructional

strategies, learning theories, service learning, curriculum development, classroom management, and related educational topics. During the decade he was a full-time consultant, Dr. Dunn was an author, trainer, and consultant for several educational and business agencies including USAID Mission in Bosnia-Herzegovina Education Department Brcko District; International Youth Foundation in Skopje, Macedonia; Quest International and Lion's International throughout the United States and in Iceland, Poland, and Lithuania; Skylight International Renewal Institute throughout the United States; Ted Anders Company from Atlanta, Georgia; National Children's Educational Reform Foundation in Hartford, Connecticut, and Dallas, Texas; American Management Systems and Army JROTC in Hampton, Virginia; National Endowment for Financial Education (NEFE) in Denver, Colorado; and Church of God Hispanic Educational Ministries in Cleveland, Tennessee. Dr. Dunn earned his bachelor's and master's degrees from Utah State University, and his EdD from Brigham Young University. He was a high school English teacher and coach at Weber High School in Ogden, Utah. He has also taught on the faculties of Bowling Green State University in Bowling Green, Ohio, and Utah State University in Logan, Utah. Dr. Dunn currently teaches graduate education courses at Newman University.

Introduction

TOOLS OF THE TRADE

A lesson design is to a teacher what a recipe is to a chef, a blueprint to an architect, or a game plan to a coach. Not only does the recipe tell the chef what ingredients are needed; it also prescribes the amount of each ingredient, the sequence for combining the ingredients, and the preparation techniques required to prepare the dish. In similar fashion, an architect creates a construction blueprint on which are the types of materials needed to construct the building, the amount of each material, the construction plan, and the guidelines for construction. Coaches follow a similar process while preparing their teams. They choose the offense and defense that are most likely to counter the strengths of the opponents, they assign each athlete to the best playing position, and they rehearse the strategies to insure that their athletes have the competence and confidence to execute well.

Likewise, lesson plans guide teachers in selecting activities that work best for helping students understand lesson concepts and acquire new information, in determining how long to spend on each learning activity, and in deciding when each activity should be included during the learning process. Lesson plans are the recipes, blueprints, and game plans for engaging students in a successful learning process.

However, lesson plans are just that—plans. What really makes lessons come alive are the skillful strategies employed by teachers. The underpinnings for each successful lesson plan are the brain-compatible teaching or instructional strategies that work best to provide appropriate learning experiences for students. These strategies are the teacher tools. Not only do teachers need to select the tools for each lesson, they need to become more skillful in the use of these tools. A comparative analogy is the architectural blueprint. Competent construction workers not only know how to read the blueprints, but they also know which tools to select for each part of the construction job, and they have the skills to use those tools correctly. Their ability to choose the appropriate tools from their "tool belt" for each part of their job and their expertise in the use of those tools will determine the quality of the finished construction project. The same principles apply to teachers. The lesson plan is lifeless until skilled teachers bring it to life by selecting their best tools from their teacher tool belts.

The emphasis throughout this book on brain-compatible learning is an effort to capitalize on the latest brain research and on its implications for the classroom. Learning how information gets into the brain and what the brain does with that information can be very helpful in making sure lessons in the classroom have the best chance of being understood and have the best chance of getting into long-term memory.

Brain-Compatible Learning for the Block is a highly practical resource for teachers, not just as a blueprint but as an instructional guide to creating one's own blueprints (lesson and unit plans). Each of the first five chapters provides a detailed sample Four-Phase lesson, which includes standards identified by James S. Kendall and Robert J. Marzano (1997) in their *Content Knowledge: A Compendium of Standards and Benchmarks for K–12 Education.*

The four phases of the lessons are inquire, gather, process, and apply, a design built upon the concepts of the "three-story intellect" and the processing model.

The purpose of the inquire phase is to help learners identify what they already know about the concept(s), information, or skill(s) to be covered in the lesson. Students explore what they know by determining past experiences that relate to the topic, by retrieving from long-term memory previously formed associations with the topic, and by identifying skills they have previously acquired. During this phase students discover what other students know about the lesson content. And just as important, students discern how they feel about the lesson topic, how motivated or reluctant they are, and what they would like to learn. Some may even be clear how they would like to go about learning what that would like to learn.

The primary purpose of the second phase of the lesson design, the gather phase, is to help students collect new information related to the lesson topic, to create a new schema or mental model, and to refine an existing schema. Strategies teachers employ during this phase need to engage students in learning experiences that add to or enlarge their knowledge base and that connect the new information to what they already know or understand. Teachers need to select tools that will guide students through the process of creating new schemas and refining previously formed schemas.

As a function of the processing phase, students experience activities that will assist the brain as it stores new information into long-term memory (Sprenger, 1998). Teachers guide students beyond the process of rote memorization and help them create their own meaning. Comparing examples, targeting the similarities among examples, and helping students encode and organize the similarities among examples help students learn contextually.

To engage in thinking without acting upon what the brain is thinking about is antithetical to what the brain is designed to do—think and act (Sylwester, 1995). During the processing phase, students are provided with an opportunity to knead and manipulate the knowledge and concepts, data, skill, techniques, or behaviors, ultimately molding them into a tool that they can use to carve out meaning from that which they encounter in real life. Strategies selected during this phase include complex activities that engage the whole student—cognitive, affective, and psychomotor—as part of the processing experiences (Bruer, 1998). Such things as speaking, reading, writing, interacting, performing, planning, problem solving, and organizing need to be part of using all new information and skills.

The purpose of the apply phase is to use the tools forged in the previous phases in a relevant and practical context to create something new. The focus in this phase is to help students improve their proficiency under a variety of conditions or situations. The teacher engages in the direct teaching of transfer. Transfer can be presented as the ways the lesson content is connected to other disciplines, such as how a music lesson on fugues has applications to a math class or how the language arts lesson on Shakespeare's Julius Caesar is related to a speech or debate class. Transfer can also be related to the multiple intelligences, such as how an understanding of a math concept like trigonometry (logical/mathematical) can be used in solving problems related to putting a shot, platform diving, or uneven bars in gymnastics (bodily/kinesthetic). Generalization and transfer are recognizing problems in new and different settings. The apply phase connects the material to the real life of the student.

Brain-Compatible Learning for the Block is presented in six chapters. The first five chapters acquaint the reader with the tools (strategies and techniques) that will help them implement and ultimately design their own Four-Phase lesson and unit plans as set forth in the sixth chapter and in the samples provided throughout.

Chapter 1: "Physiology and Philosophy" provides an in-depth discussion of what recent research in the area of neuroscience seems to indicate about the brain's structure and multi-functionality and the implications for education.

Chapter 2: "Four-Phase Lesson and Unit Design" suggests the fine points of this innovative and dynamic design scheme. An outline of a sample unit is included.

Chapter 3: "Time for Brain-Compatible Learning" explores various alternative scheduling formats and the impact time has on learning.

Chapter 4: "Content and Curriculum" examines the weighty issue of content coverage and makes several practical suggestions for using the gift of time that alternative scheduling provides to delve deeply into content.

Chapter 5: "Instruction: The Art and Science of Teaching in Alternative Time Periods" focuses on brain-compatible educational principles and strategies that help teachers build a robust and exciting learning climate. In addition, ways in which an alternative schedule can make time for ongoing professional development are discussed.

Chapter 6: "Assessment: Measuring Achievement and Growth in Alternative Time Periods" balances the reality of standardized testing with the opportunity that authentic assessments provide to "catch" students learning.

Some may wonder how this new edition has been revised and updated. Since the first edition of this book was written, brain research has been made even more available to the education community. We included quite a lot of that research in this revision. In addition, we added vignettes based on actual classroom situations to help bring to life the approaches we are recommending. These vignettes are found in the sample lessons at the ends of Chapter 1 and Chapters 3 through 6. We have added new material on differentiated learning and schema development and have included additional activities highlighting the bodily kinesthetic. Finally, we have added several figures illustrating instructional strategies and their connection to the four-phase lesson plan, to multiple intelligences, and to the structure of practical, analytic, and creative—Sternberg's structure. We believe that all teachers will find this material valuable. With this in mind, we have used not only the term *block scheduling* but also the term *extended time formats* to clarify the book's relevance for anyone teaching in a period that is longer than thirty to forty minutes. We hope that this new edition challenges and inspires educators with concrete and practical ideas, and the promise of an enriched learning environment for both students and teachers.

Physiology and Philosophy 1

Edelman's model of our brain as a rich, layered, messy, unplanned jungle eco-system is especially intriguing . . . because it suggests that a junglelike brain might thrive best in a junglelike classroom that includes many sensory, cultural, and problem layers that are closely related to the real-world environment in which we live—the environment that best stimulates the neural networks that are genetically tuned to it.

—Robert Sylwester, 1995, p. 23

THE BRAIN'S STRUCTURE AND FUNCTIONS

Because of the complexity of the brain's physiology, it is logical to assume its functioning is at least as complex. The brain has a myriad of interconnecting systems made for figuring out complexities. Current neuroscientific research appears to reveal that many of the traditional assumptions about how people learn, which researchers based largely on behavioralist theory, are faulty. As people understand more from research about how humans learn, it will become increasingly possible to discover better methods of facilitating learning (see Chapter 5).

All attempts to summarize how the brain works fall short of both the complexity and the magnificence of how the brain is structured and how it functions. Any such effort will oversimplify the intricacies of the brain. However, it is important for teachers to be aware of the basic physiology of the brain in order to understand what neuroscience has to say.

Education has come to benefit greatly from the findings of brain research in these last few decades. Revelations of how the brain is constructed and how the brain learns has become vital information for all teachers today. "The human brain is an amazing structure—a universe of infinite possibilities and mystery. It constantly shapes and reshapes itself as a result of experience, yet it can take off on its own without input from the outside world" (Sousa, 2001, p. 1). Research informs us that the brain weighs around three pounds and is about the size of a small grapefruit. It looks somewhat like a walnut with all of its outer folds. While it may be as little as 2 percent of a human's body weight, it requires around 20 percent of our calorie intake to get the energy it needs in order to function well (p. 15).

Hemispheres

Researchers divide the brain into two hemispheres, which have developed decidedly distinct functions.

Researchers recognize the left hemisphere as the logical, analytical hemisphere. It examines information systematically and literally. The left hemisphere controls the right side of the body. This hemisphere allows people to use language. It is quite sensitive to time, looks at parts, and tends to examine the words it hears very literally.

Researchers recognize the right hemisphere as the intuitive and creative hemisphere. This hemisphere is more sensitive to space, while also considering the whole picture. It looks for patterns. The right hemisphere, while listening to the words people speak, is paying more attention to the context, the emotions being expressed, the person's tone, and, of course, the body language. Figure 1.1 shows these two hemispheres.

A four-inch cable of over 250 million fibers called the *corpus callosum* connects the two hemispheres. The hemispheres use this cable to send information back and forth to each other. Since the hemispheres have discrete tasks, the corpus callosum helps to coordinate and integrate these tasks (Sousa, 2001, p. 19; Wolfe, 2001, pp. 44–45).

Brain Cells

Simply speaking, there are two kinds of cells in the brain: nerve cells and glial cells. Researchers suggest that there are about one trillion cells altogether with nerve cells making up about one tenth of the total (Sousa, 2001, p. 20).

Nerve Cells or Neurons

The nerve cells or neurons have many parts that figure in the transmission of information from nerve cell to nerve cell. These neurons are the heart of the action in the brain and the whole nervous system. Figure 1.2 shows a diagram of the nerve cells with their components.

◉ Figure 1.1 Hemispheres of the Brain

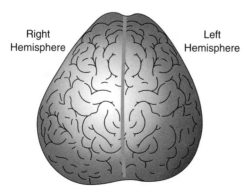

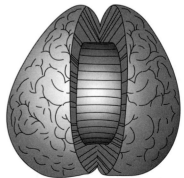

Right Hemisphere   Left Hemisphere

View of the Brain from above

Hemispheres separated to show the corpus callosum

◉ **Figure 1.2** Brain Cells

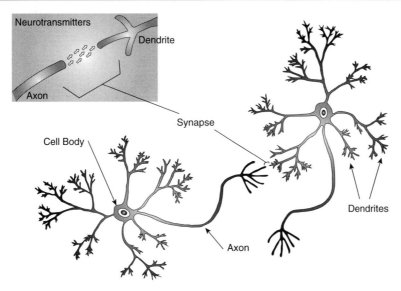

NEURONS or NERVE CELLS

Each nerve cell or neuron includes an axon, dendrites, synapses, and neurotransmitters. Table 1.1 offers a description of each of these.

For a long time, researchers assumed that the brain could not regenerate new neurons. Lately, researchers are suggesting that the brain can produce new neurons. They are yet to discern exactly how this happens and how these new cells function (Wolfe, 2001, p. 14). The brain grows new

◉ **Table 1.1** Descriptions of Brain Cell Parts

DENDRITES	Coming from the Greek word for "tree," the word *dendrite* describes the many branches coming from the neuron cell. One cell may contain thousands and thousands of dendrites. The brain can continue to grow dendrites. The function of the dendrites is to pick up impulses from other neurons and transmit them through the axon of the nerve cell. Within the cell, these impulses are electrical.
AXONS	Each nerve cell contains only one of these extensive fibers. The function of the axons is to transmit chemicals that then connect with dendrites in another neuron.
SYNAPSES	The axons do not directly touch a dendrite. This small space is where chemicals called *neurotransmitters* are sent to receiving sites on the dendrite. The function of the synapses is to allow impulses to travel from neuron to neuron.
NEUROTRANSMITTERS	Almost 100 different chemical neurotransmitters have been discovered. Some of the common ones are serotonin, dopamine, and epinephrine. The function of the neurotransmitter is to excite or inhibit the neuron it links to.

(Sousa, 2001, p. 20–22; Wolfe, 2001, pp. 14–16; Sprenger, 1999, p. 2)

dendrites as neurons make more and more connections. The more times the brain encourages these connections, the stronger the synapses get (Sprenger, 1999, p. 3). This is how learning takes place. *Plasticity* is the name given to this ability of the brain to grow and alter itself (p. 10). The implication of this is that, no matter how old one is, one's brain can learn more and, in fact, learning more helps the brain to stay healthy and active.

One often hears how exercise can release positive neurotransmitters; however, research is showing that affirmations of touching or smiling or being in the midst of important relationships can release these very neurotransmitters (serotonin, dopamine, etc.; Sprenger, 1999, p. 25).

Glial Cells

The glial cells surround the neurons. The name *glial* comes from the Greek word for "glue." Different glial cells have different functions. One type plays a critical role in the formation of the fetal brain. Another helps in the removal of dead cells. Another type functions as filters soaking up unhelpful substances before they interfere with the neurons. Another type creates myelin that wraps around the axons of the neurons. This wrapping facilitates the transmission of electoral impulses through the axons (Sousa, 2001, p. 20; Wolfe, 2001, pp. 17–18).

Brain Sections

Many brain researchers have identified, using different names, three primary sections of the brain. Table 1.2 describes these three sections.

Table 1.2 Description of Three Sections of the Brain

EXTERIOR BRAIN OR OUTER BRAIN	• This part of the brain, which covers the inner brain like bark on a tree, has been called the *cortex, neocortex,* or *neomammalian* brain.
	• Most of the higher order thinking functions occur in this part of the brain.
INNER BRAIN OR MID-BRAIN	• This inner section of the brain has sometimes been referred to as the old mammalian (*paleomammalian*) brain, as it is similar to the brain structure and functions of early mammals.
	• Many of the functions of this part of the brain have to do with emotions and memory.
BRAIN STEM	• Sometimes this has been called the *reptilian brain* because it closely resembles very early brain structures.
	• Some say this appeared as long as 500 million years ago.
	• The primary function of this part of the brain is survival.

Exterior Brain (Outer Brain)

Covering the brain is a layer of cells about six cells thick. It is about the size of a page from a newspaper. It is wrinkled to fit into the size of a human skull. The major parts of this exterior brain or "cerebral cortex" (Wolfe, 2001, p. 31) are four lobes—occipital, parietal, temporal, and frontal—and a strip across the top of the brain called the motor cortex. All of the parts of the exterior brain, as well as the parts of the interior brain, are present in each hemisphere. Figure 1.3 illustrates the parts of the exterior brain. Table 1.3 describes these parts.

At the very front of the brain is a part called the prefrontal cortex. This houses what some have called the "executive functions." People who are highly organized, find it easy to use logic and reason, are good at planning ahead, accurately assess risk and danger, can multitask, can foresee consequences, and can control their emotions are all people with extremely well-developed executive functions. A poor environment while one is growing up can stall the growth of these executive functions (Caine, Caine, McClintic, & Klimek, 2005, p. 7). This happens to be the last area of the brain to receive the process of myelination, the covering of parts of the axon with a fatty white material that speeds the transmission of signals. Since this does not happen until one is in his or her early twenties, this has implications for what we can reasonably expect in the level of thinking maturity of young people.

Figure 1.3 Parts of the Exterior Brain

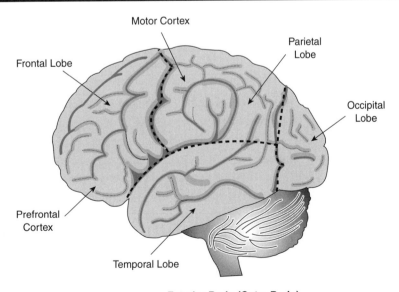

**Exterior Brain (Outer Brain)
view of the left hemisphere**

◉ Table 1.3 Description of the Parts of the Exterior Brain

OCCIPITAL LOBES	The *occipital lobes* can be found in a central lower location toward the back of the brain. They handle the visual messages from the eyes. These lobes actually have designated cells for processing motion, color, lines, and depth perception. They also compare information with previously stored visual information.
TEMPORAL LOBES	The *temporal lobes* are located above the ears and curve from the occipital lobes to the frontal lobes. They handle all of the auditory messages, and they have discrete sections to handle hearing, language, and memory.
PARIETAL LOBES	The *parietal lobes* are located at the top of the brain and have two sections: anterior and posterior. The anterior section of the parietal lobe receives information from all over the body. The posterior section analyzes the information and coordinates the implications of this information for body and spatial awareness. The parietal lobes assist in keeping us focused or helping us shift attention to as body stimuli shift.
FRONTAL LOBES	The *frontal lobes* are found from behind the forehead to the top of the head. They carry out many higher order thinking functions such as reflecting on the past, projecting to the future, focusing attention, decision making, and problem solving. In addition, this part of the brain enables us to be conscious of our thoughts and actions.
MOTOR CORTEX	The *motor cortex* is a band of cells located at the back of the frontal lobes going across the top of the head from ear to ear. It initiates the neural signals for body movement that then get sent to the cerebellum for implementation. Crucial motor areas such as the fingers, lips, and tongue are given more space in the motor cortex. In front of the motor cortex are areas which form words to be spoken and then allow them to be spoken (Wernicke's Area and Broca's Area).

(Sousa, 2001, p. 16–17; Wolfe, 2001, pp. 31–34)

Inner Brain (Midbrain)

This area of the brain includes the limbic system and the cerebellum. Figure 1.4 illustrates the parts of the limbic system and shows the location of the cerebellum.

The thalamus, hypothalamus, amygdala, and hippocampus compose the limbic system. Table 1.4 describes the parts of the limbic system.

It is especially important for teachers to note that the two parts of the brain most concerned with memory production are located in the limbic system, often called the emotional system of the brain (Sousa, 2001, p. 19). This emphasizes how crucial it is to include feelings and emotions in teaching as a way to enhance the formation of long-term memories.

The cerebellum is located above the brain stem at the back of the brain. It is so important that it makes up 11 percent of the total weight of the brain. The cerebellum monitors all body movements. It plays a role in maintaining balance, monitoring posture, and regulating the body's

Figure 1.4 Parts of the Inner Brain

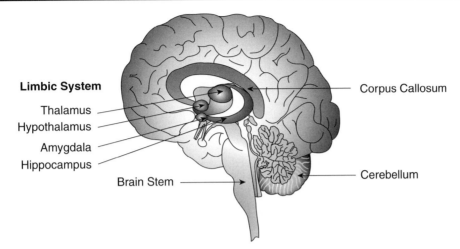

Cross section of the left hemisphere of the brain

muscles. The cerebellum receives messages from the motor cortex to initiate a movement. The cerebellum carries the signals through to the appropriate muscles. The cerebellum stores muscles' memory, which allows one to remember how to ride a bicycle, keyboard, and play a musical instrument, even after periods of not doing these things. This permits the con-

 Table 1.4 Description of the Parts of the Inner Brain

THALAMUS	The thalamus is a small, plum-shaped structure found toward the center of the brain. All incoming sensory information except smell goes here first.
HYPOTHALAMUS	Below the thalamus is the hypothalamus, which is the size of a thumbnail. It is a control center for many body functions. Bodily responses to fear are controlled by the hypothalamus.
AMYGDALA	The amygdala is almond-shaped and located close to the center of the brain. It plays a critical role in regulating and controlling emotions, especially fear. Emotional memories are stored here. When the thalamus sends sensory information to various places in the cortex, it also sends that information to the amygdala. Danger or harm causes the amygdala to alert the hypothalamus. The amygdala relays emotional information.
HIPPOCAMPUS	The name *hippocampus* came from the Latin for seahorse. Others say it appears like two animal paws facing each other. It is found near the base of the limbic area. The hippocampus permits a person to store conscious memories. The hippocampus relays factual information. Memories of the recent past are stored here until the memories are sent to the cortex. It is always comparing working memory with stored memory. Thus it is crucial for creating meaning. Once the final encoding of the memory occurs, the hippocampus no longer is needed for retrieval purposes.

(Sousa, 2001, pp. 18–19; Wolfe, 2001, pp. 25–29)

scious mind to focus on more demanding tasks. Lately, researchers are exploring the cerebellum's role in dealing with thoughts, emotions, and memories (Sousa, 2001, p. 20; Wolfe, 2001, pp. 23–25).

Brain Stem

As this part of the brain is deeply concerned with survival, it automatically controls necessary functions such as respiration, digestion, heartbeat, and body temperature. "Of the 12 body nerves that go to the brain, 11 end in the brain stem (the olfactory nerve—for smell—goes directly to the limbic system, an evolutionary artifact)" (Sousa, 2001, p. 17). Consequently, its sensory filtering function is crucial. The sensory filtering function, or "sensory register" as Sousa (2001, p. 40) called it, or the "reticular activation system as Wolfe (2001, p. 22) called it, makes the initial decision to let data go or to send information to the thalamus or, if the data is threatening, to the amygdala. Finally, the brain stem produces many of the chemical messengers needed for brain functioning (Wolfe, 2001, p. 23).

As this chapter unfolds, there will be references to these sections of the brain and how they impact learning and memory. What is becoming clear is that, while education is extremely concerned about academic content and higher-order thinking (much of which involves the exterior brain or cerebral cortex), for learning to occur the learning process needs to engage all parts of the brain.

With this background on the brain and brain cell physiology, it will be easier to grasp the significance of all this for memory and learning.

Memory

Crucial for the teacher now is the question how does memory take place? Without memory, there can be no learning. Yet, this is the task of the teacher: to facilitate learning. The terms *short-term memory* and *long-term memory* are familiar to most teachers today. It has become more and more apparent that teaching needs to focus on enabling material to get into long-term memory—that is, to go beyond the teacher. The question one might pose is the following. Which is more beneficial: "covering" ten chapters of material and perhaps getting the equivalent of four or five chapters into long-term memory or enabling six or seven chapters' worth of material to get into long-term memory through the use of teaching strategies that are brain compatible?

Short-Term Memory

Sousa (2001) suggested that one break short-term memory into two parts: immediate and working (p. 41).

Immediate Memory. So much information is flowing through our senses that immediate memory can hold data for only about thirty seconds. Most of the data is inconsequential and is dropped quite quickly. In other words, high-priority data will take precedence over low-priority data. Data indicating a threat and emotionally charged data are examples of high-priority data. Data that indicates a survival threat causes the reticular activating system to shut down almost all brain activity so that the brain's full attention can be on survival. The brain immediately sends emotional and threatening data to the amygdala to handle it. Other data goes to the thalamus to be processed (Sousa, 2001, pp. 41–42).

Working Memory. Whereas immediate memory can be both conscious and subconscious, working memory processes consciously. The activity of working memory occurs primarily in the frontal lobes using other parts of the brain as necessary. There are both space limitations and time limitations to working memory. The time limit for adolescents and adults is from ten to twenty minutes. The space limit is only a few items at a time. The telephone company figured out that seven was the ideal space limit, so except for area codes our phone numbers are seven digits. If the brain does not do something rather quickly to the information, it disappears. Linking the data to preexisting information and using the data immediately in a practical situation are two ways that the brain can shift data into long-term memory (Sousa, 2001, pp. 44–46).

Another criterion is novelty. Something that is unusual and different captures the brain's attention. An additional factor is intensity: the more intense stimuli get the most attention. Finally, movement causes the brain to pay attention. This puts a heavy demand on teachers to innovate continually, to develop intense learning events, and to create situations where both the students and the teacher are moving (Wolfe, 2001, pp. 82–83).

Perhaps now it is easy to understand that the brain retains material presented visually with colors better than it retains material presented in just black and white (Sprenger, 2003, p. 7).

Long-Term Memory

Sousa (2001) liked to make a distinction between long-term memory and long-term storage: "This is a good place to explain the difference between the terms *long-term memory* and *long-term storage*. As used here, long-term memory refers to the process of storing and retrieving information. Long-term storage refers to where in the brain the memories are kept" (p. 50).

A crucial criterion for information to get into long-term storage is whether a person can make sense and/or create meaning out of that information. Without either of these, there is very little likelihood of information getting into long-term storage. When a person can both make sense and create meaning out of the information, the chance of long-term storage is tremendously increased (Sousa, 2001, p. 47).

Needless to say, one of the key implications of this is for teachers to pay attention to enabling students to create their own meanings out of information. Finding ways to connect information to students' own experiences helps in this. Assisting students to make connections with material studied in other subject areas also enables long-term storage.

Material gets into long-term storage when the hippocampus sends it there. As there are many possible storage areas, the hippocampus decides where it will go. Most of this occurs during sleep (Sousa, 2001, p. 49).

Table 1.5 Description of Nondeclarative Memory

NONDECLARATIVE MEMORY

PROCEDURAL	MOTOR SKILL	EMOTIONAL
Driving a car, solving an equation, writing a business letter, reading, and playing chess are all tasks that require a lot of "how to's," which gradually become very unconscious and automatic—even after a period of time when they haven't been performed.	Skills of grooming oneself, playing a musical instrument, and preparing a meal are motor skills that once we had to be very conscious about, but now we can do without much conscious thinking.	Emotional events can rapidly cause a long-lasting memory of the event. Where and when you heard about the 9/11 attacks may always be part of your memory.

(Sousa, 2001, pp. 82–83; Wolfe, 2001, pp. 115)

There are two types of memory storage: nondeclarative and declarative.

Nondeclarative Memory Storage. Nondeclarative memory helps people remember how to do certain things. After learning these activities, nondeclarative memory allows people to carry them out quite unconsciously (Sousa, 2001, pp. 82–83; Wolfe, 2001, pp. 113).

There are three types of nondeclarative memory: procedural, motor skill, and emotional. Table 1.5 describes each of these.

Declarative Memory Storage. Declarative memory helps people remember information, names, music, and objects. The hippocampus and the cerebrum process all of this. Declarative memory stores things about which people can speak or write (Sousa, 2001, p. 83; Wolfe, 2001, p. 116).

There are two types of declarative memory: semantic and episodic. Table 1.6 describes these two types.

Research informs one that different places in the brain usually store nondeclarative and declarative memories. Consequently, one may remember

Table 1.6 Description of Declarative Memory

DECLARATIVE MEMORY

EPISODIC MEMORY	SEMANTIC MEMORY
Episodic memory recalls the details around one's first job, what one experienced on an overseas trip, the music played at a key event, and so forth. Episodic memory is focused on memories in one's own life experiences.	Semantic memory recalls the multiplication tables, the rules of grammar, the position of letters in the alphabet, the meaning of words, and so forth.
One can refer to this as *contextual* or *spatial* memory. Surrounding space or location is associated with this kind of memory.	

(Sousa, 2001, p. 83–84; Wolfe, 2001, pp. 116–117)

how to play a musical instrument and forget what the name of the instrument is (Sousa, 2001, p. 84).

It is possible, knowing these different memory paths, to designate specific instructional strategies that will be compatible with each memory path. Table 1.7 describes the memory process for each memory path and offers some suggested instructional strategies to help material get into these specific memory paths.

 Table 1.7 Memory Paths With Instructional Strategies

MEMORY PATHS WITH INSTRUCTIONAL STRATEGIES

PATH	MEMORY PROCESS	STRATEGIES
SEMANTIC	Brain stem to thalamus to hippocampus to temporary storage to prefrontal cortex (working memory) to long-term memory. This takes many repetitions in order to get material into long-term storage.	Graphic organizers Peer teaching Questioning strategies Summarizing Role-playing Debates Outlining Time lines Mnemonic devices
EPISODIC	The key part of the brain used in episodic memory is the hippocampus.	Creating bulletin boards Changing desk arrangement Accessorizing Using one color of paper for all the handouts in a particular unit Teaching from a specific area in the room
PROCEDURAL	Since this kind of memory is sometimes called *muscle memory*, the key part of the brain for this is the cerebellum.	Repeating a procedure frequently Using hands-on techniques and materials (manipulatives) Using movement (role-playing, debate, dances, marches, and games)
MOTOR SKILL	Again, the key part of the brain used for motor skill is the cerebellum. Sometimes this memory stimulates more about it in other parts of the brain.	Putting information to music Creating raps and poems Using flash cards Oral conditioning Developing quiz shows
EMOTIONAL	The key part of the brain for this memory path is the amygdala. It is important to know that emotional memories are the most powerful memories we have.	Music Celebrations Presentations involving emotions Role play involving emotions Display your enthusiasm as a teacher

(Sousa, 2001, pp. 82–83; Wolfe, 2001, pp. 115)

Needless to say, when more than one memory path is used to get material into long-term storage, the stronger the memory of the material becomes (Sprenger, 1999, pp. 62–63).

Schemata

The brain organizes information into schemata.

Description

Learning is a scaffolding process. As we learn, we progress in our understanding from declarative knowledge and propositions, including images and linear ordering, through procedural knowledge and to the creation of schemata. Cagne (1993) supported the learning model of schema development. His work demonstrates the component parts of schema formation including declarative knowledge, propositions, images, linear orderings, and procedural knowledge.

Declarative knowledge. Declarative knowledge consists of a proposition(s), a single unit of information or idea, and its underlying semantics. Propositions can include facts, theories, experiences, events, objects, and so forth. Propositions of related topics can be linked in memory to form propositional networks. For example, one can know that the 9/11 World Trade Center disaster was the result of religious zealots who flew passenger planes into the Twin Towers. Or, one can know that the exploding planes carried enough fuel to create a fireball of intense heat.

Images. Images are mental pictures of what the information looks like and includes spatial and/or continuous information. Images can help reinforce declarative knowledge particularly when visual information is important. For example, one can picture the passengers aboard the doomed airplanes and imagine their emotional states. This mental image generates sympathy for their plight and raises questions about the means the religious zealots used to accomplish their goals. Or, engineers can visually reconstruct ways in which the steel beams of the buildings responded to the firestorm.

Linear orderings. Linear orderings are sequences, rankings, or primary orderings of information. For example, one can recreate how the zealots prioritized and followed essential steps to synchronize their attacks so fighter planes could not intercept them before they hit their targets. Or, engineers can identify what happened structurally and in what sequence in order for the complete collapse of the Twin Towers.

Procedural knowledge. Procedural knowledge consists of knowing how to perform or execute something including motor, cognitive, and problem-solving skills. For example, students with procedural knowledge would be able to determine which Web sites contain the most accurate and timely information on world events; how to use the computer to access that information quickly and efficiently; and how to determine which information source is most reliable, objective, and comprehensive. Or, engineers can study the weaknesses in high-rise buildings evidenced by the collapse of the towers and design structures that could withstand another such firestorm.

Students need to engage in learning activities that include declarative knowledge (propositions), images, linear orderings, and procedural knowledge. All of the just mentioned are essential elements included in the creation of a schema.

Schemata Development

Storing declarative and procedural knowledge as discreet, unattached, or disconnected bits of information is too cumbersome and inefficient for the brain. Imagine your brain trying to manage all the information it receives daily without a way to organize this huge volume into a format that is readily accessible, retrievable, and usable. Fortunately, the brain automatically and subconsciously takes those discreet bits of information, perceives a relationship among them, and links them together in an organizational form that it can easily store and recall. When the human brain develops concepts, identifies values, and establishes relationships through the creation of hierarchically organized information, the result is called a schema or mental model.

Schema theory addresses how we actively make meaning of information and experiences. For example, if one were to overhear the following conversation, he or she would most likely be able to understand it because his or her brain would would be able to access the appropriate schema.

Tim: What happened after I left?
Ann: We scored one more time, one minute to go, a fluke pass.
Tim: How long?
Ann: 45 yards. Crazy run, too. You wouldn't have believed it.
Tim: Did they go for two?

From this conversation, one can probably surmise that the game was football. One can probably also identify the score as a touchdown, and one can probably guess that the score was close because the scoring team had a decision to make about the extra point(s). Embedded in this conversation is the schema of the game of football because without a schema of football, one would not be able to interpret the conversation. The schema of football includes one's declarative knowledge of team size, game rules, offensive and defensive positions, and so forth. One's images include the size of the playing field; number of men on the field; the skills required to play football, including passing, blocking, running, catching, punting, defending; and so forth. One's linear knowledge includes number of downs, importance of field position, when to call a time-out, how to use the clock, and so forth. One's procedural knowledge would include setting up plays to capitalize on the opponents' weaknesses and strengths, deciding which play to call based on field position, following the procedures to call a time-out, and so forth. For all of the just mentioned information to be retrievable and usable, it must be organized into a schema labeled "football."

Schemata are formed when the brain processes information and experiences and organizes these together into units and images that are stored in memory and recalled as fundamental knowledge. This stored knowledge can be used to solve problems, recognize similarities and differences, draw inferences, and so forth. We form schemata for everything, such as what makes good fiction, what distinguishes a dog from a cat, what is a right-angled triangle, what is effective teaching, why the product of a negative number multiplied by another negative number is a positive number, what defines happiness, what is a scientist, how gravity works, and so on.

Function of Schemata

Schema (singular) and schemata (plural) are the blueprint or lens for our future pattern recognition, interpretation, and thinking about new information, ideas, and experiences. Our schemata drive our abilities to attend to new ideas, interpret our experiences, understand our emotional reaction, and achieve a particular level of motivation. Once our brains create and store schemata, we rarely question what we *think* or *feel* unless something forces our brains to confront their own schemata. The reason schemata can be so different from person to person is that our brains form schemata based on our individual experiences, our interpretations of those experiences, the amount of information we attend to, and the varied connections the brain makes in an attempt to make sense of the information or experiences. When someone says, "I tell it the way it is," he or she is really describing the schema his or her brain created and, subsequently, his or her interpretation of what "it" is. Certainly, his or her "it" is not the "way it is" for everyone in every situation; therefore, "I tell it the way it is—for me" would be a more appropriate statement.

Creating accurate schemata or refining existing schemata appropriately becomes a formidable challenge for both students and teachers. We can help students reflect on each new learning experience and guide the process of connecting, interpreting, understanding, and creating new or refining existing schemata. We can ask our students to explain what they think or understand related to the lesson concepts then work to refine or modify the inaccuracies of the schemata. We can also provide examples that place information into familiar contexts or settings, we can create a feeling of cognitive dissonance to help students question what they think they know or understand, and we can help show the relevance and importance of the lesson material.

Implications of Schemata for Teaching

We need to help our students recognize their faulty schemata before adding new information or providing new learning experiences. As we share information or provide new experiences, students with an existing inaccurate schema may either reject the new information because it does not match their existing schema, become confused because the new information does not make sense, or alter the new information to match their existing schema thus perpetuating the inaccurate schema. All these situations can frustrate the learning process. Science and math teachers regularly try to dispel the myths and misunderstandings students bring with them before they begin to impart new information.

We can help students refine or modify a schema by

- sharing verbally and/or visually our own unique organization of complex information;
- helping students organize new information with the use of graphic organizers, class discussions, charts, and so forth;
- demonstrating curricular and real-life connections with what the students currently know and understand;
- clarifying the information through matched and nonmatched examples.

In order to refine inaccurate or inappropriate schemata, teachers can provide multiple examples that are similar yet different in important details. Students effectively learn new information and with greater long-term retention when examples are shared, relationships among elements are shown, and the context or setting is provided. Conscious processing through metacognition and higher order thinking skills coupled with examples, examples, and more examples are the keys to helping students form appropriate schemata.

To refine a schema, learners must be actively involved in the processing of information and recognize the need to modify or refine their schema. Teachers need to provide examples that vary in essential points, called "matched nonexamples." Telling their students to change their ideas or offering them more information is not as effective as providing disparate examples that are closely matched but different in critical points. A child may initially understand "chair" as being made only of wood, having four legs, and having a straight ladder-back. To refine the child's chair schema, we can (a) provide examples of chairs made of plastic, leather, cloth, grass, bamboo, or twigs and (b) show different styles and functions of chairs like rockers, stools, folding chairs, settees, or chaise lounges. Students, armed with a variety of examples, can explore different uses of chairs, discuss the effectiveness of each design, and consider alternative chair proposals that differ significantly from their original schema. These examples forever alter their understanding of chair, their schema, or their mental model. Without visual, relevant, and contextually appropriate matched nonexamples, appropriate and accurate schemata are difficult to form and refine.

Learning

All of this helps us to clarify what the process of learning is all about. The brain research sheds light on how learning happens and on ways to improve the chances that learning will happen. There is a difference between learning and memory. "Learning is the process by which we *acquire* new knowledge and skills; memory is the process by which we *retain* the knowledge and skills for the future" (Sousa, 2001, p. 78). While learning does not add to the number of brain cells, it does increase the number of dendrites in each cell, thereby increasing the number of connections and networks created (Sousa, 2001, p. 79).

It is clear that enabling students to make sense of new information and to create meaning out of it means helping the students to connect new learning with past learning and experiences. The brain has a limited capacity to retain material that does not make sense to the learner.

Furthermore, the brain wants to use what it is learning rather quickly. The challenge is to find ways for students to take material and rather quickly do something creative with it or create a useful product with it (Sousa, 2001, p. 40).

"Active emotional engagement appears to be a key to learning" (Sprenger, 1999, p. 60). This is one reason why teaching is becoming more challenging. The task is to find ways to tap into the differing emotional motivations of each student. In addition, using as many of the different senses as possible can assist in the learning process.

Emotions

"Emotions interact with reason to support or inhibit learning" (Sousa, 2001, p. 43). This succinctly describes the growing understanding of the role of emotions in the learning process. Fear or threat causes the amygdala to shut down cognitive thinking and concentrate on survival. On the contrary, a supportive environment enables the higher order thinking processes to thrive. In this way, a supportive environment causes the amygdala to release signals encouraging the brain to strengthen the memory (Sousa, 2001, p. 42).

The challenge in the classroom is to create emotionally rich learning environments. Generally, education has tried to eliminate emotion in the classroom, thereby creating very sterile surroundings particularly at an age when adolescents are teeming with emotions. Having emotions acted out in role-plays of material being covered can bring emotion into the classroom. Asking questions about the emotions going on in a novel character or an historical person can do this. Allowing students to write about their emotions is another way to do this.

This is why Goleman (1995) said, "IQ and emotional intelligence are not opposing competencies, but rather separate ones" (p. 44). To push this even further, the research is telling us that emotions can be highly supportive and even necessary for effective cognitive processes.

Movement

If we really believe in the phrase "all students can learn," then to reach many of our students, it is necessary to incorporate movement into teaching. We know that many of our students are "kinesthetic" learners. Yet, it may seem that we are wasting time if we use strategies that involve movement and action in the classroom.

What we are learning from the brain research is that body movement enhances the working of the brain. "Integrative movement improves learning by maintaining communication and developing all parts of the brain" (Heiberger, Wilson, & Heiniger-White, 2000, p. 14).

Brain research educator Eric Jensen (2000) echoed this. "Brain research confirms that physical activity—moving, stretching, walking—can actually enhance the learning process" (p. 34). Movement encourages an increase in one's heart rate and one's circulation that, in turn, impacts the brain. Initiating a movement activity right after an input session can allow the brain to carry out its tasks of processing the information. Even simple stretching can enable more oxygen to get to the brain and keep it alert (p. 34).

There are so many ways to implement "structured movement" in the classroom. Cooperative learning group tasks, such as working on a graphic organizer together or creating a poster together, allow students to get up and move around the table as they contribute to the product. "People search" activities around topics currently being studied can get people out of their seats, moving around, and learning at the same time. Acting out simple skits and role-plays are other ways of allowing movement in the context of learning.

What may seem difficult for those who learned mostly from books and lectures is that some people actually learn by using their body. Some people internalize facts and concepts using their bodies. "The brain learns best and retains most when the organism is actively involved in exploring physical sites and materials and asking questions to which it actually craves answers. Merely passive experiences tend to attenuate and have little lasting impact" (Gardner, 2000, p. 82).

Environment

Sprenger (2003) gave us a most practical look at factors in the environment. While her main topic had to do with differentiation, it is quite relevant to our focus on the brain research. She noted three major elements: the physical environment, the social/emotional environment, and the cognitive environment. Table 1.8 puts into chart form the suggestions she makes.

Table 1.8 Three Major Elements of the Environment

ENVIRONMENTAL FACTORS

PHYSICAL	SOCIAL/EMOTIONAL	COGNITIVE
Lighting	Self-awareness	Predictability
Temperature	Self-management	Feedback
Color	Social awareness	Novelty
Nutrition	Relationship management	Choice
Music		Challenge
Humor		Reflection
Water		
Physical safety		

(Sprenger, 2003, pp. 4–24)

When a teacher incorporates these factors into the classroom environment, it intensifies and facilitates focus on learning. When a teacher ignores these factors, it can result in boredom or chaos. Discipline problems may increase. Classroom management may deteriorate.

Multiple Intelligences

When Howard Gardner came out with his book *Frames of Mind* in 1983, he proposed two radical thoughts. Contrary to the thinking until then that human beings had a single intelligence and had it in varying degrees, Gardner suggested there were several intelligences. He initially listed seven intelligences, adding an eighth intelligence in the late 1990s (Gardner, 1999, pp. 41–44, 48–52). He provisionally added a ninth one (Gardner, 2006, pp. 18–21). The important point is that a human being has more than one intelligence. More to the point, every human being has all of them in varying degrees of strength.

The second radical thought is a definite implication from the previous one. One can modify weak intelligences. Perhaps one will never become an expert. However, one has the possibility of becoming more comfortable with a particular intelligence.

The identification of an intelligence is an explicit and seriously thought-through process for Gardner. Part of this identification process depends on Gardner's extensive knowledge of the brain and his examination of people with normal brains and people with damaged brains. Overall, he applies eight specific criteria before naming a separate intelligence:

- The verbal/linguistic intelligence is strong in skillful verbal communication, learning languages, and expert in writing. This intelligence learns well through reading and listening to talks and lectures.
- The logical/mathematical intelligence is comfortable using mathematical and scientific processes. This intelligence is often organized and thinks through things in a logical, step-by-step manner. This intelligence can often recognize patterns easily. This intelligence learns well through highly organized material presented very explicitly and in a linear progression.
- The visual/spatial intelligence presents ideas, concepts, and emotions through the visual or through the spatial. This intelligence learns well through visually presented material. This intelligence can easily imagine things without actually seeing them directly.
- The musical/rhythmic intelligence appreciates, creates, or performs musical or rhythmic patterns with great ease. The musical/rhythmic intelligence learns material when presented through songs, raps, or rhythm.
- The bodily/kinesthetic intelligence expertly uses the body to work through challenges. This is clear both in athletics and in dancers. This intelligence learns information by using the body.

- The interpersonal/social intelligence displays great gifts at understanding the inner workings of others and understanding how to connect well with them in work and in play. This intelligence learns well when information is shared with or garnered from others.

- The intrapersonal/introspective intelligence understands inner emotions and inner workings well. This intelligence learns well alone. This intelligence is adept at self-motivation and learning independently.

- The naturalist intelligence embodies extreme sensitivity to the surrounding environment. This may manifest itself in abilities to distinguish characteristics among the animal and plant kingdoms as well as in deep concerns about ecology, the environment, and the well-being of the planet. This intelligence learns well when material is presented in a way that connects with the surrounding environment. (Gardner, 2000, pp. 41–48)

Provisionally, Gardner (2006) considered what he called the existential intelligence. This intelligence concerns itself with big questions of life, how life began, the purpose of life, what happens after death, and so forth. This intelligence learns well when material is presented in the context of depth issues and concerns (p. 21).

Obviously, this theory has dramatic implications for the teacher. It suggests that using only one teaching style or one teaching approach cannot possibly reach the spectrum of intelligences represented in the classroom. It also suggests that we ask the wrong question when we ask, "How smart is James?" Rather, through using the multiple intelligences screen, we could be asking, "How is James smart?" "Adopting a multiple intelligences approach can bring about a quiet revolution in the way students see themselves and others. Instead of defining themselves as either 'smart' or 'dumb,' students can perceive themselves as potentially smart in a number of ways" (Moran, Kornhaber, & Gardner, 2006, p. 23).

Finally, it is very possible that one can use a strong intelligence to shore up a weaker intelligence. In an age when the verbal/linguistic and the logical/mathematical are of supreme importance, how can a teacher use the bodily/kinesthetic or the musical/rhythmic to increase a student's ability in language, math, or science (Moran et al., 2006, p. 24)?

A Child's Brain

Brain research is clarifying how a child's brain is different from an adult brain. Very early on, the infant's brain is incredibly busy as its neurons are making connections at unbelievable speeds. The more different experiences the infant has, the more connections the infant's brain can make. Researchers are affirming that the more a parent talks to the child, the more the linguistic area of the brain can develop. Larger vocabularies and increases in intelligences can occur just by the hearing of language from the parent (Sousa, 2001, p. 23, 26).

Between twenty-four and thirty months, the young child can develop healthy emotional control. There is a battle at this point between the rational system in the cortex and the emotional system as to which will win out. If emotional outbursts and tantrums get the young child what it wants, then that will predominate. If rational thinking begins to win, that determines whether the child grows in emotional control. No wonder we call these the *terrible twos*. One can alter the emotional outburst pathway later in life, but it will take a great deal of effort to undo what was learned at this young age (Sousa, 2001, p. 25).

Motor skill development occurs most naturally until the age of six. When one neglects motor skill development, this can have a significant impact on learning when the child begins schooling (Sousa, 2001, p. 25).

At ten to twelve years of age, two significant processes occur. Neural connections that have proven useful to the child become more permanent. The brain then eliminates unused or unuseful neural connections. This begins to pave the way for the turbulence of the adolescent years (Sousa, 2001, p. 23).

Male Brains/Female Brains

Some documented evidence shows differences between male and female brains. These differences show up early in a child's development. Table 1.9 lays out some of these differences. Table 1.10 adds some reflective implications about these differences.

Table 1.9 Differences Between Male and Female Brains

DIFFERENCES BETWEEN MALE AND FEMALE BRAINS

MALE BRAINS	FEMALE BRAINS
1. More area of the cortex for spatial-mechanical functions	1. More area of the cortex for emotional and verbal processes
2. Boredom shuts down the brain.	2. A more active prefrontal cortex
3. The corpus callosum develops at a different rate in males.	3. Frontal lobes develop earlier than they do in males.
4. The male brain tends to compartmentalize and focus.	4. Even in boredom, the female brain can function.
5. If the frontal lobe is not fully developed yet, the male brain will be more susceptible to responding emotionally through the amygdala.	5. The two hemispheres appear more interconnected in the female brain. This can result in more ability to multitask.

(King & Gurian, 2006, pp. 56–61; Brozo, 2006, pp. 71–74; Ripley, 2005, pp. 51–56)

◉ Table 1.10 Reflections on Differences Between Male and Female Brains

REFLECTIONS ON THESE DIFFERENCES

MALES

1. When it is time to read, boys often want to roam the room rather than sit and read.

2. Boys naturally bring a lot of impulsivity, single-task focus, kinesthetic learning, aggression, and competition to the classroom. Teachers often view these as problems.

3. When studying sentence parts, an alert teacher will have boy students arrange cards representing the parts on the floor.

4. An alert teacher will use storyboards with pictures to spark the visual in the brains of boys.

5. An alert teacher will plan an activity or content material that is full of action with many heroes.

6. An alert teacher will make sure the real-life connection is obvious and clear for male students.

7. An alert teacher will invite men to talk in the classroom, especially having them emphasize books and reading.

FEMALES

1. Girls often like the verbal-emotional emphasis in the classroom.

2. Girls often find it easier to sit still, listen, and write down notes.

3. Girls often find it easier to multitask.

4. Girls can often pay more attention to more information about different subjects.

5. Because the frontal lobes in female brains develop earlier, they may possess less impulsivity.

6. Girls can transition more easily from one task to the next.

(King & Gurian, 2006; Brozo, 2006; Ripley, 2005)

Understanding the previously mentioned can really assist teachers in the creation of curriculum materials and instructional strategies that will have a chance to get through to the differing male and female brains in any classroom. In no way does this call for any watering down of content. Rather it calls for exploring alternative ways of getting material in front of all students and alternative strategies for helping them grasp the content and make it their own.

Adolescent Brains

There was a time when brain researchers thought that the brain was fairly well developed by the time a child reached the beginning of adolescence. Current brain research has dramatically challenged this view. At least two processes are continuing through adolescence. One is the continuation of the pruning that removes unused connections between neurons in the cortex. The other is the ongoing process of myelination. This process of coating the axons facilitates the working of the neurons. Now it is clear that this whole process is not completed until a person reaches the early twenties (Price, 2005, p. 24).

This helps to explain why many adolescent cognitive processes appear severely flawed. The very seat of those cognitive processes is in the prefrontal cortex, the very part of the brain that is undergoing the previously mentioned changes toward the end of the total change process going on in the adolescent and early adult brain. "No matter how a particular brain turns out, its development proceeds in stages, generally from back to front" (Willis, 2004, p. 59).

As we know, in the midst of all this, sex hormones are raging through the brain's limbic system. Without the strength of the judgment center, which is still developing, the hormones and the emotions can go relatively uncontrolled (Willis, 2004, p. 61).

All of this presents a challenge to the teacher of adolescents. There are at least three needs that are to be addressed: the need for autonomy, the need to belong—and yet be oneself, and the need for personal meaning (Inlay, 2005, pp. 42–43). The need for autonomy calls for a safe, structured environment that allows for more responsibility and decision making. This strengthens the adolescent's own sense of personal power and reduces the tendency to follow peer pressure unquestioningly. The need to belong and yet be oneself calls for an environment that allows students to develop and display their growing senses of selfhood while also supporting meaningful connections with both adults and peers. The need for personal meaning calls for a teacher to present the curriculum in ways that can enable adolescents to connect with it and see its relevancy. No longer can a teacher assume that just because the material is mandatory or just because the teacher loves the material that students will automatically see personal meaning in it. The teacher of adolescents is called on to understand the current adolescent world as well as to be knowledgeable about subject matter.

Autistic Brains

The occurrence of autism has dramatically increased. "In 1970 the estimated incidence of autism was 1 in 2,500. Today it's 1 in 170" (Wallis, 2006b, p. 65). Autistic brains are showing distinct differences from other brains. What is unclear is whether the autism caused these differences, or the differences caused autism. "The frontal lobes, home to higher reasoning are greatly enlarged, due mainly to excess white matter, the brain's connector cables. The brains of kids who develop autism are growing at an unusual rate by age 2 and have puzzling signs of inflammation" (Wallis, 2006a, p. 45). Some researchers have documented that the brain of an autistic four-year-old is as large as the brain of a thirteen-year-old without autism (Wallis, 2006a, p. 46).

In addition to this, the corpus callosum, the connector between the right and left hemispheres, is smaller than it is in other brains. On the other hand, the amygdala is much larger. Just like the frontal lobes, the cerebellum is enlarged with much myelin or white matter (Wallis, 2006a, p. 45).

In general, in an autistic brain, there are intense local connections causing high local brain activity. Because the connectors to other parts of the brain are not as strong or as present (e.g., the corpus callosum is smaller), there is not enough communication from brain section to brain section. This results in a lack of synchronization or coordination. Because the amygdala is larger, the sensitivity to potential threats is highly increased. A simple act of looking at another face may trigger an emotional reaction. As the cerebellum has a great deal of myelin, there is difficulty in smooth physical coordination and the carrying out of motor responses (Wallis, 2006a, p. 45).

Since there is so much potential threat to the autistic brain, creating solid, structured, safe environments is paramount. Needless to say, showing anger or displeasure can really ignite the sense of threat. Keeping tasks small and focused also is important. As in many situations, each autistic brain is different and challenges the teacher to figure out exactly what will work.

BRAIN COMPATIBILITY AND MULTIFACETED LEARNING

The brain-compatible classroom, therefore, is a classroom that is student-centered rather than teacher-centered. In other words, the action is happening with the students instead of all the students watching only what the teacher is doing or listening to what the teacher is saying. In a brain-compatible classroom, the teacher is using multiple approaches to get information and concepts across to the students. Consequently, the students have choices about how to learn and how to show what they have learned. Each student in the class experiences appropriate challenges within a nonthreatening environment.

The brain-compatible classroom depends upon, among other things, the teacher becoming a "brain-compatible" teacher. Teachers need to recognize each facet of an enriched learning experience (the learner, the content, and the activity) to bring the concept of brain-compatibility into focus.

Nine Facets of Brain-Compatible Learning

I. Learning becomes relevant through personal context.

II. Learning is dependent upon motivation.

III. Learning is reinforced through hands-on experience.

IV. Learning requires linking new information to prior knowledge.

V. Learning is achieved more efficiently when information is "chunked."

VI. Learning is enhanced with time for reflection.

VII. Learning is retained longer when it is associated with senses and emotions.

VIII. Learning occurs for the greatest number in an environment that fosters and accommodates various ways of being smart.

IX. Learning is a high-energy activity.

Figure 1.5, "Brain Compatibility in Focus," illustrates the interaction and relationship between brain-compatible learning, the learner, the content, and the activity.

The Learner

Most teachers are well grounded in the content before setting foot in the classroom. Once there, however, the primary focus needs to be on the learners they encounter. Who are they? What are their strengths and gifts? What are their weaknesses? What are their life experiences? What makes them tick? It is important to look not only at the characteristics and dynamics of the group but also at those of each individual. Without some sense of who these learners are, it is impossible to create a brain-compatible classroom.

Figure 1.5 Brain Compatibility in Focus

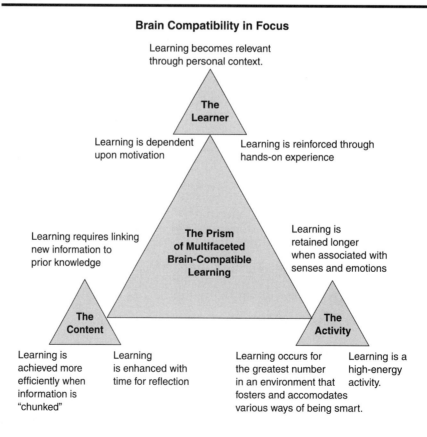

I. Learning Becomes Relevant Through Personal Context.

"Our brain is most efficient at recalling and using episodic memories that have important personal meanings" (Sylwester, 1995, p. 96). Students are better able to understand information when they integrate learning with their own life experiences. The brain responds best in a learning environment when it can make the connection between the learning going on and real-life applications.

When one connects learning to material that students perceive to be useful in real life, the brain is more alert and pays more attention to that learning. It is more feasible to introduce a lesson or subject with a demonstration, video, or case study that "shows the relevance of the new topic to real-life concerns; and stimulates serious questions in each student's mind" (Fitzgerald, 1996, p. 20) in an extended time format. Teachers need to draw the connections explicitly to real-life even when they may seem obvious. An aura of importance that automatically provides its own motivation to the student thus surrounds new material. In fact, the more the process of seeing the meaning and connection of the material presented to everyday life engages the student, the better it is.

Teachers preparing lessons for use in an expanded time block need to work hard at making crystal clear the connections and the relevancy to real life. Teachers can introduce units or lessons with a simple hook that helps the students see the connections to real life. A short video; a reference to a current news event; a reference to a TV character, to a music star, or to a movie star; a line from a piece of popular music; or a recent neighborhood or community event can all help students make the content material relevant.

Teachers can create thought-filled questions to help students make these connections. Engaging, complicated tasks can also energize student thinking so they can discover the relevancy on their own. With the help of their colleagues, teachers can come up with the kinds of "complex, interactive tasks" that require the student to grapple with the content.

Students come to school immersed in real life. Their own lives, television, and movies make it inescapable. Real life fills their brains before they walk into school. A student's real life context creates a tableau that educators can use by showing how what they have to teach can assist the student in the journey through life.

II. Learning Is Dependent Upon Motivation.

Students will file information in long-term memory when new information motivates and interests them. Attending to this new information does take energy and concentration; therefore, teachers need to design learning activities to enhance motivation and pique student interest. "Memory is impossible without emotion of some kind, that emotion energizes memory. The practical consequence is that the enthusiastic involvement of students is essential to most learning" (R. N. Caine & G. Caine, 1991, p. 57). Understanding what is motivational for students is critical to their successful learning.

Teachers can discern what motivates their particular students by doing the following:

- simply asking individual students directly;
- paying attention to what the students like to write about;
- listening to the conversations going on in cooperative groupings;
- speaking informally with students before or after class;
- providing options, alternatives, and choices in assignments.

III. Learning Is Reinforced Through Hands-On Experience.

Hands-on experience can incorporate many different skills, including practical, physical, and metacognitive, engaging students in discovery. Simulated or real experiences can elicit critical thinking as it applies to real-life situations. Hands-on experience can place the learning process into a context that students understand. Experience allows students to take concepts, skills, and information apart to understand how each part works and then put the parts together into a working whole. Long recognized as an integral part of the science curriculum, laboratories are crossing curricula. Technology/computer labs, science labs, language labs, art and music studios, school radio stations, TV-video production, and online and real-life writing labs are just some of the meaningful and authentic ways to demonstrate what students know in the fashion that best suits the way(s) they are smart.

The Content

The content has to do with the curriculum, the standards that the teachers want the students to learn. Once teachers are acquainted with the students in their classrooms, they need to find the appropriate context in which to present the content so that it will connect with those students. Skillful and effective teachers

- find out what students already know about the content;
- give the content material an illuminating framework;
- decide on a structure that speaks to their particular group of students.

IV. Learning Requires Linking New Information to Prior Knowledge.

Exploring and asking questions about previously learned and understood material helps students build a bridge from their current knowledge to new information. The key is to help students make connections between the new material and the knowledge they already possess. The brain has a limited capacity to take in unrelated, disconnected facts. On the other hand, the brain has an almost limitless capacity to incorporate material it can connect and relate to knowledge already learned. To ignore this natural memory capacity is to abandon what the student can bring to the learning.

The brain's natural memory capacity is enhanced when the individual becomes engaged in the process of organizing or creating the connections. Very often teachers deliver material without connecting it to that which students have previously learned or without engaging the student in making the connections. Stating beforehand to the student what the connections are without engaging the student in making the connections is not helpful. The effort a student uses to make his or her own connection helps make the material the student's own. More time coupled with appropriately crafted lessons offers more opportunities for students to relate new information to old information.

V. Learning Is Achieved More Efficiently When New Information Is "Chunked."

The brain automatically connects information that appears related. The brain searches for patterns in the new information it receives, and if something appears familiar, the brains connects it to what is already stored. By chunking information together, the brain begins to form a concept, a schema, an idea, or an understanding of the experience or information. The brain's ability to form patterns is unlimited and includes such things as how a nonfiction book is different from fiction, what makes an animal a dog and not a cat, what a right angle triangle is, what the characteristics of a good teacher are, what defines happiness, what the purpose of science is, and so on.

The brain has a natural drive to discern meaning in information and events as well as to discern patterns and to create order out of what seems like chaos. When the brain is given permission to seek out patterns and meaning, a great deal of learning occurs.

A key point is how much the brain resists the forcing of patterns that do not make sense. The brain's inclination is to find the patterns and create the meaning that makes sense for itself—not what makes sense to someone else. Another key point is that these are qualities of every brain. How a brain creates patterns, what patterns it creates, how a brain figures out meaning, what meanings it creates—all of this will vary greatly from brain to brain. What is consistent is that every brain is wired to create patterns and to figure out meaning (R. N. Caine & G. Caine, 1991).

VI. Learning Is Enhanced With Time For Reflection.

Reflection and metacognition can greatly aid in the whole effort of finding the patterns and drawing out the meaning of information and events (R. N. Caine & G. Caine, 1997). Metacognitive activities, which on the surface may appear to take time away from learning valuable content, are actually activities that can enhance content learning and cause the material that has been reflected upon to become part of the learner's long-term memory system. Metacognitive questioning delves into what process a student used to arrive at an answer, what thinking skill aided the student in grasping a particularly difficult concept, where a breakthrough occurred for a student, and so forth. Group discussions, metacognitive questioning, logs and journals, and graphic organizers are helpful processing tools and, perhaps, can be most efficiently employed during extended time blocks. For some students, it is only when time is allowed for reflection that lasting connections to the material are made.

The Activity

Taking into account the learner and the content, the teacher needs to think about the particular strategies and tactics that will best carry out the instruction of the content. Teachers might ask themselves the following questions: How does this content link to the senses and the emotions? (One can link all content, in some way, to the senses and emotions.) How can a teacher utilize the various intelligences to capitalize on the many ways these students are smart? What kind of energy and intensity will assist this learning? What visual tools will help the learning?

VII. Learning Is Retained Longer When Associated With the Senses and Emotion.

One retains new information, when associated with sight, sound, smell, and emotion, for a longer period.

There are many ways to make senses a part of the learning experience. Students can

- share what their perceptions or impressions of India, Pakistan, or other countries on the subcontinent are at the beginning of a lesson or unit while the teacher burns incense;
- gather information about the parts of a flower using artist Georgia O'Keeffe's paintings of flowers;
- gain a sensory and emotional connection to the 1920s, or any other time, by listening to music, wearing clothing, or playing with toys or sporting goods from that period;
- taste or make simple foods eaten in Latin America as a part of a lesson or unit on that region.

Sensory experiences provide more stimulus input that increases the chance that material will move into long-term memory.

Emotions play a crucial role in the process of learning and getting information into memory systems. Emotions are central to eliciting attention, and attention is crucial to effective learning and memory (Sylwester, 1995). Unfortunately, schools have had great difficulty understanding the role of emotion. In fact, educators have often banished emotion from the classroom, leaving the classroom a passionless and sterile place. Within the confines of the core curriculum, educators have seen emotion and the show of emotion as a transgression. Emotion was left to be explored in noncore subject areas such as "the arts, PE, recess, and the extracurricular program[s]" (Sylwester, 1995, p. 72). In so doing, educators leave out of the learning process the very necessary component of emotion. "When we ignore the emotional components of any subject we teach, we actually deprive students of meaningfulness" (R. N. Caine & G. Caine, 1991, p. 58). In other words, emotions play a vital role in the entire process of creating meaning. On a more elemental level, "Emotions are also crucial to memory because they facilitate the storage and recall of information" (Rosenfield, 1988, p. 92).

All of the just mentioned suggest that recognizing and embracing the power of constructive emotion is the key to enhancing student motivation and learning in the classroom. One reason why it is so crucial for educators to pay attention to the role of emotions is the power they can hold over cognitive abilities. According to brain researchers, this is because of the nature of the connections between the emotional systems and the cognitive systems.

Paying attention only to cognitive activities in the classroom neglects a crucial factor now becoming clear to contemporary brain research: "emotion and cognition are best thought of as separate but interacting mental functions mediated by separate but interacting brain systems" (LeDoux, 1996, p. 69). So the call is clear: paying attention to the role of emotions is a way not only to care for the students but to facilitate their learning as well.

The teacher can pose the following questions to elicit classroom discussion or can use them as "rhetorical" questions that students can respond to in their reflection journals:

- Which part of the lesson today did you like? In which part of the lesson did you struggle most?
- If you were to select a piece of music to play as background for this story, lesson, or experiment, what would it be? Why would you choose that?
- How do you suppose the Reverend Dr. Martin Luther King, Jr., felt while incarcerated in the Birmingham jail? What would have been your feelings if you had been there with him? What would your feelings have been if you were Dr. King?
- What emotions did Pablo Picasso likely experience when he created the masterpiece Guernica?
- What emotional shifts did you notice in this character? What enabled or caused the emotional shifts? What causes shifts in your emotions (positive to negative as well as negative to positive)?

VIII. Learning Occurs in an Environment That Accommodates the Multiple Intelligences.

Howard Gardner (1983), very early in his psychological research, became concerned with the narrow definitions of intelligence that educators and researchers were using. The more he researched persons possessed of full brain capabilities as well as with those impaired by brain injury, the more he began to see different intelligence capabilities emerging in different persons. Eventually, Gardner (1995) identified eight intelligences, which include visual/spatial, logical/mathematical, verbal/linguistic, musical/rhythmic, bodily/kinesthetic, interpersonal/social, intrapersonal/introspective, and naturalist. He provisionally added a ninth: the existential intelligence. See Figure 5.5, "Gardner's Eight Intelligences."

There is both good news and a profound challenge for educators in Gardner's theory. "The good news is that each of us has all of these intelligences" and "we have the ability to enhance and amplify our intelligence" (Lazear, 1991, p. ix). The challenge lies in the need for educators to perceive and encourage the rich intelligence gifts of every student in their classrooms and to discover ways to strengthen the less developed intelligences in these same students.

Expanded blocks of time may give the teacher additional opportunities to create learning activities that take advantage of more than just the logical/mathematical and verbal/linguistic intelligences in any given class period. In fact, creating activities that connect with several of the intelligences in one period can be precisely what will keep all students interested and attentive. Consequently, the content can come alive in ways not possible when a student is just listening (using verbal/linguistic intelligence) to thirty to forty minutes of a teacher lecture. Such a use of a variety of learning strategies is another way to help the students make the content in the classroom their own.

IX. Learning is a High-Energy Activity.

"The brain is about two percent of an adult's body weight, but demands about twenty percent of the body's energy" (D'Arcangelo, 1998, p. 21). Short-term memory, the process in the brain where associating, connecting, categorizing, and meaning making of new concepts occurs, requires concentrated focus and attention. New information begins to decay after thirty seconds if no rehearsal is applied. Therefore, it is important that new information be revisited several times in a variety of different ways. A time of lower intensity reflection needs to follow the high intensity of receiving new information. Pulsed learning follows the natural pattern of high-energy attention and low-energy processing or mental meanderings.

While learning requires a great deal of energy from students, the energy present in the classroom must spark and sustain that energy. Teachers who welcome the student, lessons that incorporate a variety of activities that are in tune with content objectives, and teachers who model enthusiasm can increase the energy present in the classroom, which in turn helps fuel student concentration and attention.

BRAIN-COMPATIBLE LEARNING CLIMATE

One of the critical aspects of learning that comes from brain research is that throughout history human learning has taken place in a complex environment (Bruer, 1998). A complex environment is one that is filled with limitless wonders, surprises, experiences, and observations, whether that environment is government buildings in Washington, DC or a small private farm in South Dakota. The brain is adapted for making meaning out of the complexities of its environment. When the classroom is a complex, dynamic environment, students can engage in activities that demand several brain and thought processes simultaneously. When this occurs, energy rises, motivation intensifies, and learning increases. Such things as engaging in debates, working with a small group of students to synthesize notes onto a graphic organizer, taking field trips to museums, small businesses or factories performing laboratory and field experiments, and constructing models are all examples of complex environments.

Seeing the linkages between the emotional and cognitive centers of the brain makes it clear that the atmosphere for learning is more crucial than may have previously been understood. An emotionally supportive environment can actually enhance the higher thinking processes of the brain. Expanded time formats can enable more activities and learning experiences that engage higher order thinking and problem solving. A school needs to consider the block if it believes that an alternative extended schedule could involve more and more students in significant learning activities.

Greater variety and flexibility occur in the classroom as more choices are offered to the student. In order to harness students' interests and skills, schools need to begin to match the variety, flexibility, complexity, and vitality of life outside the classroom (R. N. Caine & G. Caine, 1991).

Expanded blocks of time can permit the teacher, often focused only on the content nature of the curriculum, to add multiple intelligences arenas, thinking skills, and social skills to the focus in the classroom. Once again, this has the potential to reshape the classroom into a dynamic, interactive center of learning. Teachers working in the block report that in their experience a greater percentage of students want to come to school when this kind of dynamic, lively center of learning is taking place in classrooms. An additional comment is that such a classroom engages students who were never able to be engaged in thirty to forty minutes of lecture—thus creating classrooms compatible with the rich diversity of student populations.

The first sample Four-Phase Lesson plan acknowledges the way the brain processes information and makes the most of time in the expanded time formats by utilizing brain-compatible learning techniques as they relate to multifaceted learning. Note the four phases mentioned in the introduction: inquire, gather, process, and apply. The activities in the inquire phase of the lesson plan each raise consciousness of the brain as well as explore what students already know about the brain. Both of the activities in the gather phase encourage the students to amass and pull together relevant information. In the process phase, students discern the meaning from the information by using a graphic organizer. Finally, in the apply phase, they go one step further in higher order thinking by creating a rubric for a student presentation of the material.

"What's on Your Mind?" is a biology lesson, with curriculum connections to psychology, technology, and physical education. The biology teacher may invite a psychology or physical education teacher or a local therapist, sport psychologist, or social worker to participate in the class. The integrated curricular focus for this lesson is psychology and physical education; however, the focus could be chemistry and drugs or health issues like Alzheimer's. The reflect component of the process phase can be used as a springboard to a service-learning project. The authentic assessment tool built into the process phase is a rubric for evaluating student presentations.

Sample Four-Phase Lesson Plan

 **WHAT'S ON YOUR MIND?**

Level: Secondary

Curriculum Integration: Biology (Anatomy and Physiology), Psychology, Technology, and Physical Education

Multiple Intelligences

- ❑ Bodily/Kinesthetic
- ☑ Interpersonal
- ☑ Intrapersonal
- ☑ Logical/Mathematical
- ❑ Musical
- ❑ Naturalist
- ☑ Verbal/Linguistic
- ☑ Visual/Spatial

Content Standards

LIFE SCIENCES

Knows the general structure and functions of cells in organisms

BEHAVIORAL SCIENCE

Understands that interactions among learning, inheritance, and physical development affect human behavior

LIFE SKILLS

Understands and applies basic principles of logic and reasoning
Performs self-appraisal

TECHNOLOGY

Uses methods of information-gathering on the Internet
Identifies capabilities and limitations of technology
Uses safe and ethical behavior on the Internet

PHYSICAL EDUCATION

Uses movement concepts and principles in the development of motor skill

GRAPHIC ORGANIZERS

Inquire Phase: Chart of visuals and/or K-W-L
Gather Phase: Matrix or Concept Web
Process Phase: Students choose from several graphic organizers
Apply Phase: Students share their graphic organizers

LESSON USE OF TECHNOLOGY

Internet research of additional information on approved and recommended Web sites

ESSENTIAL QUESTION

How can an understanding of brain biology and relationship among thoughts, feelings, and behaviors help you maintain positive mental health?

The Teacher

Ms. Haws is a high school biology teacher. She wants to add more depth to her lessons, so she decides to coordinate with the psychology teacher. They work together in order to connect brain biology and function with mental health, demonstrate how thoughts influence emotions, and clarify how human behavior is a result of the combination of thoughts and emotions. Ms. Haws peruses the Internet to gather appropriate sites to recommend to her students for their Web searches. The students will create visuals to represent the information they find on such topics as Martin Seligman's Positive Psychology and Authentic Happiness Theory and Aaron Beck's Cognitive Therapy and Cognitive Behavioral Therapy. Because of their research and presentations, students will be able to analyze and identify the biological and cognitive causes of such ubiquitous stressors as actors and stage fright, students and test panic, athletes and choking, and crime victims and freezing.

INQUIRE PHASE
TWENTY MINUTES

Inquire Activity 1

Objective: Students participate in "Student Tic-Tac-Toe" energizer.

ATTEND

The teacher asks

- What happens to your thoughts when you are excited, nervous, or scared?
- What happens to your actions or your skills under the same situations?

The teacher suggests

- As you play this energizer, observe what happens to the other students. What emotions do you recognize? What behaviors do you see? What do you hear students saying?
- What feelings do you experience?
- What behaviors do you exhibit?

Experience: "Student Tic-Tac-Toe"

Figure 1.6 "Student Tic-Tac-Toe" describes the rules and game format.

REFLECT

The teacher asks

- How did students respond when they were unable to form a line and lost a round?
- How did they respond when they won?
- What happened to your thoughts and your feelings as you competed for a square and tried to form a line? How did you behave? Why?
- What kind of relationship exists in the human brain among thoughts, feelings, and behaviors?

◉ Figure 1.6

Student Tic-Tac-Toe

The teacher or student leader prepares for the game by . . .

- Creating large tic-tac-toe grids on the floor using masking tape—one grid for every two groups created. Each quadrant should be large enough to comfortably accommodate a standing person with both arms outstretched.
- Asking for two or three volunteers to serve as game referees. (The number of referees should be based on the number of students playing the game. Additional referees can be used and rotated in to make sure the teams have an equal number of players.)
- Forming teams (of six to ten persons) of equal size.
- Instructing students to count off within their teams.
- Directing teams to choose a grid and stand across from another team on that same grid.

Informing teams of the rules of the game as follows:

- The teacher or student leader randomly calls out three numbers one through six (or one through the largest number present on the team). The numbers should be written down.
- The three players from each team run into the grid and try to form a vertical, horizontal, or diagonal line. Players may not attempt to create a line directly parallel to the side where they were standing.
- Teammates outside the grid may yell out encouragement to their teammates but not disparaging remarks to their opponents.
- Referees settle all disputes over who was there first.
- When a tic-tac-toe line is formed a point is awarded to that team.
- All persons leave the grid.
- The process is repeated by calling out different number combinations.
- The referees assigned to each grid keep score for both teams.

Inquire Activity Option A (When two options are offered, choose one.)
Objective: Students draw from memory several brain structures.

ATTEND
The teacher asks
- What are the parts of the brain that you can recall?
- Is the brain's structure and function more like a computer, a jungle, or a tossed salad? Why?

EXPERIENCE: "PICTURE THIS"
Students
- in small groups of three to four, work together to draw the brain and several brain and central nervous system structures they have previously studied including Brodmann's areas, precentral and postcentral gyrus, brain stem, motor units, and any other parts they recall;
- combine their small group with another small group to share their visuals;
- repeat the sharing process one or two times.

The teacher
- asks a group to present their visual to the class and leads a short discussion on the various areas;
- clarifies any misconceptions and reinforces the connection between thoughts, physical movements, and behavior.

Inquire Activity Option B
Objective: Class prepares a KWL chart on the multifunctional brain.

ATTEND
The teacher poses the following questions, reinforces correct responses, and mediates misconceptions:
- What is a KWL chart?
- How is it used?
- When have you used it before?

EXPERIENCE: "GROUP KWL"
The teacher
- leads the students in creating a class KWL chart on the multifunctional brain;
- asks the students HOW they want to learn the material in the WANT column.

Figure 1.7

KWL Chart		
K	W	L

Students
- offer responses to the KNOW column and WANT to know column, leaving the what you LEARNED column to be completed later.

REFLECT

The teacher asks the following questions:
- What new insights have you gained already about the multifunctional role of the brain?
- How do you know when you have learned something? In other words, how do you know you know?
- How might understanding various brain structures and functions help you understand yourself and others?

② GATHER PHASE

TWENTY-FIVE MINUTES

Gather Activity

Objective: Students engage in an information gathering of specific brain terms and mental health concepts on the Internet.

The teacher
- divides the class into two small groups of three or four students, A and B (or students select a group). The teacher assigns group As, small groups of three or four students, a neuroanatomy Web site and group Bs a mental health or psychology Web site. Both A and B groups gather information at the same time.
- locates and bookmarks appropriate neuroanatomy and mental health Web sites in advance of beginning the lesson. The number of sites the teacher provides should exceed the number of small groups. Please note that teachers need to explore and monitor any Web sites they want their students to visit in advance of assigning the task.

ATTEND

The teacher focuses student attention by giving the following direction:

- Think of ways you could visually represent the information you find on the Web sites.

EXPERIENCE: "INTERNET INVESTIGATION PART 1: ALL A GROUPS"

Students

- are assigned a neuroanatomy Web site to explore in groups of three or four, and each group may explore only one site (jigsaw) or may explore each site;
- study new information on the brain and prepare a demonstration of their understanding; take notes on, download, or print out information of importance/relevance; and organize the information in a way that makes sense to them by using a graphic organizer (see Chapter 5).

ATTEND

The teacher asks students the following questions and creates a group definition of depression, anxiety, and disorder:

- What is the difference between the brain and the mind?
- What does mental health mean?

EXPERIENCE: "INTERNET INVESTIGATION PART 2: ALL B GROUPS"

Teachers assign students a mental health related Web site to explore in groups of three or four. Each group may explore only one site (jigsaw) or each group may explore each site. If a jigsaw activity is chosen, an additional gather experience would have to occur so that the groups could share information.

REFLECT

Teachers ask the following questions:

- What are the functions of some specific brain structures you can identify?
- How do you perceive the brain differently as you learn more about its many functions?
- How did the various Web sites help you understand the various brain structures and functions?
- Which sites were most helpful to you? Why?

③ PROCESS PHASE

THIRTY MINUTES

Process Activity 1

Objective: Students prepare a graphic organizer on the multifunctional brain and mental health (see Chapter 5, Figure 5.10).

ATTEND

The teacher asks the following question to focus on the next experience:

- What immediate connection can you make between the structure of the brain and the mental health of the mind? Are these direct or indirect connections?

EXPERIENCE: "THE BRAIN/MIND EQUATION"

Students

- prepare a graphic organizer (sequence or flow chart, matrix, fishbone, concept map, mind map, or any other appropriate form) by working in groups of four (two students from group A and two from group B) that shows the interplay between the multifunctional brain and mental health.

REFLECT

The teacher asks the following questions:

- How did preparing the graphic organizer with your group help you understand the information more clearly?
- What did you learn about the brain and cognitive therapy that you think most people do not know?
- What will you be more aware of regarding your brain and your thoughts, feelings, and behaviors?

Process Activity 2

Objective: Students, along with the teacher, decide on the criteria for a well-presented distillation of the information students worked with in this lesson.

ATTEND

The teacher asks

- What would an excellent presentation that sums up the lesson's content look like?

EXPERIENCE: "PERFORMANCE CRITERIA"
As a class, students

- decide upon a presentation rubric that the audience and the teacher will fill in during the apply phase to evaluate students' group presentations (see Chapter 5). Table 1.11 "Group Presentation Rubric" provides a blank of such a rubric.

Table 1.11 Group Presentation Rubric

Element	Not Quite (1)	Okay (2)	Way Cool! (3)
All group members participated	One person dominates the presentation	Assignments are distributed unevenly	Each person contributions significantly
Information presented is accurate	Several inaccuracies are included	Minor information errors are included	Information is accurate and current
Information is deliberately organized	Information is disjointed, illogical, and incompatible	Information is at times contradictory or random	Information is sequential, consistent, and logical
Presentation is logical and sequential	Presentation was random and hard to follow	Flow of presentation is at times inconsistent	Presentation is logical, understandable, and easy to follow
Visuals are clear and easily seen	Visuals are cluttered, incomplete, and unclear	Visuals support the presentation but lack depth	Visuals are eye-catching, compelling, and support the presentation
Presentation is creative and informative	Information is presented in a didactic way and lacks depth	Presentation is planned but lacks enthusiasm and interest	Presentation is energetic, interesting, and unpredictable
Presentation connects previously presented information	Lacks earlier references and continuity	Connections are at times not obvious or proper	Information is connected seamlessly and appropriately
One main concept is explored	Several ideas are presented without focus	Main concept is at times obscured	Main concept drives all the information and presentation
Includes audience participation	Presenters do all talking, participants appear disengaged	Audience members are engaged infrequently	Participants are included throughout the presentation

Comments:

Total Score

A = 27-30
B = 24-26
C = 21-23

REFLECT

The teacher asks the following questions for students to contemplate and answer in their metacognitive journals:

- What will you have to do to help your group have a successful presentation?
- What have you learned from previous presentations that will help you with this one?
- How do you think your group will perform?

 **APPLY PHASE**

FIFTEEN MINUTES

Objective: Students present the information they recalled and uncovered in the lesson in a creative and interesting way.

Apply Activity

ATTEND

The teacher

- calls on one to three small groups of four to present their graphic organizers to the class (The remaining groups will do their presentations during the next class session.);
- separates the small groups into two or three divisions (two to three small groups in a division and each small group presents to the other one or two groups in their division.

EXPERIENCE: "PRESENTING"

Students present their graphic organizers.

REFLECT

The teacher chooses from the following questions that students may answer as part of a class discussion if time allows or in the students' reflection journals:

- What excites you most about what you learned today?
- What do you want to do differently in your life because of your new understandings?

- How can you help someone who is having trouble handling his or her negative thoughts, emotions, and behaviors?
- What group could benefit from seeing your presentation? Why?

Teachers instruct students to complete the *L* column (what you LEARNED) on the KWL begun in the inquire phase at the beginning of the day's lesson.

Students complete the following activity at home:

- Identify the brain anatomy and physiological mechanisms involved in these four scenarios: (1) actor's stage fright; (2) athlete's choking; (3) student's test panic; and (4) crime victim's freezing.
- Include what happens to people cognitively, emotionally, physiologically, and behaviorally when they suffer the just mentioned conditions.

REFLECTIVE QUESTIONS

1. What are three things that struck you as you read this chapter?

2. Why is it helpful for teaching to be brain compatible?

3. What are some of your teaching strengths? In other words, what are you doing now in the classroom that is brain compatible?

4. What would you like to add or change in your teaching repertoire?

Four-Phase Lesson and Unit Design

2

Whereas short lectures and memorization play a part in learning, much more learning takes place when learners are constantly immersed in complex experience; when they process, analyze, and examine this experience for meaning and understanding; and when they constantly relate what they have learned to their own central purposes. When teachers assist students in engaging their own purposes, teachers may find that skill development, with its emphasis on practice, rehearsal, and refinement, becomes more effective. The challenge, therefore, is to fit skills and content to the learner, rather than fit the learner to the curriculum.

—Renate Caine and Geoffrey Caine, 1997, pp. 18–19

INQUIRING—GATHERING— PROCESSING—APPLYING

The challenge of lesson and unit design is to package curriculum and instruction in a way that both engages students in significant curriculum and stimulates high-level thinking skills. Information and concepts are crucial to student understanding, but just as crucial is the ability to think and to manipulate the information and concepts in ways that demonstrate that the students know how to use and apply the sum of their experience to new situations.

The four-phase lesson and unit design mirrors both the processing model (see Figure 2.1) and the natural progression of the learning process (see Figure 2.2) and is thus both brain compatible and well suited to teaching in the block.

Many of the prevailing lesson plan models are not brain compatible and do not necessarily work well as the organizational structure of a lesson in an extended time format because they

- promote one major activity during a lesson rather than several "pulsed activities" (see Chapter 5);
- do not incorporate brain-compatible activities;

◉ **Figure 2.1** The Processing Model and the Four-Phase Lesson Design

What?	Inquire Phase	• What do students know about the lesson content? • What experiences have students had? • What do others know? • What would students like to know?
So what?	Gather Phase	• So what else do students need to know? • So what are the important ideas, knowledge and skills needed? • So what do the students need to do to understand the information or improve their skills?
Now what?	Process Phase	• Now what can students do to remember this information? • Now what activities will clarify the concepts and ensure students learning and understanding? • Now what can students do with the information that will help them know it?
What else?	Apply Phase	• What else can students do with the information and skills? • What else is related to what students are learning or experiencing in their daily lives? • What else is done with this knowledge that the students can try?

- do not recommend/accommodate mediation, metacognition, or processing;
- reinforce the outmoded concept that the teacher's principle function is to disseminate information;
- lack real problem-solving and higher-order thinking focus.

◉ **Figure 2.2** Natural Learning Progression

Identify past, related student experiences and their impact on student knowledge and perception of the topic at hand.

Provide new insights and information, complex interrelated concepts, extensive concepts, and an opportunity to understand relationships and make multiple appropriate connections.

Engage students to act on the information, to reinforce concepts through involvement in various problem solving, to participate in complex tasks that require open-ended strategies, and so forth.

Consider various ways that concepts, information, and skills can be applied in settings that are new and dynamic.

On the other hand, the four-phase lesson design begins with the inquire phase, in which questions are posed that the study of the particular curriculum lesson or unit can answer. It is in the first phase that the teacher discovers what prior knowledge is present and hears the questions students would like to see answered throughout the study of the unit. Beginning connections are established here that help the class see the applicability of the content area. It is in this phase that the teacher helps to generate the kind of interest that can catalyze enough motivation to begin the serious study of the curriculum content.

The remaining three phases are built on Bellanca and Fogarty's (1991) work on the three-story intellect as described in *Blueprints for Thinking in the Cooperative Classroom.* In the gather phase, information is presented; data and concepts are researched and amassed; material is observed and described; and stories are summarized or narrated (p. 88).

In the process phase, the gathered information is analyzed, compared, prioritized, and categorized in ways that make sense for the student. It is in this phase that students begin to internalize the material of the curriculum unit and can practice a procedure, produce a product, or prepare a performance (Bellanca & Fogarty, 1991, p. 90).

In the apply phase, the internalized information is used to create a new product, is built upon to figure out the next steps, is used to imagine a different outcome, and is applied to something concrete and real in the students' lives (Bellanca & Fogarty, 1991, p. 92).

The dimensions of inquiring, gathering, processing, and applying may not flow precisely from one to the other. For example, the gathering and processing may go back and forth for awhile before actually moving on to the applying. It is crucial, however, that all four phases be included, even as they spiral back on themselves, and that the lesson and unit culminate with the students' application of the knowledge gained in the other three phases through an authentic activity or experience. It is the apply phase that helps students discern why all the effort of learning and studying is going on. When the application phase is shortchanged or skipped altogether, motivation is squelched. The four phases work together to create informed students who can utilize the material learned.

In addition to the four phases, Figure 2.3 includes space to write in the particular lesson focus, the two or three multiple intelligences to target that day, and the specific thinking skill and specific social skill targeted that day. The last line is for the lesson wrap-up, which could simply be concluding remarks by the teacher such as "Tomorrow we'll explore how the information you gathered today has implications for playing sports" or "As you can see, the insights we reflected on today reveal that the character in this play is very much like some of your friends."

Figure 2.4 describes the following three aspects relative to each phase:

- the relative potential student benefits;
- the teacher's role;
- brain compatibility.

Figure 2.3 Lesson Plan

Lesson Topic:		
Content Area(s):		

Lesson Benchmarks/Goals	Focuses Multiple Intelligences	Assessment Methods

Inquire Phase ———— Minutes	Gather Phase ———— Minutes	Process Phase ———— Minutes	Apply Phase ———— Minutes
Attend:	Attend:	Attend:	Attend:
Experince:	Experince:	Experince:	Experince:
Reflect:	Reflect:	Reflect:	Reflect:

Wrap-Up

◉ Figure 2.4 Four Phases for Lesson and Unit Planning

	Inquiring	Gathering	Processing	Applying
Function	• Raises questions the unit will answer • Discovers prior knowledge	• Information is presented • Data and concepts are amassed • Material is observed and described	• Gathered information is analyzed, compared, prioritized and categorized	• Now understood information is used to create a product or applied to something concrete in the student's life
Student Benefit(s)	• Teacher checks what they want to get out of the lesson • Student's own knowledge is affirmed	• The students collect information by various means that accommodate each student's unique multiple intelligences	• Organizing, classifying, and categorizing new information and concepts • Making connections with prior material and experiences	• Explores ways to apply the data and concepts in ways that connect with the student's real life
Teacher's Role	• Teachers assess what the students know • Teachers assess the content and skills the student need to grasp	• Prepare mini-lectures • Model learning and thinking strategies • Invite experts • Develop learning opportunities	• Organizes individual and group activities to help construct the meaning of information	• Enables the students to express their knowledge in various ways • Catalyzes applications beyond those in one content area
Brain Compatibility	• Draws on what the students know and have experienced • Calls upon the emotions to generate involvement	• Require the *students* to become immersed in data gathering • Offers interaction with peers	• Asks students to create the meaning and significance • Students teach each other to help clarify the data	• Encourages transfer and application of material learned • Occasions reflecting on the learning process

The Inquire Phase

Brain research suggests that students must bring previously formed patterns from long-term memory to working memory so the brain can connect new information with stored schemas as well as modify and expand them.

In the inquire phase, students benefit from

- constructing meaning of lesson content from their past experiences and stored information, knowledge, and understanding;
- identifying what they know about the lesson content, what they want to know about the subject, and eventually, what they actually learned;
- participating in "communities of practice"—the learning theory that states that everyone learns as part of a group and that the collective knowledge of the group elevates each member's understanding and learning—to identify the collective knowledge, skills, and expertise of the learning group through discussions and sharing;
- demonstrating or sharing what they know or think they know about the lesson content so the teacher can identify strengths and weaknesses of the group and adjust activities and time accordingly;
- gauging their level of motivation and emotional involvement in the lesson content.

The Teacher's Role in the Inquire Phase: Consultant

The role of the teacher varies within each phase and among the phases; no role fits with each phase perfectly. All four roles can be used during each phase or combined in a variety of configurations for each phase. Teachers can select the roles they feel are most appropriate for the learning experience of students. Descriptions of the teacher's role in each phase are generalizations.

The teacher acts as a consultant by assessing what the students know, what they misunderstand, what they have experienced, and what they need to improve their understanding and develop appropriate skills.

Brain Compatibility in the Inquire Phase

The activities in this phase are brain compatible because they

- draw on what the students know and have experienced;
- call upon the emotions that are linked with the knowledge;
- elicit input from peers and cooperative groups;
- help students assess themselves and others;
- begin the connection-making process with new information and skills;
- do not require a prescribed set of responses or outcomes.

The Gather Phase

In the gather phase, students benefit from

- thinking through concepts to arrive at an understanding that they construct—instead of being supplied with—information without having to think about the basis or genesis of the information;
- beginning to connect new ideas and understandings to those they previously learned;
- beginning to organize, classify, and categorize new information and concepts;
- beginning to identify patterns and relationships among new concepts and skills;
- participating in group investigations;
- collecting information by various means that accommodate each student's unique learning style and multiple intelligences.

The Teacher's Role in the Gather Phase: Presenter

As a presenter, the teacher can prepare mini-lectures, model recommended learning and thinking strategies and behaviors, present students with experiences that can teach or reinforce content, require students to present their data and/or their processes, invite experts to share their insights, and develop opportunities for students to learn from a variety of sources including technology, resource materials like books, magazines, television, the Internet, their peers, and any other appropriate sources.

Brain Compatibility in the Gather Phase

The activities in this phase are brain compatible because they

- require students to become immersed in information gathering or data collecting;
- ask students to think through the information to identify processes and to make meaning;
- offer students an opportunity to interact regularly with peers, teachers, and others who can answer questions, share information, and reinforce understanding;
- allow students a chance to learn in their preferred way without prescribing one technique or strategy;
- assist students in looking for patterns and recognizing appropriate examples;
- do not require a prescribed set of procedures for making sense of the information, so students can start with wholes and look for parts or study parts to construct wholes.

The Process Phase

In the process phase, students benefit from

- rehearsing skills in a context that is familiar and relevant;
- exploring concepts through a variety of processes, with a particular focus on the multiple intelligences;
- practicing concepts in new and challenging ways that may differ from earlier models;
- observing others as they practice to develop competencies and compare their own processes with those of others;
- receiving immediate and appropriate feedback;
- engaging in a variety of different ways of teaching and helping others understand and learn.

The Teacher's Role in the Process Phase: Facilitator

The facilitator's role is to guide learning and to help students acquire knowledge and skills. The facilitator utilizes the constructivist approach to learning by designing cooperative learning activities, group discussions, and individual reflection time. The constructivist model of learning relies on the group, the group process, and individual involvement for constructing meaning from experiences and prior knowledge. The facilitator

- organizes group activities where the synergy of group interaction discovers and constructs meaning and learning from experiences;
- leads processing and open discussions with the group(s) as they explore their understandings from experiences;
- asks participants to personally reflect on each experience.

Brain Compatibility in the Process Phase

The activities in this phase are brain compatible because they

- require students to challenge themselves;
- ask students to think through the information again and again;
- offer students an opportunity to teach others, to clarify both understandings and misunderstandings;
- allow students a chance to learn in their own preferred way without prescribing one technique or strategy;
- assist students in giving and receiving feedback;
- allow students to deviate from a prescribed set of procedures to follow the process where it takes them.

The Apply Phase

In the apply phase, students benefit from

- looking for other curricular connections with the skills, knowledge, and concepts they learned;

- exploring ways to apply the lesson material that are different from what was used in the lesson;
- choosing various ways to express their understanding or demonstrate individual competence;
- evaluating the effectiveness of the learning and the validity of the information or skills they have acquired;
- completing the homework assignments;
- engaging others to explore and compare their understanding.

The Teacher's Role in the Apply Phase: Mediator

The mediator's role is to guide, realign, and focus students' thinking and attention through learning experiences. The mediator uses metacognition activities, diagnostic/prescriptive assessments, and techniques that occasion transfer. The mediator

- guides the direction of students' reflective or introspective thinking;
- identifies students' problems or concerns, helps them realize their particular challenges, and assists and encourages them to modify their understandings and behaviors;
- focuses students' attention on key ideas, main themes, or critical issues by eliminating distracters such as side issues or extraneous information;
- explores with students the personal meaning and the various applications of each experience or episode;
- encourages students to transfer their new knowledge to broader applications.

When fulfilling the role of mediator, teachers need to

- label and draw attention to their instructional strategies and behaviors;
- think "out loud" as they perform cognitive functions like problem solving, making conceptual or informational connections, recognizing patterns, or identifying relationships;
- discuss how their experiences lead to new understandings or insights that occurred through self-reflection, introspection, and personal evaluation;
- provide feedback to the group;
- reveal their own strengths and challenges;
- explore other applications of what has been learned by teaching students how to transfer their understanding to related disciplines and concepts;
- encourage students to do the same things modeled by the teacher.

Whichever role teachers assume throughout the course of a lesson, they select the teaching strategies that will help them accomplish the role and facilitate student learning. Appropriate instructional strategies keep students focused and engaged in making meaning of the learning experiences.

Brain Compatibility in the Apply Phase

The activities in this phase are brain compatible because they

- require students to look for ways to transfer the information, concepts, and/or skills to activities outside the classroom;
- ask students to search for curriculum connections, allowing the brain to make numerous links;
- offer students an opportunity to scaffold learning by engaging in homework activities that require them to extend concepts or create guidelines;
- allow students a chance to demonstrate, in a variety of ways, their understanding of the lesson content;
- assist students in reflecting on their own learning processes;
- allow students to become independent in designing additional learning activities.

FOUR PHASES ASSIST IN SCHEMATA FORMATION

One needs to design learning experiences with schemata in mind. It is necessary to determine the accuracy and inaccuracy of students' existing schemata, the depth and breadth of their existing schemata, and the number and quality of their past experiences. In addition, you can help your students generate and refine schemata, acquire the general knowledge and experiences they need to create and refine schemata, and help them become competent in procedural knowledge. Table 2.1 is a chart of schemata development guidelines and relevance of schema in each phase.

Table 2.2 provides additional assistance for the teacher as the teacher prepares a four-phase unit or lesson.

When teachers use the four-phase lesson plan, they have an opportunity to differentiate their instruction by selecting a minimum of four best practices to help students engage with the lesson content in several different ways and help students participate in a natural learning progression. For each phase, teachers can select the most appropriate instructional strategies to help students accomplish the purpose of the phase. Refer to Table 2.2 for best practices options.

⦿ **Table 2.1** Schemata Development Guidelines

Teacher: Schemata Development Guidelines	Lesson Phase	Learning Activities
Provide experiences for students to help them generate general knowledge and understand basic concepts. Students with learning difficulties often lack adequate general knowledge or have very different experiences based on cross-cultural backgrounds. Students understand abstract concepts best when these concepts are built upon a foundation of general knowledge consisting of concrete and relevant information. General knowledge provides the framework for the creation of schemata.	Inquire and Gather	Students can watch video clips, go on field trips, participate in authentic experiments, engage with guest speakers or experts, watch demonstrations, interview other students, explore concepts on the Internet, listen to relevant tapes, TV or radio programs
Help students build schemata and make connections among ideas. Students can use a variety of multiple intelligences learning activities for each concept including connections to real-life situations. Engage students with experiences and information that can help them acquire the prerequisite knowledge they need in order to form appropriate schemata.	Process	Students prepare a product or performance through graphic organizers, class discussions, student-generated songs or poems, student-acted role-plays or skits, illustrations on charts or other visual aids, examples or models of applications
Assess prior knowledge. Helping students bring their schemata into working memory is essential for students to comprehend new information, refine or modify incomplete or inaccurate schemata, and establish new connections.	Inquire	Students participate in or complete: K-W-L charts, agree/disagree statements, preassessment quizzes or tests, class discussions of related experiences, student demonstrations
Require students to identify what they already know every time you present new content.	Inquire	See above
Assist students to become conscious of the processes they use to attend to new information or participate in new and relevant experiences as they develop or expand schemata.	All	Students reflect on metacognitive questions and higher order thinking questions, construct categories, develop procedures, generate theories, identify connections and applications
Challenge students with contradictory yet accurate and relevant information that questions their suppositions. Provide examples and matched nonexamples to help students create viable schemata. When students feel internal conflicts or contradictions to their perceptions, they will attend more closely to the constructs of the schemata they are creating or modifying. Recognize the tension and be sympathetic.	Gather and Process	Students collect and prepare examples, matched nonexamples, real-life problems (problem-based learning), debates, projects, jigsaw, reciprocal teaching
Dare students to examine their long-held and strongly believed schemata. Some students will find it difficult to modify their schemata. Many may prefer to live with inconsistencies rather than to change a deeply held value or belief.	Process and Apply	Students engage in peer teaching, tutoring, action research, service-learning projects, portfolios, integrated curriculum connections, lab experiments, simulations

◉ Table 2.2 Guidelines for Using the Four Phases

Phase 1—Inquire

Remember that the purpose of the **inquire phase** is for students to clarify their current level of expertise, evaluate the competence of their peers, and establish a meaningful purpose for the lesson.

- Determine what students already know or don't know concerning the lesson
- Ask what students want to know
- Assess what students misunderstand
- Identify students' past experiences related to the lesson
- Share the purpose of the lesson
- Measure how motivated the students are to learn the content

Phase 2—Gather

Remember that the goal of the **gather phase** is to engage students in gathering information, collecting important data, and participate in fact-finding research that will complete the lack of information, adjust the misunderstandings, and improve the weak skills identified during the inquire phase.

- Research and collect information from a variety of sources
- Synthesize information from connections and associations
- Evaluate existing information modified with new information
- Accumulate data and observe procedures
- Evaluate ideas and make sense of new information
- Observe new skills

Phase 3—Process

Remember that the goal of the **process phase** is for students to take the information they have gathered and to make sense of the new information by manipulating it in significant ways, such as with the use of the following three Ps: (1) Practice a skill or procedure, (2) Prepare a performance, or (3) Produce a product

- Provide the students choices of several ways to act upon the concepts or skills
- Engage in a variety of activities that help students store information in their long-term memory
- Use the new information so students can demonstrate understanding
- Show relationships among data points and/or concepts
- Practice and improve new or more complex skills
- Manipulate the concepts or skills to reinforce thoughtful processing

Phase 4—Apply

Remember that the goal of the **apply phase** is for students to reflect on their new levels of understanding and skills, to identify real-life applications, to make broad connections, and to perceive other functions or uses.

- Explore real-life applications of the new concepts or ideas
- Think about ways to integrate the lesson concepts or skills with other curriculum content
- Plan ways to transfer students' learning or skills into personal use outside the classroom
- Consider what else can be done with the information
- Identify ways to make the information usable and practical
- Participate in activities that apply the concepts or skills in unique ways

ESSENTIAL QUESTIONS

Another element of the lesson design that can help students focus on the purpose of the lesson is for teachers to formulate a question that captures the key concepts of the lesson. The question, when answered at the end of the lesson, will demonstrate to the teacher and students alike that the students have achieved an understanding of the lesson concepts. See the following example questions:

- In the lesson "What's on Your Mind?" a question the teacher might pose is "How can an understanding of brain biology and the relationship among thoughts, feelings, and behaviors help you maintain positive mental health?"
- In the lesson "Can Prejudice Kill a Mockingbird?" a question the teacher might write is "How can the process of overcoming prejudices and negative biases improve intelligence and creative thinking?"
- In the lesson "Circles That Cycle" a possible question might be "How can scientific thinking help you understand key applications of circles?"
- In the lesson "Gender, Age, and Pyramids—Only Your Sarcophagus Knows for Sure!" an insightful question might be "How can statistics influence an understanding of critical historical health issues among different countries?"
- In the lesson "Science Schmience or Who Framed Sir Isaac Newton?" a key question could be, "How can connecting historical events with scientific discoveries reinforce a deeper understanding of those events?"

Teachers can post the key question or write it on the board and refer to it during the lesson. Of course, asking students to reflect on the question at the end of the lesson will be an important measure of the effectiveness of the lesson design.

Teachers can ask several important questions during the four phases of a lesson to assess, diagnose, and focus the learning experience for the students. In the following tables, the first three columns (Student Assessment, Student Diagnosis, and Student Focus) are the questions teachers should ask about their students. In the fourth column (Student Reflection) are questions students should ask about their own learning. Table 2.3 covers the four categories for inquiring phase. Table 2.4 covers the four categories for the gathering phase. Table 2.5 covers the four categories for the processing phase. Table 2.6 covers the four categories for the applying phase.

◉ Table 2.3 Guidelines for the Inquire Phase

Inquire Phase

Student Assessment	Student Diagnosis	Student Focus	Student Reflection
• What do the students already know, understand, or believe regarding the lesson?	• What misperceptions or misunderstandings do the students have?	• What information should the students attend to or focus on?	• What do I know about the lesson topic?
• In what skills and at what skill level can they demonstrate competence?	• What gaps in knowledge or skills are they missing?	• What new or improved skills or strategies should the teacher model for students?	• What do I partially understand or what don't I understand?
• What experiences have they had related to the lesson concepts?	• How motivated or resistant are they to learning the new concepts?	• How are the lesson concepts related to the students' lives and life experiences?	• What do I assume, take for granted, or believe as fact?
		• What is the context of the lesson concept(s)?	• How do others think differently about the lesson concept than I do?
			• Which student(s) is knowledgeable on the topic and would be a helpful resource?

◉ Table 2.4 Guidelines for the Gather Phase

Student Assessment	Student Diagnosis	Student Focus	Student Reflection
• What is the main concept, topic, or theme of the lesson?	• What new schema should be created?	• How can the new information be connected to what students already know?	• What don't I understand?
• What new content, information, or skills should the students know?	• How can already existing schemas or understanding be refined?	• What experiences will clarify and reinforce student learning?	• With which concept, information, or skill do I need help?
• What are the best ways to help students learn the lesson content?	• What new skills are required or need improvement?	• What information should be committed to memory?	• What "aha's" (I realize I understand or know the concept or skill) did I have?
		• What and where are the best sources of information?	• How do other students understand or learn the content?
			• What is the teacher doing and why is the teacher doing it?
			• How do I know that I "know" the information?

Table 2.5 Guidelines for the Process Phase

Process Phase

Student Assessment	Student Diagnosis	Student Focus	Student Reflection
• What complex and integrated experiences will facilitate students' learning?	• How many students can participate at one time in practicing or rehearsing the skill or investigating the information?	• What activities will help me clarify the information or concepts?	• What skills do I need and want to practice?
• What is the social context for the skill or information?		• What is the best way for me to learn and understand the information?	• What mistakes do I continue to make and how can I correct them?
• What will clarify the skills as pertinent or the information as relevant to the present lives of the students?	• What projects or activities will replicate the way the skills and information will be used outside the classroom?	• How will acquiring these skills or understanding these concepts benefit me?	• What new information or insights have I gained as a result of the activity I just engaged in?
• How many practice opportunities do the students need?	• How many different practical options or choices do the students need to help them make meaning of the lesson content?		• Am I satisfied or dissatisfied with my current level of expertise or understanding?
• What practice activities or rehearsal experiences will simulate "real-world" applications?			

Table 2.6 Guidelines for the Apply Phase

Student Assessment	Student Diagnosis	Student Focus	Student Reflection
• What skills or concepts can students transfer to new, real-life applications?	• What additional understandings do they need?	• What skills do I need to solve problems or perform classroom tasks?	• What can I do to apply these skills and concepts in my life?
• Can students use the information and concepts to invent new applications?	• Are the activities limiting students' progress by requiring them to do the same tasks again and again without transferring them?	• What examples are others providing that can help me make connections and see applications of the lesson?	• Where do I observe others using these same skills and drawing on the same information?
• Can students transfer their new skills?	• Are students bored with the tasks because they are too easy or are they resistant to the tasks because the tasks are too difficult?	• What skills will I need to excel in my work, in managing my life, or in maintaining my relationships?	• How is this or similar information used in my other classes?
• How have they practiced previously taught skills?			
• How competent or how expert are the students' new skill levels?			

ATTEND—EXPERIENCE—REFLECT

Three components—attend, experience, and reflect—are central to each of the four phases and are discussed in the following sections. These three components are a suggested flow through each of the four phases.

Attend

In the attend component, teachers help students understand and appreciate what they are learning and experiencing by guiding them through each learning activity. Students learn how to think about information, how to filter out unimportant or irrelevant details, how to organize their thoughts, how to make sense of new experiences, and how to connect new information with what they already know or understand. Teachers help students focus their concentration and raise their level of consciousness or mindfulness by asking discerning questions and by assigning students specific cognitive tasks. For example, (a) if students watch a video, the instructor encourages students to focus on specific elements of the video; (b) if students read a chapter in a book, the instructor identifies the details that the students should consider while reading; and (c) if students research the Web, the instructor clarifies the research topics or important information students need from their research.

The purpose of the attend section within each phase is for students to begin to make meaning of each learning experience or new information. During every experience, students should focus on the meaning of the experience by reflecting on or thinking about particular aspects of the experience as they occur. Thinking during the experience is as important as the experience itself. And helping students filter out extraneous information or helping them focus their attention is itself an important learning process.

Experience

Learning is ultimately active and experiential; therefore, the learning activities, instructional strategies, and experiences presented to students in the experience section will affect students' perception, thought processes, and ability to process the activity's content.

The learning activities of each phase are student centered. The activities are based on best practices and on brain-compatible learning processes. The variety of activities in each phase taps into the different learning styles of students and their different multiple intelligences. Because the activities are "active," students remain engaged throughout the lesson. Students become responsible for their own learning while the instructor assumes the role of facilitator, coach, mediator, guide, encourager, mentor, and observer.

Reflect

Reflection, as used here, is a thinking process in which teachers lead students through intrapersonal reflections and group discussions to assist students in a meaning-making process. Reflecting on a learning experience requires students to revisit the thinking they were encouraged to attend to throughout the learning activity. Reflection gives students a chance to process and discuss what they have just learned or experienced. As students encounter new information, they need time to make sense of it and to connect what they have learned with other things they already know or understand. When students share their perceptions and understandings, they offer insights to each other. Such social interaction reinforces what the students learned or challenges what they think they learned. As students verbalize or write down what they understand, they are forming an observable expression of their comprehension for themselves, their classmates, and/or the teacher, depending upon the reflection activity. They are able to consider again and again what they just experienced. Revisiting the learning activity assists students in creating meaning from the information, and consequently, in strengthening brain connections with prior knowledge and experience.

As students share their perceptions, understandings, and insights, they reinforce their learning or challenge their thinking. As students express what they think they understand, they are required to express their comprehension of the material and to consider again and again what they just experienced. Revisiting the learning activity assists students in formulating the meaning of the information and in strengthening connections with patterns they have already established. Reflecting also helps the brain store the information as long-term memory.

INTERNAL STRUCTURE

Inherent in the four phases is the idea that at least four different activities are included in each lesson. However, teachers may include additional activities in selected phases, or even revisit that phase at a later time in the lesson, depending on the desired emphasis or the needs of the students. By engaging in at least four different activities, students

- participate in four beginning-end-middle (BEM) cycles (see Chapter 5);
- cycle through at least four attend-experience-reflect sequences;
- benefit from pulsed learning;
- interact with the information in four different ways, allowing different learning styles and intelligences to be used;
- stay on task within the recommended "age plus or minus two minutes" time frame;
- receive feedback at least four different times from the teacher, from peers, or through self-evaluation;

- take time to build understanding through the use of multiple examples or experiences;
- engage in metacognition and processing of the lesson at least four times throughout the lesson.

INTEGRATED ASSESSMENT

The attend and reflect sections of the attend-experience-reflect sequence of each phase of the lesson plan are ideal for integrating assessment and learning. (See sample lessons at the end of the chapters.) During the attend activities, students can focus on the requirements of a job well done illustrated by a criterion-based rubric. Keeping the requirements in mind as a standard, students can monitor themselves during each learning experience. The reflect strategies can serve as the checkpoint for students to reflect on how their performance compares with the rubric. The continual evaluation helps students determine how closely their behavior approximates the ideal standard. The extended time format provides teachers with the opportunity to engage regularly in the attend and reflect activities critical for integrating authentic assessment tools into a teaching design.

COMPARE/CONTRAST FOUR-PHASE LESSON WITH TRADITIONAL LESSONS

When teachers learn about the four-phase lesson design, they readily identify ways in which their traditional lesson plans are both similar and dissimilar. Table 2.7 compares and contrasts the four-phase lesson with a traditional lesson. Notice that the similarities between the two models can make for an easy transfer for teachers moving from the traditional lesson model to the four-phase lesson model.

BENEFITS OF FOUR-PHASE LESSON DESIGN

According to Michael, an athlete and education major, after learning the four-phase lesson design, "It makes designing lessons so easy. I finally understand how to create learning experiences that really help kids learn. I like it a lot."

After learning how to use the four-phase lesson format, Cindy, a veteran teacher, reflected, "I used to include many of the same elements in my lessons, but never in this sequence, and rarely did I include all of them. This lesson format is a great reminder to include all the important steps in learning. It also encourages me to change what I do in the classroom and not get stuck doing the same things."

Table 2.7 Comparing and Contrasting a Four-Phase Lesson With a Traditional Lesson

4-Phase Lesson	Similarities	Traditional Lesson
• Logical sequence of learning activities	• Graphic organizers	• Students focus on the teacher during the lesson
• Set times for frequent and in-depth reflection of learning activities	• Research-based teaching strategies	• Teacher works hardest during the lesson
• Multiple and diverse teaching strategies	• Cooperative learning activities	• Students primarily listen during the lesson
• Focus is on students engaged in generating information and data	• Student outcomes assessed	• Students read teacher-assigned materials
• Teacher prepares beforehand for the learning activities the students will experience	• Student performances, projects, presentations, and so forth.	• Teachers and students alike typically use verbal/linguistic and logical/mathematical intelligences during the lesson
• Students construct their own meaning out of the data, information, and concepts they collect		• Primary assessment tool is a paper/pencil test or quiz
• Brain-compatible instructional strategies		

Carlos, a student teacher, described using the four-phase lesson design: "I was having a hard time with the lesson plan I was taught in college. It seemed so complicated and hard, and I got confused. The four-phase lesson plan is simple. It helps me think through the steps that will really help my students learn. They're having fun with my lessons, and so am I."

Keiko, a young teacher, shared that, "I used to rack my brain trying to come up with ways to differentiate my instruction. The four phases make that process so easy. I'm really starting to change my role in the classroom, and I am enjoying my students a lot more."

These comments are typical of what many educators think when they have used the four-phase lesson format. The critical elements from the lesson design and from the comments of teachers using the four-phase lesson format are that it

- is simple to follow;
- provides meaningful direction to the teacher and students;
- supports differentiation in instruction and learning activities;
- is based on best practices and learning theory;

- changes the teacher's role for each phase;
- engages students and teachers in fun and challenging learning experiences;
- focuses on student learning and growth.

PLANNING A UNIT AND A LESSON

Unit Design

A unit is a division of information for study supported by state and/or national benchmarks and standards. (See Chapter 3 for a discussion of the development and impact of standards on curriculum.) The underpinnings for the teaching unit are formed by standards that are knowledge related, that support understanding of major concepts, and that provide required skill development. Units can be centered on the following:

- Themes (human rights or life)
- Concepts (gravity or democracy)
- Issues (women's suffrage or religious differences that lead to political and social crises)
- Skills (short story writing or the use of a protractor or other measurement device)
- Problems to solve (any shortage or scarcity or pollution)
- Knowledge to relate (historical events and their contemporary counterparts)

Units follow a developmental process to ensure the acquisition of both skills and understanding. Figure 2.5 provides an outline for teachers to construct four-phase unit plans of their own. In addition to the four phases, the blank "Unit Plan" page includes space to note the unit standards and curriculum goals, the particular multiple intelligences to be stressed overall, and the assessment tools and methods for the unit. The wrap-up could include remarks by the teacher concerning how the unit will connect to the next one; a mention of how this unit has implications for other content disciplines; or a comment on what he or she is particularly pleased with in terms of the class work on the unit.

The Lesson/Unit Dynamic

Units must be composed of an adequate number of lessons to ensure that objectives of the unit are met. The unit follows the same cycle as the lesson (inquire-gather-process-apply). It is important to remember that while each lesson within the unit has four phases the lessons themselves may be concentrated in one phase more than the others. Figure 2.6, "Emphasis at Each Phase of the Unit," illustrates the lesson emphasis at each phase of the unit.

◉ Figure 2.5 Unit Plan

Unit Topic:		

Unit Content Standard/Goals	Focuses Multiple Intelligences	Assessment Methods

Inquire Phase	Gather Phase	Process Phase	Apply Phase
___ Class Meetings	___ Class Meetings	___ Class Meetings	___ Class Meetings

Wrap-Up

Figure 2.6 Emphasis at Each Phase of the Unit

Inquire Phase		Gather Phase	Process Phase	Apply Phase
Inquire Phase	Gather Phase	Process Phase	Apply Phase
Inquire Phase	Gather Phase	Process Phase	Apply Phase
Inquire Phase	Gather Phase	Process Phase	Apply Phase

In addition, enough time needs to be allocated for student understanding and skill acquisition, as well as for student demonstration of understanding and skills. Units may last for one week or for three to four weeks. The number of lessons per week will depend on the particular extended time format used.

The school year can be separated into the following time frames:

- 36 weeks = Yearlong course; from 12 to 18 units
- 18 weeks = Semester, or one-half year, course; from 6 to 9 units
- 12 weeks = Trimester, or one-third year, course; from 3 to 6 units
- 3 weeks = Minicourse; 1 or 2 units

If a month long unit in traditional schedules has now become just two weeks in a four-by-four block scheduling format, for example, these four phases can be laid out over the two weeks.

- Day one: the inquiry phase
- Days two through five: the gather phase, pulling together all the necessary information on the unit at hand
- Days six through eight: the process phase, spent using various methods and working with the material gathered in the previous phase
- Days nine and ten: the apply phase, in which the material is applied or expanded on, or something new is created from it.

Such a plan calls for a whole new form of information delivery. It absolutely necessitates using the students to prepare and deliver some of that information, and it demands that the teacher become a facilitator in addition to being the instructor.

The four-phase unit format that encourages meaning making for each successive experience throughout the unit mirrors the cycle followed in lesson design. Each lesson of the unit is an experience, and the progression of experiences throughout the unit helps students in their individual meaning making of the unit goals and objectives.

The unit format, the lesson design, and the teaching strategies used throughout the unit are based on brain research and proven instructional techniques for facilitating learning. Four fundamental strategies serve as the basis for each unit of instruction: cooperative learning, multiple intelligences, higher order thinking skills, and graphic organizers. (See Chapter 5 for a discussion of each.)

Before designing the content flow and sequence of the unit, teachers can ask themselves these essential questions:

- What are the key concepts students need to learn during this unit?
- What skills ("know how") do the students need to demonstrate and represent their understanding of the concepts?
- What are some individual and general applications ("know why") of the key concepts?
- What experiences will provide students with not only emotional connections to the concepts, but also with the invaluable insights into the meaning and applications of the concepts?

After the framework for the unit has been set (see Figure 2.7), the teacher then determines the delivery structure. In the case of the biology unit example, thematic instruction is used in the inquire phase, problem-based instruction and case studies in the gather phase, performance learning in the process phase, and both project and service learning in the apply phase. The lessons are then "hung from" the scaffold of the delivery structure.

Inquire Phase

The purpose of the first phase of the unit is to investigate what students know about the unit concepts and what skills they possess, and to identify the goals and objectives of the unit. In addition, during the first phase, the teacher and students may decide how to assess changes in student "know how" and "know why."

Gather Phase

The goal of the gather phase of the unit is to obtain information that introduces students to new ideas, concepts, or skills. Teachers can also select activities that help students understand why they each have diverse associations or different understandings regarding the new information and skills. Students can also be assisted in linking the new information with their past experiences and connecting their new knowledge with insights and concepts they have stored in long-term memory. During this phase, teachers can select examples that place the new information and skills into context for the students. Context provides students with an understanding of how useful and practical the new information and skills can be.

Unit Topic: Cardiovascular system			
Unit Content Standard/Goals	**Focuses Multiple Intelligences**		**Assessment Methods**
Understands the major systems of the human body			

Inquire Phase	**Gather Phase**	**Process Phase**	**Apply Phase**
<u>1</u> Class Meeting(s)	<u>3</u> Class Meeting(s)	<u>2</u> Class Meeting(s)	<u>2</u> Class Meeting(s)
Video excerpt "Incredible Journey"	Describe projects	Each team creates a matrix, fishbone, or concept web on info gathered	Finish projects
Discussion	• design a video presentation for PBS on how to keep your cardiovascular system healthy	Debate	Present projects
Web graphic organizer on definition of systems		• Exercise has/has no effect	Self-evaluation in journal
Small group study of paragraphs on social, biological, ecological, and solar systems	• sculpt a detailed model of the cardiovascular system	• Tension has/has no effect	Peer performance evaluation checklist
Fishbone graphic organizer on traits of systems	• create a brochure containing guidelines for person recovering from heart attacks	• Unhealthy diet has/has no effect	
KWL on cardiovascular system	Create project plans	Quiz on important facts and details	
	Share info sources	Give time to work on projects	
	Submit project plans		

Wrap-Up
Show how this unit provides a bridge between what was studied up until now and future work

Process Phase

Processing the new knowledge and skills that students have acquired during the gather phase occurs through a variety of activities. Students can participate in practice drills, in peer tutoring, in preparing charts and graphs, or in any number of student performances that will reinforce their understandings, clarify any misunderstandings they might have, and possibly add new understandings or insights related to the unit concepts.

Apply Phase

During this last phase of the unit, the focus of the learning activities is on relating the new knowledge and skills to real-life settings. Relevance and application are the primary goals of this phase. In order for students to transfer unit concepts to their other courses and to other real-life experiences, students can be asked to look for examples of *who, how,* and *when* they have seen others use the skills and knowledge presented during the unit. They can be asked to make connections to activities with which they are already engaged. Further, they can share with each other the insights they have gained as they have reflected on the unit concepts and how they can be applied to their lives.

Function Follows Form

It is important for teachers to follow the four-phase plan presented here because it reminds them of the various components of the learning process and of the reason for using their strategies. It can help them provide diversity in learning opportunities for students. The design can help teachers remember to include successful strategies and techniques they used to use, but discarded, lost, or forgot over time. In addition, it helps teachers think about and evaluate the effectiveness of their instructional strategies. The lesson design also helps students recognize a process they can use when designing their own learning experiences.

A Four-Phase Unit Example

The following is an example of incorporating the four-phase lesson plan principles into designing a unit.

Mr. Morrison is teaching a unit on American history, 1815 to the present. He has taught this unit before and he now wants to include more brain-compatible strategies and to follow the sequence of learning identified in the four-phase lesson format. He reviews the standards and determines that he can accomplish the objectives in eight lessons. For the lessons' theme, he chooses to explore how the events of this particular time frame influenced American thought and culture. To provide the context for this unit of study, he writes a critical question that will help the students process and connect the information they will be gathering. His instruction and assignments will also reinforce the lesson context.

He poses the following unit question: How have the events from 1815 to the present changed how Americans view their responsibilities as citizens, impacted current American culture, and influenced how Americans view both federal and state governments?

Outcome: Students will have a major project to complete during this unit. They can choose from a number of assignments. The assignments include the following:

- In pairs, students will prepare a debate addressing the need for war versus the need for pacifism in resolving major conflicts (or a topic of the students' choice, approved by the instructor).
- Independently or in a small group, students will prepare a history of the musical genre that accompanied each major event.
- Independently or in a small group, students will complete a visual time line of the types of jobs available to Americans throughout this time frame.
- In a small group, students will portray the growth of the women's liberation movement, U.S. influence internationally, science advancements.

Inquire Phase of the Unit

During lessons 1 and 2, Mr. Morrison will spend a little more time determining students' level of understanding and misunderstanding regarding this unit. He will introduce the objectives of the unit and then, with the students, he will complete a KWL for the unit. He will also prepare agree/disagree statements that target students' understanding of the objectives of the unit. Both the KWL and the students' responses to the statements will help guide the role Mr. Morrison will play and how much work he will have to do to repair misconceptions and fill in the gaps in the students' knowledge.

Lesson 1: How did the Civil War, the Mexican-American War, and westward expansion impact the American culture during the formative years of 1815 to 1899?

Mr. Morrison decides that the students will spend most of this first lesson gathering and discussing information on the Mexican-American War, the Civil War, westward expansion, and nationalism. For the process activity, students will compare/contrast the differences among citizens living in the three regions of the United States during this time: the industrialized Northeast, the slavery South, and the rugged West. Students will create visuals to represent each region.

Lesson 2: What were the causes and how was the United States impacted as a result of America's involvement in World War I?

During this lesson, students will gather information on such concepts as the selective service, World War I, industrialization, isolationism, and European influences in America. For the process activities of this lesson, students will take a position—an ally or the United States—and role-play a diplomatic exchange encouraging the United States to get involved in the war. Students will also explore how the role of the United States changed in the world as a result of its involvement in the war.

Gather Phase of the Unit

For the next two lessons, 3 and 4, students will continue to spend time gathering information. During this phase of the unit, the students will gather the information they will need to prepare the projects they selected at the beginning of the unit. Mr. Morrison will remind the students of their assignments and he will meet with the groups and individuals to assess their progress and provide assistance where needed.

Lesson 3: What were the causes and effects of World War II on the American dream?

During this lesson, students will be exploring such powerful emblems of World War II as the Holocaust, Japanese American internments the atomic bomb, and Pearl Harbor.

Students, for the process activities, will create a graphic organizer comparing the tragedies and triumphs for each of the major wars.

Lesson 4: How did the Cold War change American (and world) culture?

Students will investigate the philosophy of communism and the clash with democratic principles.

To help put the Cold War into context during the process activities, students will create a simulation of the climate of fear as manifested during McCarthy's reign of suspicion.

Process Phase of the Unit

The next two lessons, 5 and 6, students will continue to gather information, but the major focus will be to process the previous lessons and finalize their projects.

Lesson 5: How did the cultural revolution of the 1960s and 1970s affect the American ideal?

The primary focus of this lesson is for students to explore how the civil rights movement, the Vietnam War, and space travel challenged and inspired the shift in American thought.

For the process part of this lesson, students will work in small groups and prepare a role-play of a stereotypical person from the 1960s and 1970s.

Lesson 6: How do the presentations change my level of understanding of the concepts explored in each project?

Students will share and present their projects to the class. All students will use an assessment rubric to evaluate the content and presentation of each project. Mr. Morrison will facilitate a discussion following each project and to culminate the impact of all projects.

Apply Phase of the Unit

For the final two lessons of this unit, Mr. Morrison will challenge students to explore applications, consider future directions, and evaluate the personal impact of the concepts explored in the next two lessons, 7 and 8, as well as throughout the unit.

Lesson 7: What are the present challenges Americans face as a people and a country?

Students will work in small groups to research then create a mini-lesson on one of the following topics:

- Computer technology
- Environment
- Health
- Global connectedness
- Space exploration
- Terrorism

Students will then teach each other about their particular topic.

Lesson 8: What will be my impact on the future history of the United States?

Students will take an area from lesson 7 or select another area and explore ways they think they will become part of history. They will identify their legacy.

To conclude the unit, Mr. Morrison will refer back to the KWL chart the class prepared at the beginning of the unit, and they will fill in the "L" column. In addition, Mr. Morrison will ask the students to reconsider the agree/disagree statements and reflect on the changes in their understanding. Finally, Mr. Morrison will ask the students the unit question and lead them in a final reflection on this unit.

Unit Question: How have the events from 1815 to the present changed how Americans view their responsibilities as citizens, impacted current American culture, and influenced how Americans view both federal and state governments?

REFLECTIVE QUESTIONS

1. In your own words, why might this suggested four-phase flow be brain compatible?

2. Which of the four phases are you competent in already?

3. Which of the four phases would you like to do more work in?

4. Broadly map out how you might teach an upcoming unit in these four phases (remember that you might alternate back and forth between gathering and processing before wrapping up with applying).

5. Taking one lesson from that unit, broadly map out how you might include all four phases in that lesson, knowing that depending on where you are with that unit, one phase would probably be especially emphasized.

Extended Time Formats Including Block Scheduling 3

TIME FOR BRAIN-COMPATIBLE LEARNING

The classroom environment that best facilitates the full development of the intelligences is sometimes called 'brain compatible.' For the brain to function fully, it is beneficial for the classroom to provide five elements: trust and belonging, meaningful content, enriched environment, intelligence choices, and adequate time.
—Chapman, 1993, p. 9

ADEQUATE TIME

The first four elements of brain-compatible learning to which Carolyn Chapman (1993) alluded (trust and belonging, meaningful content, enriched environment, and choices) are dependant upon the fifth element—adequate time (see Figure 3.1). Increasingly, educational professionals are exploring the concept of block scheduling and other extended time formats to meet the need for time.

To clarify what is meant by extended time formats, it is informative to be reminded of the traditional bell schedule. Elementary schools generally work on their own system of large time blocks, leaving the individual teachers the flexibility to pace and plan curriculum according to the needs of the class and the material. In middle and secondary schools, however, students often change classes every forty-three to fifty minutes, seven to ten times a day. (Shorter class times naturally mean more class changes.) A student attends classes in six or seven subjects a day, shifting classes and passing through the halls that many times. When a school adds a period for lunch and perhaps one for physical education, there may be eight periods a day. In contrast, extended time formats often provide sixty to one hundred minutes for each class period. In some cases, there are only four

◉ Figure 3.1   Five Elements of Brain-Compatible Learning

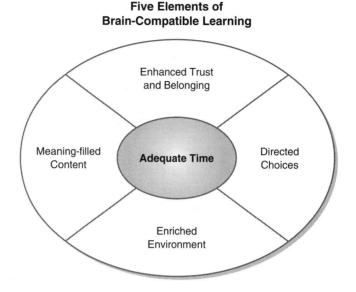

Adapted from *If the Shoe Fits . . . How to Develop Multiple Intelligences in the Classroom* by Carolyn Chapman. © 1991 by IRI/Skylight Training and Publishing, Inc. Reprinted with permission of Skylight Professional Development, Arlington Heights, IL.

class periods a day: two in the morning and two in the afternoon (see Figure 3.4, "4 × 4 Schedule"). A student may have only four subjects a day instead of six or seven.

To paraphrase Joseph Carroll (1994a), the concept of block scheduling and other extended time formats is not about time; it is about the relationship between time and learning. While more time favors brain-compatible learning, it does not necessarily in and of itself bring about greater student cognition and performance. More time is, instead, an opportunity to apply the best brain-compatible practices to instruction, thereby achieving the greatest possible results.

There is only one reason to implement extended time formats: because they meet the needs of the students. However, the resulting meaningful benefits of larger blocks of time for students include enhanced trust and belonging, directed choices, an enriched learning environment, and meaning-filled content. Following are just a few ways more time and brain-compatible learning strategies can work in concert to bring about the desired result—fully realized, thinking students (see Figure 3.2, "Expanding on the Five Elements of Brain-Compatible Learning").

Enhanced Trust and Belonging

As discussed in the previous chapter, emotion plays an essential role in the learning process. The need for an environment that recognizes and supports student comfort, confidence, and camaraderie is increasingly

⦿ Figure 3.2 Expanding on the Five Elements of Brain-Compatible Learning

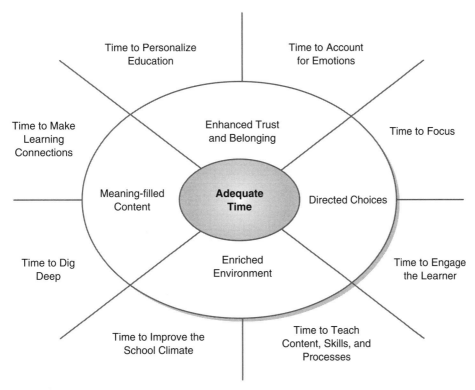

**Expanding on the Five
Elements of Brain-Compatible Learning**

important. Such knowledge informs brain-compatible teaching strategies, and extended time formats allow time for those strategies to be optimally exercised.

Time to Personalize Education

In the past, students received a great deal of emotional support from their local communities, their churches, their neighbors, and their extended families. As times have changed, such social and economic structures have themselves changed. Schools feel the ripple effect of this change in the attitudes and baggage students carry with them into the schoolroom. Now because there is often little emotional support in middle school and secondary school students' lives, school needs to be a place where that kind of support can materialize—both for the students and for the adult members of the school community. Unfortunately, the very time during which students undergo the greatest personal change—adolescence—is the same time when they are abruptly moved from the elementary school environment where they have fewer class changes per day and a greater personal connection to their teachers, to an environment where they often must deal with seven to nine different teachers per day and, conceivably, with 180 different classmates. A personal connection between an adult at school and his or her students may be the single most crucial factor in preventing students from dropping out of school (Shore, 1995). An increased level of positive student-teacher relationship actually helps "underachieving" and "at-risk" students (Brett, 1996).

Extended time formats enable the teacher to turn attention to the student as a human being. These formats can enable a human connection to occur when the teacher uses brain-compatible practices such as cooperative learning and service learning, which help develop the intrapersonal and interpersonal intelligences. Personal connections encourage lifelong learning and enhance self-esteem, both of which are more important today than ever before. Genuine, positive personal connections strengthen the school and the larger community, which is the ultimate goal of education.

Time to Account for Emotions

Research has shown the necessity of including emotions in the brain-compatible classroom. Lessons and classrooms that incorporate emotions can actually stimulate learning. One simple way to do this is for teachers to ask questions that directly relate to emotion:

- How do you feel about what this character did in this story?
- How do you feel about what this historical figure did?
- What emotions have you experienced while watching this video excerpt?
- What emotions do the characters display in this chapter?
- When have you felt something like what this character felt?

The key is for the teacher to pay close attention to students' answers, making sure that they are indicative of true emotions. "I felt confused" is more of an answer about unclear thinking than about emotions. "I was upset and angry," "I was frustrated," "I was delighted," and "I was excited." All of these answers indicate the expression of true emotion. Another simple way to tap into emotions is by learning what issues, ideas, topics, projects, or hobbies and whatever else ignite student enthusiasm. Tying learning to student interests can provide the emotional component that fuels student motivation to learn. Service learning, project learning, and case studies are profitable learning encounters because they each begin by beckoning emotions into the inquiry or exploration and then channeling those emotions into a well-defined learning task and experience. (Chapter 4 explains service learning, project learning, and case studies in depth.)

On the other hand, schools that use fear and coercion will not bring about the best results in learning and achievement. The threat of poor grades or temporary expulsion does not enhance student learning. In fact, William Glasser's (1990) research asserts that coercion can at best enable students to accomplish elemental, uncomplicated tasks and may actually impede the higher-order thinking that characterizes true understanding. Support and high challenge enable the kind of problem-solving skills and

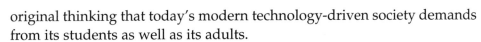
original thinking that today's modern technology-driven society demands from its students as well as its adults.

Teachers using expanded time blocks are able to create activities that can truly motivate and engage the learner because they involve the whole person. Students who

- do not handle sitting quietly for lectures have the opportunity to move around during activities and projects;
- love to talk to fellow students from time to time can do this during structured group work;
- want to share their feelings can do so during the conversations teachers lead.

Simply speaking, the goal of a strong educational program is to enable all students to learn to their capability and capacity. Students are falling through the cracks in our current educational structures. There are many reasons for this. One of these reasons is that a traditional lecture approach is not reaching some students. Some students need a more interactive, hands-on approach to learning. This can be attempted in traditional scheduling. It flows more naturally when more time allows the teacher an opportunity for input followed by an opportunity for a more interactive, hands-on activity to help students make the material their own.

Brain-compatible learning is more than just learning facts and information. Facts and information by themselves can be dry and boring. However, when facts and information become connected to practical situations, when they are rooted in real life, which naturally includes emotions, then the facts and information come alive and invite the student into more and more learning.

Directed Choices

It is becoming increasingly apparent from recent research that students learn at different paces and experience learning on their own terms. The teacher in an extended class period has the time and, one hopes, has amassed the professional resources to present students with challenging, stimulating learning experiences (options) that engage them fully in their own learning.

Time to Focus

Many teachers experience the seven- or eight-period day as rushed and hurried. Likewise, students are barely getting into material when the bell rings and it is time to go to the next class for a repeat of settling in, a dose of content, an assignment for the next day, and then another bell. "Assuming a seven-period day, a homeroom, and lunch, a typical student will be in nine locations pursuing nine different activities in a six and a half-hour school day. If the schedule includes physical education, he or she may have changed clothes twice and showered once.... It produces a hectic, impersonal, inefficient instructional environment" (Carroll, 1994a, p. 5). Traditional schools have become some of the worst environments possible for enabling concentration and focus, which is true for both the student and the teacher.

What Robin Fogarty (1996) suggested is echoed by countless teachers already teaching in some form of extended times periods. "These larger allotments of time allow students to concentrate their energies intensely on a single focus—the subject matter addressed during the block of time. In other words, the schedule itself encourages more involved, more active, and more student-initiated learning" (p. 1). Greater concentration occurs just by virtue of the fact that there are fewer hall changes. Hall changes can be unsettling and permit disorder, making it difficult for students to move into class and immediately begin focusing. In addition, the extended time block permits the kinds of activities and projects that engage students and draw forth the concentration and focus needed to accomplish learning.

Focus does not happen automatically. It does not happen automatically in a forty-five-minute class period, and it does not happen automatically in a ninety-minute class period. Michaly Csikszentmihalyi (1990) coined the term *flow* to describe a state where one's mental focus and one's emotional focus are linked together and engaged in learning. "Because flow emerges in the zone in which an activity challenges people to the fullest of their capacities, as their skills increase it takes a heightened challenge to get into flow. If a task is too simple, it is boring; if too challenging, the result is anxiety rather than flow" (Goleman, 1995, p. 93). Such a state of flow in student attention allows for the optimal and most sustainable learning experiences.

In an extended time schedule, each day the context is set, reminding the student of the direction and intention of the unit, what has happened already, and what is going to happen until the unit is completed. All of this helps the student to move from the last class and the last hall change into concentrating on the day's material at hand. Visuals can be extremely useful here to help the mind focus on the material. Many teachers find that with extended time periods, it is possible to move from material presentation to activities and projects that help make the material belong to the student. This can also enable concentration to deepen. Each of the sample lessons presented in this book follows the inquire-gather-process-apply sequence, which is most conducive to focus and is very brain compatible.

Time to Engage the Learner

The clue to engagement lies in varying what R. N. Caine and G. Caine (1991) called "states of arousal" so that interest and motivation can be sustained. While teachers may dislike the thought that the classroom could be entertaining, in order for focused rigor to take place, some interest and attraction needs to occur. In addition, without a connection to real life or the concerns the students bring to school, the content is boring, which is why teachers in extended time formats suggest the importance of a short activity that actually hooks the student into the material being covered.

"There is more time to insert such 'hooking' activities in longer class periods" (Fitzgerald, 1996, p. 20).

In the traditional schedules, teachers may feel the necessity to jump right in and get the material covered as quickly as possible. While this may serve the content and give the teacher a sense (if not the illusion) that the material is being covered, attention needs to be given to bringing the learner along. The biggest challenge for the teacher is to alter the instructional approaches so that students become engaged in choosing, directing, and fully participating in the learning process. Initially, this may seem overwhelming to the teacher accustomed to lecturing as the primary instructional strategy. Nevertheless, teachers, when confronted with the challenge of expanded time blocks, are making the effort to vary instructional approaches and create lessons that engage the learner.

The key to success in these formats is using varied instructional strategies in the classroom, which relieves boredom and maintains focus and attention. "The more closely the students are involved with the information, the more likely it will stick with them. Through research projects, collaborative activities, oral presentations, use of technology, and critiquing of one another's work, students engage more actively in the topic at hand than when simply reading or listening" (Wyatt, 1996, p. 16).

Although many teachers initially report that the shift to extended time periods takes a great deal of time and energy, they add quickly that the shift in their students' receptiveness to learning has made it all worthwhile. Brain-compatible learning is eminently engaging and, when done well, is rigorous and challenging, allowing students to pursue their greatest potential.

Teachers need to concentrate not only on the content of a particular discipline but also amass a huge repertoire of effective teaching strategies, tools, and approaches. In this way, the teacher becomes more like an artist than ever before imagined. If the content is the idea in the head of a musician, then these strategies, tools, and approaches become more like the various instruments in the orchestra from among which the composer chooses to create a piece of music. The teacher then chooses which instrument will best convey the content, will best speak to the particular class, and will ultimately captivate the learners.

Enriched Learning Environment

Expanded time scheduling is exactly the opportunity many teachers have been looking for to put into practice brain-compatible teaching approaches, which will do the job of blending content, skills, and processes. When content, skills, and processes are linked to many areas of the lives of the students, motivation for learning is enhanced.

In the past, the education system presumed that enough students would pick up high-level thinking skills on their own. Those who did not and who did poorly in school went on, if they were lucky, to find jobs in the unskilled job market. Today and tomorrow, every student will be in situations where more and more learning and relearning will be required. In the twenty-first century, it is more important than ever before that upon graduation every student have the tools to become a skilled problem solver.

Time to Teach Content, Skills, and Processes

The call today is not just for students to dig deep into the content but also for them to develop skills and learn processes that will serve them on into adult life. Some teachers report that expanded time formats permit attention to skills and processes to occur while maintaining a focus on content. Students have the time not only to process material but also to learn how to learn, without de-emphasizing content. On the contrary, there is a great need to give students a grasp of skills and processes along with the content. The content is a tool that can be used not just for its own sake but also for the sake of helping to uncover and/or to foster student problem-solving and processing skills. Content standards continue to evolve and change as new theories, technologies, and practices emerge. Emphasizing content to the exclusion of problem solving makes today's lesson obsolete by tomorrow. Students need to know how to continue learning, how to keep abreast of shifting and expanding information, and how to attain learning skills and processes to help them focus on content.

The good news is that there are teachers and schools who are implementing instructional approaches that blend content, skills, and processes. Successful teachers employ brain-compatible learning strategies such as cooperative learning, thematic instruction, and multidisciplinary curriculum in conjunction with authentic assessment tools.

Time to Improve the School Climate

"Currently, the greatest support for block scheduling appears to be related to the overall improvement in school climate and the quality of the school day for both students and teachers" (Rettig & Canady, 1996, p. 10). Teachers often comment that they recognize a dramatic positive shift in the entire school climate with the advent of extended time periods. Such teachers confirm what Canady and Rettig (1993) suggested: the mere fact of fewer passing periods encourages fewer disruptions than would normally occur during frequent passing periods. The move from many passing periods to actually just one in the morning and one in the afternoon has had a definitive calming effect in the atmosphere of schools practicing extended periods. In addition, many teachers report that a longer class period has actually enabled many students to stay focused and involved in a way not possible with the constant change of the traditional bell schedule format. An extended time format can actually reduce stress in the teaching and learning day.

As teachers become accustomed to an extended time format, they move away from their concern for how they are going to change their instruction and modify their content to working productively in a longer time format. They are then able to discern the tremendous possibilities for total change in the school climate that can occur because of well-implemented alternative scheduling. Creating a more relaxed and a more individually challenging environment can create a school where both teachers and students will want to be. Consequently, these longer formats have actually brought about a decrease in both student and staff absenteeism.

Meaning-Filled Content

True learning is more than just skin-deep. With the increasing volume of content material, teachers are in a bind. How can they enable their students to grasp all the necessary information while at the same time dealing with it in enough depth that students come away with lasting understanding and the ability to apply that understanding to new circumstances? Expanded time available to teachers and students can be just the answer.

Time to Dig Deep

Students need to grasp a huge amount of content not only to become familiar with a particular discipline but also to pass the standardized tests, to meet No Child Left Behind requirements, and to succeed in the various college boards. On the other hand, employers are asking for employees who know how to think critically, how to problem solve, and how to continue learning on the job. Exposure to material alone does not guarantee that the material has been absorbed and retained. The core curriculum is becoming ever more demanding and the volume of material massive. Gardner (2000) said succinctly what he favored: "To put it crisply, I favor depth over breadth, construction over accumulation, the pursuit of knowledge for its own sake over the obeisance to utility" (p. 39). Opportunities to make the connections, explore the meanings embedded in the material, and reflect upon and process the material are needed. Expanded time blocks can allow for significant amounts of material to be absorbed and worked with so that depth of understanding can emerge. Sadly, though perhaps not surprisingly, "much of the effort put into teaching and studying is wasted because students do not adequately process" (R. N. Caine & G. Caine, 1991, p. 84). Time to connect meaning to the material through reflective and higher-order thinking processes moves that material into long-term accessible memory. Because of the advantage more time permits, access to long-term memory may be increased. Brain-compatible learning in the context of an extended time format offers a chance for students to become genuine researchers and learners, which generates positive habits and skills that can continue into student lives beyond the final exam.

Processing and applying strategies may be practiced in the traditionally scheduled classroom; however, often, time does not allow for the presentation of learning to take place on the same day as the processing and application phases. When the processing and applying activities are presented on the following day, time must be spent going over the material presented the previous day before the processing and applying can begin. Time is actually saved when part of the longer periods is used to introduce material that is immediately followed by strategies and activities that help students process, reflect, understand, and then apply the material. The more time that elapses during which material is not processed and applied (even a span of twenty-four hours is significant), the more material that can be forgotten or lost. Conversely, when material is immediately processed and applied (as is possible most times only in the context of an extended time blocks), students have a chance to immediately realize the importance and relevance of the content.

When time for reflection and active processing is allowed, actually more material is firmly established in the brain than when vast amounts of content are rapidly covered. Teachers are finding that longer time blocks offer a great flexibility and dynamic rhythm to instruction when a high intensity activity such as team presentations is followed by one of lower intensity like journaling (see the discussion of pulsed learning in Chapter 5).

Time to Make Learning Connections

In a traditional scheduling context, subjects and curricula are discrete, fragmented pieces, which communicates to students that the world is just as fragmented and disorganized. The reality is that "[e]verything is connected to everything else," as Robert Sylwester (1995, p. 140) asserted. While Sylwester was talking about the way human brain cells and sections are interconnected, it is also true about the world teachers and students inhabit. Students are done a disservice when connections are not facilitated. Teachers in the extended time blocks have an enhanced opportunity to help students perceive the implicit connection between concepts. Conveying the big picture is difficult in traditional scheduling, and relating material to other disciplines is even more difficult.

A related concern is finding the schedule that allows the teacher to guide students to make the kind of intellectual and practical connections that well-presented material can foster in the classroom. The time spent enabling students to make such connections results in more lively participation and deeper motivation on the part of the students. Teachers themselves report experiencing elevated morale and renewed motivation when working with extended time blocks.

Reflective questions can start the connections cooking in the minds of the students. Many times teachers feel they can ask these kinds of questions only at the end of the lesson, at the end of the class period, or at the end of the unit. Instead, these connection-generating questions can be used throughout the time block and throughout the lesson. As the research is suggesting, the more connections get made, the more real learning occurs.

Examples of reflective questions teachers may pose include the following:

- What does this concept remind you of?
- Where have you heard something like this before?

- How does this remind you of something we worked on last semester?
- How could you apply this concept we have discovered in history to science, math, or language arts?
- In what ways have you encountered this principle in your daily life?

The attend-experience-reflect circuit of each phase of the four-phase lesson plan offers a built-in opportunity for ongoing reflection.

ALTERNATIVE SCHEDULING FORMATS

In 1996 eminent block scheduling researchers Michael Rettig and Robert Lynn Canady reported that more than 50 percent of high schools in the United States were using or thinking about using some form of extended time blocks. In a separate study the same year, Sadowski (1996) found that after the first year or two of adjustment, 80 percent of both students and teachers taking part in alternative scheduling prefer the extended time blocks to traditional scheduling.

More recent studies are finding that block scheduling increases student retention and achievement when the instructors vary their instructional strategies during that extended time (Gaubatz, 2003). A conclusion from research by Lewis, Dugan, Winokur, and Cobb (2005) indicated score gains in reading and mathematics from students in the block 4 × 4 plan were greater than the gains from students in a traditional schedule or a Block 8 plan.

Block scheduling can take many forms, but the following represent those most widely used. It is important to keep in mind, however, that the key to alternative scheduling is to find and modify a schedule type that best suits the particular school environment and population it is to serve.

Block 8 Plan

Some schools hold four classes one day, alternating with four different classes the next day. Such schedules are sometimes referred to as "Block 8" (also called the alternating, or the A/B, plan), and they maintain the advantage of longer class times while enabling teachers to meet regularly with students yearlong (see Figure 3.3). Consequently, the Block 8 avoids some of the sequential gaps in math and foreign language course studies that concern many people with the 4 × 4 plan discussed next. It seems that teachers can buy into the Block 8 more readily than other plans. Highly sequential subjects such as foreign language and mathematics may be best taught continually throughout the year without taking a semester or session off between classes. The Block 8 also reduces the apprehension some persons have relative to student performance on standardized tests. The concern has been that material learned in the fall will not be retained by the time the spring standardized tests come around.

◉ Figure 3.3 Block 8 Schedule

Monday	Tuesday	Wednesday	Thursday	Friday
Class 1	Class 5	Class 1	Class 5	Class 1
Class 2	Class 6	Class 2	Class 6	Class 2
Lunch	Lunch	Lunch	Lunch	Lunch
Class 3	Class 7	Class 3	Class 7	Class 3
Class 4	Class 8	Class 4	Class 8	Class 4

In any given day, students need to focus only on four classes. Many students report that they like this ability to concentrate on just four classes.

4 × 4 Block Plan

In what is also called "an accelerated" or "Block 4" plan, some schools hold the same four classes every day, completing an entire year's course in a semester. The following semester these schools hold four different classes, also completed in a semester (see Figure 3.4). What teachers like

◉ Figure 3.4 4 × 4 Schedule

Monday	Tuesday	Wednesday	Thursday	Friday
Class 1 90 min.	Class 1 90 min.	Class 1 90 min.	Class 1 90 min.	Class 1 90 min.
Class 2 90 min.	Class 2 90 min.	Class 2 90 min.	Class 2 90 min.	Class 2 90 min.
Lunch 30 min.	Lunch 30 min.	Lunch 30 min.	Lunch 30 min.	Lunch 30 min.
Class 3 90 min.	Class 3 90 min.	Class 3 90 min.	Class 3 90 min.	Class 3 90 min.
Class 4 90 min.	Class 4 90 min.	Class 4 90 min.	Class 4 90 min.	Class 4 90 min.

about such a plan is the opportunity to have only 90 students at a time (as opposed to 150 or more). Students also benefit from teachers having fewer students. It is far more likely that a teacher will get to know 90 students per semester well than would be possible with 150, resulting in a potentially much deeper student-teacher connection. Such connections have been shown to mitigate students' tuning out or dropping out.

The Copernican Plan

The Copernican model was named by its innovator, Joseph M. Carroll, for the sixteenth-century scholar Nicolaus Copernicus, who revolutionized thinking during the Middle Ages with his notion of the movements of the planets around the sun rather than vice versa. At its inception, this scheduling model may have seemed as revolutionary. It combines longer blocks of time (in ninety-minute, two-hour, or four-hour partitions—called "macroclasses") with smaller blocks of time in an extremely varied and flexible schedule. This model has tremendous advantages in terms of flexibility. When the schedule is done well, it allows students to get the classes they want at some point during their time in school. The Copernican plan, however, is complex (see Figure 3.5). Schedulers might find it a bit more challenging than they bargained for until they gain experience with it. Some educators have found that this plan is too complex to be efficiently implemented in a middle school environment.

Figure 3.5 The Copernican Schedule

Possible Day A	Possible Day B
Class 1—All Morning for 30 Days	Class 1—1/2 Morning for 60 Days
	Class 2—1/2 Morning for 60 Days
Class 2—Music/Art 70 Minutes and LUNCH 35 Minutes	LUNCH 35 Minutes and Class 3—Music/Art 70 Minutes
Class 3 Seminar or PE/Study/Help	Class 4 Seminar or PE/Study/Help

The School Calendar

Modified instructional terms can produce more time for learning. Seventy-five-day terms in conjunction with interim or mini-terms of fifteen days are one way to alter the school calendar. Intensive short courses taught during the interim terms can include enrichment, remediation, or structured review for college board or advanced placement tests, among other subjects (for an example of structured review, see Sample Four-Phase Lesson: Who Framed Sir Isaac Newton). The fifteen-day (or three-week) term can also be used for rotating teaching assignments with staff development courses. Moving from semesters to trimesters and year-round schools can also allow for greater flexibility in scheduling (Cushman, 1995).

Before- and afterschool workshops, seminars, explorations, tutoring sessions, and service-learning projects have found their way formally and informally onto school schedules with increased regularity. It seems obvious that to maintain or enhance the richness of the educational experience in or out of the block, some alteration of the school day (and even the school year) is close at hand (National Education Commission on Time and Learning, 1994).

Finally, moving to an alternative scheduling is not a magic wand that once waved over the system will automatically bring about the desired result. However, "by partitioning the school day into larger chunks of time, by looking at the concept of flexible, modular scheduling that accommodates learning, school faculties create a framework that favors the needs of the learner" (Fogarty, 1996, p. v).

The sample Four-Phase Lesson, like each of the lessons shown here, exemplifies the best practice in an extended time format setting by making the most of the time at hand. It is a middle school language arts lesson on the book *To Kill a Mockingbird* and deals with the impact of prejudice on justice. Notice the use of visuals to reinforce students' understanding of complex issues and concepts. Some of the skills developed and practiced include improving as reading and synthesizing information, recognizing bias in writing and speaking, writing a persuasive argument, debating issues, and improving critical thinking—the careful analysis of qualities and an evaluation of their comparative worth. Other topics that may be selected for this lesson include the exploration of such topics or issues as jury dynamics, human relationships, historical fiction as a genre, bigotry, tolerance, ethically principled behavior, and civil disobedience. The curriculum integration is language arts with civics and technology.

Sample Four-Phase Lesson Plan

CAN PREJUDICE KILL A MOCKINGBIRD?

Level: Middle

Curriculum Integration: language arts, civics, and technology

Multiple Intelligences

- ❑ Bodily/Kinesthetic
- ☑ Interpersonal
- ☑ Intrapersonal
- ☑ Logical/Mathematical
- ❑ Musical
- ❑ Naturalist
- ☑ Verbal/Linguistic
- ☑ Visual/Spatial

Content Standards

LANGUAGE ARTS

Demonstrates competence in general skills and strategies for reading a variety of literary texts

CIVICS

Understands issues concerning the disparities between ideals and reality in American political and social life

TECHNOLOGY

Evaluates electronic sources of information
Uses the Internet to communicate and "publish" original material

GRAPHIC ORGANIZERS

Inquire Phase: Analogy
Gather Phase: Venn diagram
Process Phase: Teacher created T-Chart of affirmative and
               negative positions
Apply Phase: Matrix

ESSENTIAL QUESTION

How can the process of overcoming prejudices and negative biases improve intelligence and creative thinking?

Can Prejudice Kill a Mockingbird?

Mr. Rodriguez is a middle school English teacher. He and his team of four core teachers work with a racially and socioeconomically diverse student population. Tensions among these factions continue to impact the school climate negatively. The team decided to adopt the theme: tolerance and intelligence—the critical link. Their goal is to show how opening one's mind to differences in perspectives, experiences, cultures, ideas, and beliefs can expand the intelligence of everyone. The math teacher has worked with the social science teacher to demonstrate the struggle between scientific advances and long-held beliefs. The math teacher also explores how statistics and other objective measures can reinforce intolerance and how math has been used to either advance critical thinking or stifle it. Mr. Rodriguez is using this lesson to teach students about the power of words and stories in creating prejudices and in opening minds and expanding thinking. Through the novel, *To Kill a Mockingbird*, Mr. Gates is helping students to research information on the Internet and other sources and helps students to recognize accurate and appropriate Internet sources.

① INQUIRE PHASE
TWENTY-FIVE MINUTES

Inquire Activity Option A
Objective: Students define terms related to prejudice, justice, and bias.

ATTEND
Students write their responses to the following reflective questions regarding bias, prejudice, and justice in their personal journals.

- What does the word *bias* mean to you?
- What are some of your biases?
- What does the word *prejudice* mean to you?
- When have you acted prejudiced? Why?
- When did someone act prejudiced against you? What happened?
- Is "justice for all" a myth? Is it possible to attain? Under what conditions/circumstances is it possible?
- How is the quality of justice related to bias and prejudice?
- On a scale from one to ten (one being completely unjust and ten being absolutely fair and equitable), how would you rate yourself? What circumstances can or have had an impact on how fair you are?

EXPERIENCE: "MIX AND MATCH"
Early in the unit, students were instructed to create an index card for each character they encountered and every incident they felt was significant in *To Kill a Mockingbird*. (The cards could have also been used to study the plot of the novel in a previous lesson.)

Students
- form groups of four and select a "secretary";
- as a class and guided by the teacher, create definitions for the following words: bias, bigotry, ethics, injustice, intolerance, justice, morality, prejudice, racism, stereotype, and tolerance.

Each secretary

- records the collective definitions on index cards for his or her group.

Students

- working in their small groups, recall or cite a specific incident from the book that represents or depicts each of the eleven vocabulary words (there may be more than one character or incident per word).

The teacher

- debriefs each group by leading a brief discussion of the examples students identified.

Inquire Activity Option B
Objective: Students create a graphic organizer analogy chart.

ATTEND
The teacher directs student attention to a quote by Victor Hugo by asking the students to

- look for the images Victor Hugo uses to express universal problems of prejudice;
- think about how Hugo might define prejudice;
- imagine a simile that illustrates your definition of bias.

EXPERIENCE: "HAUNTED BY PREJUDICE"

Superstition, bigotry and prejudice, ghosts though they are, cling tenaciously to life; they are shades armed with tooth and claw. They must be grappled with unceasingly, for it is a fateful part of human destiny that it is condemned to wage perpetual war against ghosts.

—Victor Hugo from *Les Miserable*, 1862

The teacher

- models how to create the analogy chart using the Hugo quote; and
- asks students to identify three supporting reasons for Hugo's analogy (Figure 3.6 provides an example).

 Figure 3.6 Prejudice Is Like a Ghost Because...

Prejudice is like a ghost because...

1. you can feel it; you know that it exists, but you cannot touch or see it.

2. the ghost's purpose is to frighten, haunt, and make life miserable.

3. many people believe ghosts persist, and it seems that, unfortunately, people will continue to believe in ghosts.

The teacher

- assigns students to groups of three or four and instructs them to create an analogy chart of the word *bias* or *prejudice*.

◉ Figure 3.7 Analogy Chart

Prejudice is like a _____.
Because (Include at least three supporting reasons for your comparison) 1. 2. 3.
Draw a visual representation of the simile you created above.

Students

- in the same small groups, create their own analogies of prejudice;
- share their analogies with the whole class;
- post their analogies on the wall.

REFLECT

The teacher asks the following questions:

- What similarities did you notice among the various analogies? What differences?
- What has changed in your definition of bias and prejudice?
- How might you identify bias or prejudice in yourself and others?

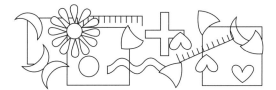

 **GATHER PHASE**

TWENTY-FIVE MINUTES

Gather Activity

Objective: Students create a Venn diagram comparing characters' personalities or actions.

ATTEND

The teacher focuses student attention on the next task by asking the following questions:

- Do you recall what a Venn diagram looks like? (The teacher draws two intersecting circles on the board or chart paper.)
- What are Venn diagrams used to illustrate? (The teacher refreshes students' memories about using Venn diagrams—see Chapter 5.)
- Do you believe the adage that "actions speak louder than words"? Why or why not?

EXPERIENCE: "CHARACTER COMMONALITY"

Students

- working with a partner or independently, use a Venn diagram to compare/contrast elements in the novel *To Kill a Mockingbird* that show bias or prejudice (a diagram considered "advanced and sophisticated" demonstrates creativity with the shape of the Venn diagram—a girl's head overlapping a boy's head or a dog's head with a man's head—and compares more than two characters on one diagram; see Figure 3.8, "Rubric for a Venn Diagram");
- choose one of the following character pairings:
  (a) Scout with Jem,
  (b) Arthur "Boo" Radley with Tom Robinson,
  (c) The Cunningham family with the Finch family,
  (d) Poor "black folks" with poor "white folks,"
  (e) Rabid dog with Mr. Robert E. Lee Ewell (Mayella's father),
  (f) Mayella Violet Ewell with Calpurnia (the Finch's housekeeper),
  (g) two or more other characters of student's choice;
- share their Venn diagrams with the class;
- post their diagrams on the wall after they present them.

Qualities Evaluated	Not Yet (1)	Emerging Understanding (2)	Accomplished Work (3)	Advanced and Sophisticated Work (4)
Diagram Design	unevenly drawn from circles	two intersecting circles neatly drawn	intersecting pictures/ shapes other than circles	very unique and creative intersecting figures and/or more than two intersecting figures
Points of Comparison (Area Intersection)	2 or 3 superficial points of comparison	4 or 5 basic points	6 or 7 points that evidence understanding of novel's characters	more than 7 points that evidence synthesis of character traits and actions and the themes of justice and prejudice
Points of Contrast	superficial details in unequal in number for each character	an equal number of physical characteristics for each character	at least 8 total attributes showing both physical and internal elements characteristics	at least nine total attributes that evidences deep understanding and a unique and informed point of view
Accuracy of Information	seems to misunderstand relationships between characters	some inaccuracies or supported by the reading or student's presentation	all points were accurate	all points were accurate and relied upon a combination of information

REFLECT

The teacher

- asks students to revisit the entries they made in their metacognitive journals in the inquire phase of the lesson and revise their answers where necessary.

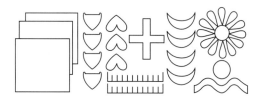

③ PROCESS PHASE

TWENTY-FIVE MINUTES

Process Activity 1

Objective: Students engage in a debate on prejudices then and now.

ATTEND

The teacher

- posts the following quote: "Thinking is what a great many people think they are doing when they are merely rearranging their prejudices" (William James, *The Will to Believe*);
- asks the students the following as part of a class discussion:
  - describe a time when you observed or heard about someone doing exactly what the quote describes;
  - how can a debate be useful in generating new thoughts not just rearranging or reinforcing prejudices;
  - how should you prepare for a debate?

EXPERIENCE: "RELATE THROUGH DEBATE"

The teacher

- posts the following statement: "Students today are less prejudiced than students living in the 1930s";
- divides students into groups of three or four persons and randomly assigns one group to the affirmative position or to the negative position.

Students

- identify four key points in their small groups, to support their assigned positions;
- engage in the debate by alternating statements supporting the affirmative side with statements supporting the negative side;
- support their positions by citing personal examples, points raised in the novel, or information they have studied.

The teacher
- moderates the debate by calling on both sides and recording the main points raised by creating a T-Chart on the board or chart paper;
- facilitates a brief discussion at the end of the debate to help students decide, by vote, which two points are most convincing for both sides.

REFLECT
Teacher poses the following reflection questions as student pairs discuss them:
- What position do you personally support—affirmative or negative?
- Did you change your position during the debate? If so, what influenced your thinking?
- How can listening to opposing sides of an issue help you minimize the effect of your biases and prejudices on your thinking?
- What do you think it takes to change someone's bias or prejudice?

 **APPLY PHASE**

FIFTEEN MINUTES

Apply Activity
Objective: Students prepare a survey, write interview questions, or formulate questions for a later visit to a Web site to determine others' opinions regarding bias and prejudice.

Students
- form groups of three or four persons based on which of the following projects each would like to undertake.

Project A
Prepare a survey to determine the attitudes, biases, or prejudices of classmates on one of the following topics and record the results using a matrix or some other appropriate graphic organizer:
- race and intelligence;
- family annual income and popularity;
- most respected professions;
- good looks and leadership;

- GPA and common sense;
- athletics and preferential treatment;
- other relevant topic approved by the teacher

Project B

Prepare interview questions to assess the opinions, prejudices, or perceived biases of two or three adults, a combination of female and male respondents, in school or out in the community, on the following issues:
- working women and the "glass ceiling" in education, business, and government;
- white males and reverse discrimination;
- minority worker wages and job opportunities;
- violence and the media;
- other acceptable topic approved by the teacher.

Project C

Prepare to visit a Web site(s) reviewed by the teacher and participate in a discussion, chat group, or blog site or post questions regarding the themes of honor, prejudice, and justice as they compare in 1930s America and America today.

REFLECT

The teacher
- posts the following quote: "Injustice anywhere is a threat to justice everywhere" (Martin Luther King, Jr., "Letter from Birmingham Jail," 1964);
- asks the following questions as part of a class discussion:
  — What condition or conditions prompted Dr. King to make this statement?
  — How can injustice to someone on the other side of the country impact justice in your community?
  — In the novel *To Kill a Mockingbird,* how could the injustice Tom Robinson faced impact justice for the Finch family?
  — How has injustice to another person impacted either directly or indirectly on your family?

REFLECTIVE QUESTIONS

1. What insights made sense to you as you read this chapter?

2. How do you currently use whatever time period you have? In other words, what is the general flow of your class periods?

3. How might you improve the general flow of your class periods?

4. How might such changes affect your students?

Content and Curriculum 4

Curriculum is the heart of why we do what we do as teachers and what we leave as our legacy to the next generation.

—Kovalik, 1997

TO COVER OR TO CATALYZE LEARNING?

Perhaps one of the most exciting aspects of moving to—or even considering—extended formats is that it stimulates dialogue about prioritizing curricular content. As is becoming increasingly clear, it is necessary to balance the massive amounts of content prescribed by fifty states, thirteen of the national subject-area associations, and district mandates with the instructional time available to present it. More and more curriculum is being added, causing many teachers to feel they are drowning in a sea of information (Chapman, 1993). Numerous school systems burden teachers with the untenable notion that "covering" vast amounts of material is the only way to prepare students to score well on the standardized tests and entrance examinations that ensure their respective academic futures. (See Chapter 6 for an in-depth discussion of assessment, achievement, and testing in extended time formats.) A profound realignment of the conventional paradigm is needed—from one in which content is "covered" to one in which students are given the time and tools to draw their own meaning from the material. While teachers may not cover as much content after such an adjustment, the content that is covered is really the students' own material in a way that has not previously occurred. "By covering less content but learning it better, students in the long run have an overall greater level of mastery" (Wyatt, 1996, p. 17). Students are then better prepared for lifelong learning instead of just for the next big test.

Many questions have been posed about the relationship of extended time formats or brain-compatible learning and No Child Left Behind. Some educators are concerned that there are often time gaps between material learned and the time of yearly standardized tests. Needless to say, there are huge implications for schools that do not perform well in these tests. The whole point of extended time and brain-compatible instruction is that more material has a chance to get into long-term memory. Furthermore, by teaching students to be thinkers, they are more skilled at thinking through answers when at first they felt they did not know how to respond.

Ultimately, educators are left with three options: increase instructional time, decrease the breadth of the content in favor of more depth, or integrate content area study to address multiple content standards simultaneously.

As discussed in Chapter 3, multiple class changes per day deeply cut into instructional time, as does time spent reviewing material presented the previous day. Moving to an extended time format schedule can actually provide more time for learning within the confines of the conventional six-and-one-half-hour school day. Extending the school day or school year and eliminating electives from the course offerings are perhaps some of the most controversial ideas for creating more time.

Robert J. Marzano and John S. Kendall (1997) of the Mid-Continent Regional Educational Laboratory have identified, after an inventory of the 116 documents constructed by thirteen subject-area associations, "200 separate standards that address 3,093 more specific topics, commonly referred to as benchmarks" for grades K–12. They have extrapolated from this number and the average number of days per year that a student attends school in the United States (180) that conventional instruction in this

◉ Figure 4.1   Prioritizing Curriculum in Extended Time Formats

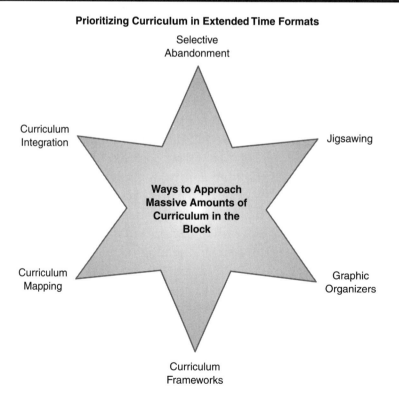

content would require twenty-one years of education (eight more than the thirteen years students now attend). In addition, the core curriculum is more demanding than ever. At the same time, mandates have added additional material to be covered: contemporary health topics, conflict management, violence prevention, and other subjects. Teachers are being called upon to make choices in what they teach and how they teach to make the most of the allotted time.

As illustrated in Figure 4.1, "Prioritizing Curriculum in Extended Time Formats," selective abandonment, jigsawing, graphic organizers, curriculum frameworks, curriculum mapping, and curriculum integration are ways that teachers can confidently prioritize curricular content.

PRIORITIZING CURRICULUM IN EXTENDED TIME FORMATS

Selective Abandonment

What can a teacher do to help students work smarter, not harder, in the flood of information? One answer, suggested by Arthur Costa (1999), is the selective abandonment of portions of content. Selected content can be carefully and thoughtfully cut without negatively impacting student learning. In fact, pruned content often results in fuller student understanding. Selective abandonment, or streamlining the curriculum, calls for serious examination of the curriculum and deciding what to keep and what to leave out.

Marzano and Kendall (1997) suggest that school districts survey local community members and organizations to determine what content standards, and which benchmarks for attaining those standards, are priorities to that particular community or district. They contend that a grassroots local approach to identify standards would be able to do what the subject-matter experts could not: identify a workable set of standards in terms of their practical application. Such an approach would indeed substantially involve the community but may not be palatable to some educational professionals. A more realistic model would be for teachers to take the data derived from the completed surveys and use that to influence team decisions on curriculum and content. An additional challenge for states, districts, and communities is figuring out how to integrate No Child Left Behind mandates into existing standards and objectives.

On the other hand, Rettig and Canady (1996) have asserted that defining curricular priorities is the role and responsibility of the teacher. The expertise of the teacher is needed to discern what is absolutely crucial for the student versus what can be eliminated or lightly acknowledged. Because of the immensity and difficulty of this task, it is most appropriate for departments or teams of teachers to work together. Many perspectives generate a more balanced result than that of only one teacher working on a course alone. The first step for teacher teams in this process is to ask the following questions in relation to potential course material:

- What is the essential concept?
- What content material best facilitates the understanding of what is essential?
- What activities employing what teaching tools are most appropriate?
- What are the essential concepts and standards?

The specific criteria set forth in Figure 4.2 can be used to make decisions about which material to incorporate into lesson and unit plans. Potential topics can be tested to see into which of three categories they might fall: essential, supportive, or extraneous.

Essential

Curriculum items in this category are deemed absolutely necessary by the practitioner(s) for the knowledge base of the student. This category looks to the future. It raises the question of what students will need ten, fifteen, and twenty-five years from now on their journey of lifelong learning. This category also keeps an eye on the standardized tests and includes information that the teacher knows from experience will be included on examinations of this kind.

◉ Figure 4.2 Selective Abandonment Criteria

Essential

- Has a real-life practical application
- Fundamental step in a large process
- Based in the present
- Helps students function in the real world in which they live
- District- or system-articulated benchmark directly tied to a vital concept

Supportive

- Collaterally linked to a curricular objective
- Promotes independent study opportunity
- Can be more fully developed in another curricular area
- Provokes student interest and motivation to "learn more"
- Provides additional opportunities for students to develop a wide range of intelligences

Extraneous

- Based in knowledge about theory or the past without practical application in the future or present
- Fun but not linked to a curricular concept
- Exercises only the logical/mathematical and verbal/linguistic intelligences
- Doesn't promote positive group interdependence

Supportive

This category includes material that can be covered in passing or can be touched upon lightly. It may be a simple concept or an event that needs a brief reference, and it might also include material that could be divided, studied, and shared by student teams in a class "jigsaw" strategy.

Extraneous

Such material is not unimportant; it may actually be useful and helpful. However, when compared with other material, it is not as helpful or not as useful.

Many critics of extended time formats are deeply concerned that there is less emphasis on crucial facts and information because in some situations, there will be fewer minutes spent in class than in traditional schedules. They would go so far as to talk about the "dumbing down" of curriculum (Rettig & Canady, 1996). Precisely the opposite can occur. Although a traditional class may "cover" nine chapters over the course of a semester, static instructional techniques coupled with the brusqueness of the bell schedule may actually cause students to retain only about five chapters worth of meaning because they have not had the time or experiences necessary to make the material part of long-term memory. On the other hand, when only seven chapters are presented using brain-compatible pedagogy, the students may full well be able to grasp and internalize six and one-half chapters worth of meaning, resulting in a net gain of a chapter and one half over the traditional schedule. This is, of course, an oversimplification, but it does help make clear that the streamlined curriculum as taught in an extended time format is not a digest or abbreviation, and it most certainly is not a "dumbing down."

Jigsawing

A huge number of cooperative learning strategies exist, but the focus here is on those that pertain to the issue of curriculum in extended time formats. A commonly used strategy in cooperative learning has been called jigsawing. David Johnson and Roger Johnson (1986) outlined this strategy in detail in their book *Circles of Learning*. Material to be studied is divided either among members of a group who then teach it to other group members, or among groups in the class who then present it to the whole class.

The benefits of the jigsaw technique are several. Most importantly, it can be used in that essential first step of gathering a lot of information and evaluating that information for key insights or critical points. It is only a preliminary step, not a processing or culminating step, which is why it is best used in the gather phase of a four-phase lesson plan. The technique allows students to organize the information they reviewed into words and phrases that make sense to them, in order to share the information with other students. Jigsawing is also helpful in reducing the amount of reading or data gathering that might be daunting or overwhelming for some students. The use of expert groups also allows students to have ownership of the information and feel a sense of responsibility to share that information with other students.

Teachers can use jigsawing as a means of

- introducing students to concepts;
- requiring students to become teachers;
- teaching students how to read information, synthesize key points, and explain the information to others;
- providing students with a learning technique of reading information first for concepts and then returning to it for more details and specifics.

Jigsawing doesn't works for all situations, however, particularly if the information is sequential and each part is necessary to understand the subsequent parts of the material—for instance, when studying the periodic table in chemistry. As with any cooperative learning strategy, jigsawing requires clear group roles and precise instructions for what the process and the product need to be. Choosing the material strategically and then passing it out to cooperative learning groups to study and then present to the whole class is one way to get a class familiar with a body of material.

Graphic Organizers

Another commonly used strategy in cooperative learning is the application of graphic organizers. Graphic organizers are visual tools that help students organize and process a great deal of information. They are sometimes called cognitive maps, visual displays, or advance organizers. Graphic organizers can help to make relationships and connections visible or concrete for students. Sometimes they even reveal what students are thinking or even *how* students are thinking. These visual tools can help launch the student into a writing assignment, a project, a debate, a role-play skit, or many other activities. (See Chapter 5 for a full discussion of the types and uses of graphic organizers.)

Curricular Frameworks

A curricular framework, or curriculum model, is the way a curriculum unit is organized, while instructional strategies (discussed in Chapter 5) are ways the material can be presented. The curriculum frameworks are project-oriented curricula, thematic units, performance-based learning, problem-based learning, service learning, and case studies. Brain-compatible learning recognizes that disciplines relate information for the brain to recognize and organize. Teachers need to look at the entire course to be taught (the whole semester, trimester, or mini-session) and then plan how and where they can use these curriculum frameworks. Such organizing structures can help to connect several disciplines. Resultant interconnections can even shorten curriculum time, as similar material is taught only once instead of over and over in different curriculum disciplines. Students are then able to experience relationships and see the real-life connections and applications to material being taught.

The concept of civil rights can encompass the following topics:

- The civil rights movement of the 1960s
- African American history
- Gandhi's nonviolent resistance movement in India
- Thoreau's treatise on civil disobedience
- Protest literature
- Current events issues such as gender-based discrimination
- Debates on the validity of affirmative action strategies
- Recent African struggles
- Songs and art that embody the civil rights theme

In the above example, the disciplines of history, social studies, civics, languages arts, art, and music are all linked, proving that a curricular framework is a powerful tool. Such sophisticated teaching takes work, as does anything worthwhile. Planning and communicating time for teachers is essential to success. Some—but not all—extended times formats allow for ninety minutes or more of teacher planning per day. Adequate planning time for teachers remains a huge challenge for schools that elect any extended time format. The classroom that incorporates interdisciplinary themes and connecting concepts requires a cooperation and connection among teaching staff that the very structure of the classroom and the school day has hindered up until now. Further rigid, inflexible time schedules and the traditional isolation of teachers, perhaps especially high school teachers, have permitted very few connections among those teaching in similar disciplines, let alone among teachers of totally different disciplines. Extended time formats may catalyze new connections among the staff that will genuinely help to make content material more relevant to how students experience real life.

Many teachers are discovering ways to link disciplines and save time while enriching the educational experience in the process. It is much more lifelike and brain compatible to present material in as connected a way as it occurs in everyday life. "Students don't often see the connections among separate and distinct subjects.... We need holistic ways to present information and get students involved in learning so they can apply what they've learned to their lives" (Fogarty & Stoehr, 1995, p. 21).

The following six curricular frameworks from Fogarty (1997b) illustrate some of the ways a unit can be structured to promote meaningful learning.

Project-Oriented Curricula

Projects focus the curriculum and the learning around actually creating and making something to demonstrate the learning. The following are examples of project-oriented curricula:

- Social studies—a project on a continent or a country could call for the creation of a travel brochure
- Language arts—a student might construct a model of a house in which a story takes place, making sure that the model accurately reflects the details the author included
- Algebra—a student could create models of various curves that visually represent their equations
- Physics—a student could construct various weights and pulleys or electronic circuitry

Note that all of these examples involve very hands-on projects that call for authentic demonstration of knowledge and learning.

Thematic Units

A rethinking of the common practice of isolating content-area curricula is called for. Such isolation is antithetical to how everyone experiences life. There are other ways to organize information than by placing it in discrete categories such as language arts, algebra, chemistry, social studies, music, and physical education. Another way—a more brain-compatible way—is to organize curricular concepts around themes or issues such as

LIFE	GLOBAL CHALLENGES
• birth	• polluted environment
• freedom	• racism
• relationships	• genocide
• patterns	• hunger
• careers	• shrinking natural resources
• travel	• global climate change
• the shrinking globe	• war
• entertainment	• fragmented families
• heroes and heroines	• mass migration of peoples

Figure 4.3, "Circles Make the World Go 'Round," illustrates the way in which the sample lesson plan "Circles and Cycles," found at the end of this chapter, works into a thematic unit.

If one chose to do so, the material in every content area could be taught in such a way. In time, with more communication among the teaching staff, teachers will discover more and more opportunities. One huge challenge for teachers is to get planning time with the teachers of different content areas.

A theme can be developed among various content areas or just within a teacher's own content discipline. It is the intent of thematic units to

Figure 4.3 Circles Make the World Go 'Round

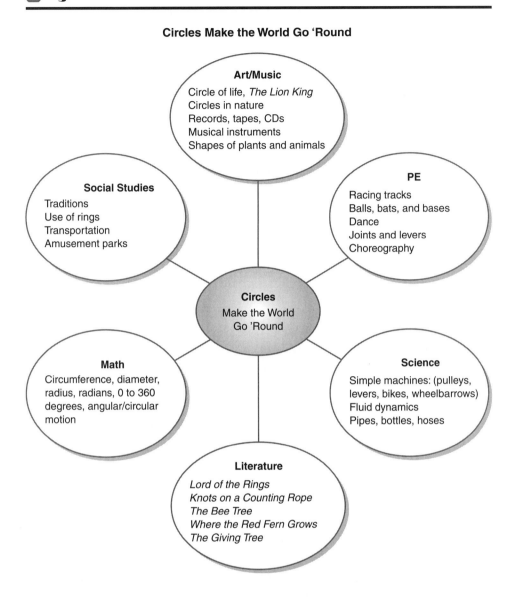

Circles Make the World Go 'Round

Art/Music
Circle of life, *The Lion King*
Circles in nature
Records, tapes, CDs
Musical instruments
Shapes of plants and animals

PE
Racing tracks
Balls, bats, and bases
Dance
Joints and levers
Choreography

Social Studies
Traditions
Use of rings
Transportation
Amusement parks

Circles
Make the World
Go 'Round

Math
Circumference, diameter,
radius, radians, 0 to 360
degrees, angular/circular
motion

Science
Simple machines: (pulleys,
levers, bikes, wheelbarrows)
Fluid dynamics
Pipes, bottles, hoses

Literature
Lord of the Rings
Knots on a Counting Rope
The Bee Tree
Where the Red Fern Grows
The Giving Tree

create organizing themes that will grab the interest of both students and teachers. Thematic units encourage teachers to prioritize, order content, and precisely define directions for students. Students can do research based on the theme to construct a paper or a cooperative team presentation or project. An extended time format allows the students time to do some of the research within class time, although many students immersed in thematic instruction will continue their process of discovery beyond class time.

Performance-Based Learning

Performances involve some authentic execution. Musical, dance, and dramatic performances are perhaps obvious, but others can include the following:

- Rewriting and performing a scene from a Shakespearean play with a different spin
- Demonstrating a laboratory experiment
- Showing a correct wrestling move
- Cooking regional or traditional dishes
- Acting out a skit in a foreign language

In each of these examples, students demonstrate what they have learned by performing an action. An extended time format demands this kind of shift to performance as another way to vary the class time and permits this direct way of embodying what has been learned.

Problem-Based Learning

Student meaning making in problem-based learning begins with a very messy problem or issue. Discussion and research are needed in order to grasp what the real problem might be. Then more research is called for before students can come up with possible solutions. The challenge for teachers is creating a problem that will genuinely grab students' attention in the classroom and that calls for awareness of what students' lives are really like. A problem in a government course might be, "You are running for political office for a congressional district in the inner city. How will you persuade the legislature to pass your recommended gun control legislation? How will you sell this position to the people you want to vote for you?" An extended time format again permits the students enough class time to do some of the research and group discussion.

Service Learning

Some teachers are linking the curricula to a defined service project that makes a concrete and visible impact in the school or community. Cleaning up a river, turning an unsightly plot of ground into an attractive flower garden, reading to senior citizens, peer teaching, and mentoring younger students are all examples of service projects. It is important for the teacher to make sure that the service project is genuinely connected to curriculum content, standards, and/or benchmarks and is also based on real needs. Because many of these service projects are carried out within class time, they fit beautifully with extended time formats. Service learning can have very positive and lasting influences on students' standards of conduct, attitudes, and understanding of course content.

Case Studies

The use of a dramatic and compelling narrative is the kick-off for a particular unit of study. The narrative raises the concept or issue in a way that grabs the students' emotions. Then, through discussion and further research, the students come to some resolution or position relative to the concept or issue. Again, the case study could raise an issue as complex and deep as racism or as personal as lying. A math class could use an issue in a case study as a springboard for studying statistics or graphs. A chemistry class could use an issue in a case study to delve into environmental pollution. An extended time format permits the research time and cooperative group dialogue time that is not impossible, but is much more difficult, in more traditional time formats.

Each of the six frameworks discussed provides ingenious ways of hooking the student into participating in the learning experience. Each finds a way to both intellectually and emotionally grab the student, at once building upon and sparking student motivation. When these approaches are well presented, the student ends up doing far more work than a teacher ever thought possible. Curricular frameworks can help create a genuine community of learners in the school environment.

Again, the more teacher teams collaborate in talking these frameworks through, the more winning insights can be gleaned relative to how such frameworks are carried out in the classroom. The nature of student involvement, the research tasks implied with each model, and finally, the demand for teamwork requires more time than forty to fifty minutes.

Curriculum Mapping

Heidi Hayes Jacobs (1997) developed curriculum mapping as a way to help teachers get a hold of what other teachers are doing and to help them grasp what they themselves are doing in the classroom. If one were to imagine a huge matrix, across the top one would lay out the months of the school year or semester, and down the left side would be categories such as particular curriculum units, needed skills, projects, guidelines and objectives, and so forth (see Figure 4.4). After teachers fill out the matrices, they share their "curriculum maps" with other teachers. "Not only did people find the calendar an honest vehicle for communication about the curriculum, but they reported it was far more efficient than reading through lists of curriculum guidelines from other departments" (Hayes Jacobs, 1997, p. 2). Though it seems too simple to work, its very simplicity is the reason why it works. "Curriculum mapping amplifies the possibilities for long-range planning, short-term preparation, and clear communication" (p. 5).

Mapping curriculum restores the big picture to a teacher, to a teacher team, or even to a whole district. The big picture is desperately needed in an environment that often focuses on minute details. Mapping curricula can reveal where duplications are occurring in methods for teaching curriculum in the classroom. In this way, it can be a tool to save time by avoiding unnecessary teaching of the same material in different courses or in different grades. While it is best for whole districts to help integrate curriculum by using curriculum mapping, even a single school, a single team,

◉ **Figure 4.4** Curriculum Mapping

Course _____ Instructor _____						
	August	**September**	**October**	**November**	**December**	**January**
Content						
Skills						
Assessment						
Standards						

Course _____ Instructor _____						
	February	**March**	**April**	**May**	**June**	**July**
Content						
Skills						
Assessment						
Standards						

or an individual teacher could make use of this tool (Hayes Jacobs, 1997). Curriculum mapping can help give the teacher a sense of control over the content, which is particularly critical when alternative scheduling is introduced. Curriculum mapping can aid the teacher in the transition to the new time organization. Finally, curriculum mapping can reveal ways that curriculum can be integrated, thus aiding in the process of making those connections for both teacher and student that can improve the long-term retention of curricular material.

Curriculum Integration

Ten different models for integrating the curriculum have been identified: fragmented, connected, nested, sequenced, shared, webbed, threaded, integrated, immersed, and networked. Many of these models can be implemented with only two teachers. Obviously, more powerful connections can be made when more than two teachers work together in the process of integration. Figure 4.5, "Toward an Integrated Curriculum," provides definition for these types and examples.

Connections not only make better use of time, but they foster the kind of learning that sticks with students and enables them to see and make real-life applications. To venture into ways to integrate the curriculum is to question the way in which curricula is organized. "We continue to add things, but we seldomly take things out. How can we possibly teach everything when information today doubles every year and a half? One answer is restructuring schools from the inside out by reviewing the curriculum and setting priorities" (Fogarty & Stoehr, 1995, p. 21).

BRAIN-COMPATIBLE CURRICULUM

Once the curricular content is identified, it must be articulated in terms of brain compatibility. No matter what group identified the content, Susan Kovalik (1997) has asserted that it is a fundamental responsibility of the district to articulate the curriculum in terms of brain compatibility. Brain-compatible curriculum is constructed and expressed in terms of concepts. Once identified at the local level, appropriate concepts must have at their core student success in life instead of student success in later schooling. She further suggests that curriculum is defined as brain compatible if it

- is conceptual versus "factoid" based;
- has flexibility with direction;
- includes the main idea (standard);
- has a rationale for inclusion, including the desired end result;
- contains clearly defined concepts, making it clear to the practitioner what is meant and not meant;
- includes expected student performance levels (criteria).

⬤ **Figure 4.5**   Toward an Integrated Curriculum

Toward an Integrated Curriculum

Ten Views for Integrating the Curricula: How Do you See It?

1

Fragmented
Periscope—one direction, one sighting, narrow focus on single discipline

Description
The traditional model of separate and distinct disciplines, which fragments the subject areas

Example
Teacher applies this view in math science, social studies, language arts or sciences, humanities, fine and practical arts

2

Connected
Opera glass—details of one discipline; focus on subtleties and interconnections

Description
Within each subject area, course content is connected topic to topic, concept to concept, one year's work to the next, and relates idea(s) explicitly

Example
Teacher relates the concept of fractions to decimals, which in turn relates to money, grades, and so forth

3

Nested
3-D glasses—multiple dimensions to one scene, topic, or unit

Description
Within each subject area, the teacher targets multiple skills: a social skill, a thinking skill, and a content-specific skill

Example
Teacher designs the unit on photosynthesis to simultaneously target consensus seeking (social skill), sequencing (thinking skill), and plant life cycle (science content)

4

Sequenced
Eyeglasses—varied internal content framed by broad, related concepts

Description
Topics or units of study are rearranged and sequenced to coincide with one another; similar ideas are taught in concert while remaining separate subjects

Example
English teacher presents an historical novel depicting a particular period while the history teacher teaches that same historical period

5

Shared
Binoculars—two disciplines that share overlapping concepts and skills

Description
Shared planning and teaching take place in two disciplines in which overlapping concepts or ideas emerge as organizing elements

Example
Science and math teachers use data collection, charting, and graphing as shared concepts that can be team-taught

6

Webbed
Telescope—broad view of an entire constellation as one theme, webbed to the various elements

Description
A fertile theme is webbed to curriculum contents and disciplines; subjects use the theme to sift out appropriate concepts, topics, and ideas

Example
Teacher presents a simple topical theme, such as the circus, and webs it to the subject areas; a conceptual theme, such as conflict, can be webbed for more depth in the theme approach

7

Threaded
Magnifying glass—big ideas that magnify all content through a metacurricular approach

Description
The metacurricular approach threads thinking skills, social skills, multiple intelligences, technology, and study skills through the various disciplines

Example
Teaching staff targets prediction in reading, math, and science lab experiments while social studies teacher targets forecasting current events, and thus threads the skill (prediction) across disciplines

8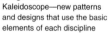

Integrated
Kaleidoscope—new patterns and designs that use the basic elements of each discipline

Description
This interdisciplinary approach matches subjects for overlaps in topics and concepts with some team teaching in an authentic integrated model

Example
In math, science, social studies, fine arts, language arts, and practical arts, teachers look for patterning models and approach content through these patterns

9

Immersed
Microscope—intensely personal view that allows microscopic explanation as all content is filtered through lens of interest and expertise

Description
The disciplines become part of the learner's lens of expertise; the learner filters all content through this lens and becomes immersed in his or her own experience

Example
Student or doctoral candidate has an area of expert interest and sees all learning through that lens

10

Networked
Prism—a view that creates multiple dimensions and directions of focus

Description
Learner filters all learning through the expert's eye and makes internal connections that lead to external networks of experts in related fields

Example
Architect, while adapting the CAD/CAM technology for design, networks with technical programmers and expands her knowledge base, just as she had traditionally done with interior designers

A dynamic classroom does not use just one or two types of instructional materials. Instead, it makes use of a variety of instructional materials at one time or another. It is lucky that extended time formats allow time for students to use multiple sources, one of which is the computer. Traditional, static educational approaches rely heavily upon students gathering information from printed material and textbooks. Such sources have a clearly delineated beginning, middle, and end, which reinforces a linear way of thinking that may help students be successful in school. For success in real life, however, persons must process information and ideas from several sources. Electronic media offers the advantage of delivering information in a way that is more lifelike and allows students to construct a structure for the information that has personal meaning and that may not always be linear. Resources that allow students to bring their own experiences to bear on information, to discover new understandings, and to construct personal meaning are patently brain compatible. In addition, electronic resources allow learning to be customized for the learner, which supports brain-compatible, learner-centered education (Tapscott, 1999).

The sample lesson plan illustrates a way that teachers can move beyond the textbook and the blackboard to illustrate a concept. In addition, it shows how the theme of circles is a magnet for content coverage. As presented here, "Circles That Cycle" is a lesson for elementary students, but teachers at any level can readily create a lesson, or even a unit, on circles (see Figure 4.3, "Circles Make the World Go 'Round," for ideas.) Teachers have a variety of options for developing student skills in measurement, understanding circular motion, and scientific investigation.

Sample Four-Phase Lesson Plan

CIRCLES THAT CYCLE

Level: Elementary

Curriculum Integration: math, science, and physical education

Multiple Intelligences

- ☑ Bodily/Kinesthetic
- ☑ Interpersonal
- ❑ Intrapersonal
- ☑ Logical/Mathematical

- ❑ Musical
- ❑ Naturalist
- ☑ Verbal/Linguistic
- ☑ Visual/Spatial

Content Standards

MATHEMATICS

Understands and applies basic and advanced properties of the concepts of measurement
Understands and applies basic and advanced properties of the concepts of geometry

PHYSICAL SCIENCES

Understands motion and the principles that explain it
Knows the relationship between the strength of a force and its effect on an object (e.g., the greater the force, the greater the change in motion; the more massive the object, the smaller the effect of a given force)

SCIENCE (NATURE)

Understands the nature of scientific inquiry

PHYSICAL EDUCATION

Uses a variety of basic and advanced movement forms

GRAPHIC ORGANIZERS

Inquire Phase: Chart of visuals and labels
Gather Phase: Matrix
Process Phase: Matrix
Apply Phase: None

TECHNOLOGY

Students evaluate the technology of bicycles

ESSENTIAL QUESTION

How can scientific thinking help you understand key applications of circles?

Circles That Cycle

Ms. Tsushima is a fifth-grade teacher in a traditional public school. She has been doing more integrating of math and science, and in this lesson, she decides to teach the students the parts of circles and relate circles to the scientific concepts of motion (linear and angular) and force. She also wants to introduce students to the concept of what it is like to be a scientist and engage in scientific thinking. The most convenient and practical hands-on example of all the concepts she will teach is a multigear bicycle. Since her neighborhood school is accessible to the students by bicycle, she has asked several student volunteers to bring their twelve- or twenty-one-speed bicycles to class. She plans to have the students work in small teams to label and analyze the bicycles. Students will compare the distances covered by the bicycle wheels compared to the sprocket size; they will also evaluate the relative force required to pedal the bicycles based on sprocket size or "gear." After the students are familiar with their bikes, they will take their understanding and go on a school field trip to find other circles and to create a matrix of information on these new circles they encounter.

 **INQUIRE PHASE**

FIFTEEN MINUTES

Inquire Activity Option A

Objective: Students physically uncover the concepts related to the parts of a circle and the distance across it versus the distance around it.

ATTEND

The teacher asks the following questions:

- What makes a circle a circle?
- What's the difference between a circle, an oval, and an oblong?
- How can we set up our chairs in a circle? Please do it.

EXPERIENCE: "ANYBODY WHO"

The teacher does the following:

- Arranges chairs in a large circle and instructs students to sit in a chair (no empty chairs should be left in the circle).
- Stands in the center of the circle to begin (the only person without a chair).

- Teaches the phrase "Anybody Who _____."
  Fill in the blank with a characteristic. Potential characteristics can include
    —Behavior: sleeps on his or her stomach, likes to dance, reads comics, and eats ice cream
    —Clothing: wears a watch, has on jewelry, wears socks
- Tells students to state a characteristic that applies to some or all of them. If the characteristic fits them, they must quickly move to another chair (at least two chairs away) as you (the teacher) also move to an unoccupied chair.
- Explains that since there is one more person than chairs, one student will be left standing. This person then repeats "Anybody Who _____" and names another characteristic.

REFLECT

The teacher asks the following questions:
- How many of you ran to a chair following the circumference of our circled chairs? The diameter? The radius?
- What was the quickest way to get to an empty chair?
- What would happen to the game if we made the circle smaller? Bigger?

Inquire Activity Option B

Objective: Students physically demonstrate the meaning of words related to the measurement of a circle.

ATTEND

While students continue to sit in the circled chairs, the teacher does the following:
- Draws a circle on the board or chart paper, assigns students to pairs, and asks them to draw and label as many parts of a circle as they can on a piece of chart paper.
- Directs student pairs to share their labeled circles with other pairs.
- Refers to the circle on the board, asks the groups to indicate the parts of a circle they identified, and writes them on the circle.
- Fills in any parts of the circle that the students don't provide, which may include circumference, radius, diameter, degrees (360, 180, 90), radian, and pi, depending on class readiness and level.
- Passes out a piece of paper to each student with five circles drawn on it.
- Asks students to "act out" the following by moving around or through the circle of chairs one by one:
    —circumference
    —degree
    —diameter
    —radian
    —radius

- Completes an observation log while students perform (see Figure 4.6).
- Asks students to then illustrate the five words by drawing and labeling each circle on their sheet of paper.

REFLECT

The teacher asks the following questions:

- Demonstrating which part of the circle took the most energy? Why?
- Demonstrating which part of the circle took the least energy? Why?
- We used footsteps to measure the length of the parts of a circle. What tool is most appropriately used to do that?

Figure 4.6 Observation Log

Focus Components	*Observation*
Parts of a circle	Audrey, Jose, and Kim remained unsure of how to act out the radius.
	Several other students were unclear regarding the concept of degrees of a circle.
	Design an experience that would mediate these difficulties, decide what phases such an experience would work into.
Student interaction	Jamal helped explain the concept of radian to Geoff and the rest of the class by stationing three students at points of the circle.
	Generally, students' demonstrations at the end of the line were modeling earlier students representations, which helped the more reluctant and unsure students be confident of their demonstration and set the state for the later phases of the lesson.
Reasoning	Most of the students were able to explain their movements and why they made them. Pam and Lewis were better able to illustrate the concepts on paper using fine motor skills than they were at using the gross motor skills of demonstrating with physical action.

② GATHER PHASE

THIRTY-FIVE MINUTES

Gather Activity

Objective: Students study a multispeed bike and the gearshift components, and then they label circle parts on the wheel, gearshift wheels, and chain. Students demonstrate how the size of a "circle" affects effort and speed. Students previously volunteered to bring multispeed bikes with gearshifting capabilities to class. One bike is needed for every four students.

ATTEND

The teacher does the following:

- Asks one student to volunteer to bring a bike to the front of the room.
- Provides students with rulers or tape measure, piece of string, masking tape, chalk, and a large protractor.
- Can model how to use the simple tools or allow students to problem solve how to use the implements.

The teacher then asks students to do the following:

- Guided by the teacher, label the parts of a circle on one of the bicycle wheels.
- Measure changes in distance the bike travels as students shift front and back gears.
- Examine their multispeed bikes in their small groups and observe what happens to the pedal speed, wheel distance, and pedal difficulty during various gear shifting positions.
- Take the bicycles outside to ride them as part of their data gathering.
- Record their observations (see Figure 4.7).
- Work with other groups after completing their observation logs to share and compare their observations.
- Participate in a teacher-led class discussion about students' bicycle observations, during which the teacher clarifies any misunderstandings or misperceptions.

◉ Figure 4.7 Student Observation Log

Group Members:			Date:
Gear Shifting	**Pedal Speed** faster/slower	**Wheel Distance** more/less	**Pedaling Difficulty** easier/harder
Front chain on largest sprocket and back chain on largest sprocket			
Front chain on largest sprocket and back chain on smallest sprocket			
Front chain on middle sprocket and back chain on largest sprocket			
Front chain on middle sprocket and back chain on smallest sprocket			
Front chain on smallest sprocket and back chain on largest sprocket			
Front chain on smallest sprocket and back chain on smallest sprocket			
Comments:			

EXPERIENCE

While still in their small groups, students do the following:

- Demonstrate the impact circle size has on effort and speed. For example, form a crack-the-whip line to show how slowly the inside person rotates compared to the person who is walking very quickly on the outside.
- Spin with arms extended compared to spinning with arms folded.
- Jump rope with a large rope compared to a small rope.

REFLECT

The teacher then asks the following questions:

- What have you learned about circles that you never knew before?
- What is the greatest thing you learned about how bikes work?
- What can you teach your friends about bikes that you think they don't understand?
- How can you use your understanding of circles when you play with friends?

 **PROCESS PHASE**

TWENTY MINUTES

Process Activity

Objective: Students prepare a quiz game on circles.

ATTEND

As a class, students brainstorm four to six categories for a Jeopardy-style game, "What's the Question?"

The teacher then does the following:

- Assigns one student group to each category to prepare at least five answers and the corresponding questions for each category.
- Monitors groups and facilitates answer and question preparation.

Students play the game by the following rules:

- One group chooses a category.
- Teacher reads the answer.
- Each of the groups has fifteen seconds to write their response to the answer.
- When time is called, students hold up their questions.
- Each group with a correct question gets the points.

REFLECT

The teacher asks the following questions:

- What did you like most about preparing and playing the game, "What's the Question?"
- How did preparing the answers and questions help clarify the information?
- What can you do to make sure you "know that you know" all that we learned today?
- If you were to tell your family one thing you learned from today's lesson, what would that be? Tell your partner.

APPLY PHASE

TWENTY MINUTES

Apply Activity Option A

Objective: Students participate in a mini field trip to "hunt" for circles on the school grounds.

ATTEND

The teacher does the following:

- Facilitates grouping students into small groups of two or three to participate in a treasure hunt for circles.
- Asks students to think of all the items that have circular shapes either in the school building or out on the school grounds. Calls on three or four students to share their ideas.

EXPERIENCE: "CIRCLE SCAVENGER HUNT"

Students then do the following:

- Find as many circles as they can and record the ways circles are used on an observation log (see Figure 4.8, "Circle Scavenger Hunt Log").
- Return to class to share the examples they found.

REFLECT

The teacher asks the following questions:

- What do you see in circles now that you didn't see before? Tell a neighbor.
- What's one thing you understand now that didn't make sense to you earlier?
- What will you do differently now that you understand circles better?

Apply Activity Option B

Objective: Students work together to create a song or design a machine using "circle" concepts.

ATTEND

The teacher facilitates grouping students into small groups of two or three students to participate in creating a song or designing a machine to reflect their understanding of circles.

Figure 4.8 Circle Scavenger Hunt Log

Names:				Date:	
For each circle you find, record the following:					
1. Describe the circle.					
2. Identify where you observed it.					
3. Note the parts of the circle that are evident.					
4. Explain the function or purpose of that particular circle.					
5. List examples of other circles you previously observed elsewhere.					
	Describe	**Where Observed**	**Circle Parts**	**Purpose or Function**	**Other Examples**
Circle #1					
Circle #2					
Circle #3					
Circle #4					
Circle #5					
Circle #6					

EXPERIENCE: "RAP UP"

Students choose to do one of the following activities:

- Make up words about circles that fit a familiar "round" and sing it. (This is more appropriate for younger, elementary-level students)
- In small groups, create a machine that uses circles. (This is more appropriate for upper-level elementary students.)

REFLECT

Students complete a self-assessment of their presentation. See Figure 4.9, "Student Self-Assessment."

◉ Figure 4.9 Student Self-Assessment

Student Self-Assessment

1. Did my song include a mention of each of the circle's five parts we studied today?

Yes	No	Maybe

2. Did I sing out clearly so the whole class could easily understand what I was saying?

Yes	No	Maybe

3. Did I work well and cooperatively with the members of my group?

Yes	No	Maybe

4. Did I make an important contribution to my group's successful performance?

Yes	No	Maybe

5. Did creating and performing our song help me to remember the parts of a circle?

Yes	No	Maybe

6. Overall how would you rate your contribution to the performance?

Excellent	Very Good	Good	Okay	Could Have Done Better

7. Explain the rating you gave yourself.

REFLECTIVE QUESTIONS

1. What curriculum formats do you currently use in your teaching?

2. What formats in Chapter 4 intrigued you?

3. What one or two changes might you might make to your curriculum formats in the next few months?

4. What marks of success might you look for?

Instruction: 5
The Art and Science of Teaching in Extended Time Formats

Block scheduling without fundamental changes in instruction is merely longer blocks of the same old stuff. If improved learning is the goal, instructional practices will have to change in order to best take advantage of the opportunity of longer blocks of time.

—Wyatt, 1996, p. 18

OPPORTUNITY FOR GROWTH AND CHANGE

Many teachers accustomed to a forty-five- or fifty-minute class period are apprehensive about the prospect of filling up twice that amount of time (or more) in an extended time block. Underlying their concern is the question of how to keep students interested and motivated for such an extended period. Both concerns find their answers in brain-compatible pedagogy.

The teacher in extended time blocks has the opportunity to orchestrate the curriculum and instruction into events, projects, environments, and graphics that can assist student learning. Such an opportunity calls for sophisticated pedagogy that goes beyond imparting data through lecturing or assigned readings. Instead, it demands strategies that enable information and concepts to be learned through challenges, questions, problems, and situations that encourage students to become interested, research the relevant and appropriate information, process it, and apply it—in other words, learning that is brain compatible. Such a dynamic, interconnected, surprise-filled, challenging environment is more feasible in extended class formats than in shorter bell schedule periods.

Students' brains are far more capable than schools have traditionally allowed for; therefore, teachers need to

- design lessons rich in sensory experiences;

- use the whole body in learning with movement and hands-on experience;
- involve a wide range of emotions and intelligences.

Not only do the previous strategies make good use of additional time, but they also make it much easier to use brain-compatible teaching principles (Fitzgerald, 1996). Further, after offering content material teachers often have had to wait until the following day for processing and application activities, often needing to review the content-heavy material previously presented before moving on to the higher-order activities.

ENERGIZING EDUCATIONAL PRINCIPLES

Although there may be others, four educational principles (pulsed learning, teaching to long-term memory, beginning-end-middle principle, and varying instructional strategies) help to energize and enhance a teacher's pedagogical repertoire (for a representation of this dynamic, see Figure 5.1, "Educational Principles Centered Around Brain-Compatible Instructional Strategies").

Pulsed Learning

Ron Fitzgerald (1996) suggested the concept of pulsed learning, which simply stated is that an activity requiring a high degree of concentration needs to be followed by an activity that is more relaxed and allows for the processing of material absorbed in the high-concentration activity. A class period of lecture, video, and a quiz is composed of all high-concentration activities. Figure 5.2 depicts the relative intensity of some activities and of how that can help teachers plot a course for learning.

In order to get a handle on high-concentration versus low-concentration activities, teachers can make a list of the kinds of activities and strategies that require a great deal of focus and intense attention (high concentration) and a separate list of the kinds of activities and strategies that are more relaxed and require less active attention (low concentration). Creating such lists is a great activity for a teacher team to engage in. The following is a sample of such lists.

HIGH-CONCENTRATION/LOW-CONCENTRATION ACTIVITIES

HIGH-CONCENTRATION ACTIVITIES	LOW-CONCENTRATION ACTIVITIES
Lectures	Think/pair/share on lecture key points
Individual reading	Team construction of graphic organizer
Watching a video	Class discussion on video
Delivering a presentation	Journal writing
Researching on the Internet	Pulling information together in a graphic organizer
Jigsawing a reading piece	Team discussions

INSTRUCTION: **123**
THE ART AND
SCIENCE OF
TEACHING IN
EXTENDED TIME
FORMATS

⦿ **Figure 5.1**   Education Principles Centered Around Brain-Compatible Instructional Strategies

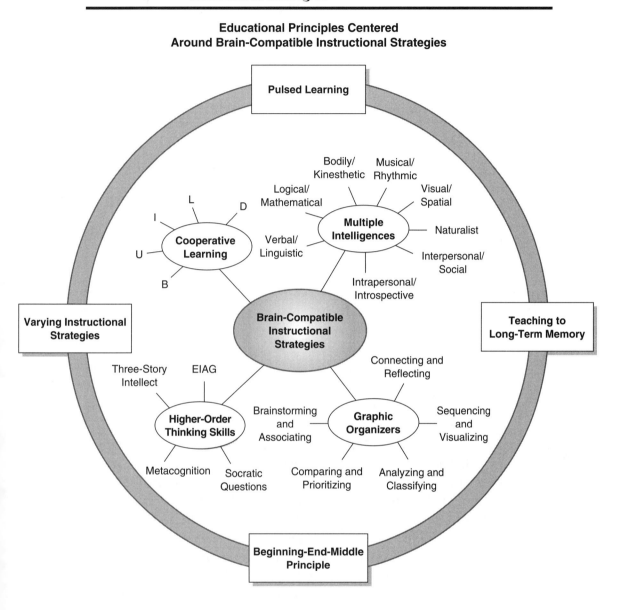

Educational Principles Centered
Around Brain-Compatible Instructional Strategies

Teaching to Long-Term Memory

As discussed in Chapter 1, memorization occurs in a part of the brain with limited holding capacity. Unless the information is connected to previously learned information, unless the information is put into some meaningful framework, or unless the information is applied to daily life in some way, then the information stays in short-term memory and gets eliminated with the next deluge of data (Sylwester, 1995). Such a simple concept, however, has obvious consequences for how curriculum is taught. This is not to suggest that discrete data and information are unimportant. Rather, it is possible to convey important data and information

Figure 5.2 Pulsed Learning

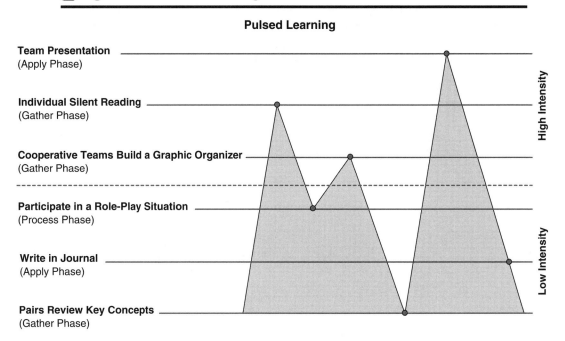

with concepts, frameworks, and connections in such a way that the brain can retain the information much longer than through rote memorization processes.

Most every discipline has core facts and crucial pieces of information that are essential for students to learn. It is part of the teacher's job to know what they are. Reading current material, attending content area classes, and maintaining a dialogue with departmental and grade-level colleagues all help teachers remain abreast of the detailed information attendant to the content area for which they are responsible. The next step is to discern what activity or experience will enable that material to be conveyed in a way that is meaningful and makes sense.

In other words, it is not enough to know what facts are important for the students to grasp. What is needed is for teachers to help content material permeate long-term memory, where it will be readily available for use in some later real-life situation or even in some later test. Figure 5.3 "Brain-Compatible Methods of Content Presentation" shows some actual course content and some alternative (brain-compatible) settings in which to deliver that course content.

The Beginning-End-Middle (BEM) Principle

Fitzgerald (1996) noted that students are most attentive at the beginning and the end of any one learning strategy and least attentive in the middle. He articulated this as the beginning-end-middle (BEM) principle. If a ninety-minute lesson has basically just one learning approach, there

INSTRUCTION: **125**
THE ART AND
SCIENCE OF
TEACHING IN
EXTENDED TIME
FORMATS

◉ **Figure 5.3** Brain-Compatible Methods of Content Presentation

Course Content	Alternative Settings
Vocabulary	Real-Life Stories by Students
Historical Dates	Timelines or Museum Trips
Factual Data	Charts or Matrices
Historical Events	Role-Playing
General Concepts	Debates or Graphic Organizers
Scientific Concepts	Lab Experiments or Cyber Field Trips to Relevant Web Sites

will be a rather large "middle" section during which attention dramatically falls off. Therefore, by utilizing more learning strategies or activities, one necessarily decreases the number of less attentive "middles" and increases the number of more attentive "beginnings" and "ends." The BEM principle aligns directly with the four-phase lesson design promoted throughout this book, which assumes that any one lesson will have a variety of activities interspersed throughout the ninety minutes. If an entire class period is devoted to one activity, energy will inevitably wane (this is especially true of a class period in excess of fifty minutes.) The four-phase lesson design builds upon this idea to propose that the activities within the lesson (as well as the lessons within the unit) should be organized to culminate in students working with the material in some authentic and meaningful way. (See Chapter 2 for an extensive discussion of constructing brain-compatible lessons for the extended time block.)

The teacher in extended time formats needs to keep several concerns in mind. When it is suggested that several strategies are used to increase the beginnings and ends, the activities still need to be meaningful and connected to the content—not simply activities for activities' sake. A variety of strategies that illuminate the desired curriculum objectives, however, can actually make the content come alive in ways not experienced by students before. Furthermore, diverse strategies can enable the teacher to reach a broader base of students than perhaps has previously been touched.

Varying Instructional Strategies

What is done with the time is more important than the length of time itself. The key to increasing student attention is expanding the variety of instructional strategies and approaches (Rettig & Canady, 1996). Learning and attention are enhanced when there are shifts from one approach to another within the extended period, or even within a fifty-minute period for that matter. Blending cooperative learning strategies, multiple intelligence theory, higher-order thinking tasks, and information managing tools such as graphic organizers call forth the very attentiveness and desire to learn from students that teachers want to capture.

BRAIN-COMPATIBLE INSTRUCTIONAL STRATEGIES

In brain-compatible instruction, students become fully involved in their learning. The teacher guides or leads students to the sources of knowledge. Consequently, students and teachers are traveling companions on the journey of learning. In this way, students discover how to solve real-life problems, how to find the answers when the answers are not immediately available, and how to adapt when yesterday's answers no longer fit today's problems. Using brain-compatible learning strategies can help aid in the advance of information from the short-term working memory system to the long-term memory system, promoting learning for life and not just for a test.

Cooperative Learning Approaches

Robert Sylwester (1995) stated it well that the central reason for the success of cooperative group activities when used well is that "[s]uch activities…place students at the center of the educative process, and thus stimulate learning" (p. 132). Consequently, motivation runs high, learning runs deep, and time passes quickly. Ultimately, the skills students gain from working in a cooperative fashion are the very same skills that have become inextricably woven into a great number of the jobs and careers students are in training for today (Fitzgerald, 1996). Cooperative skills are becoming as important in the world of work as knowledge and technological skills.

D. W. Johnson, R. Johnson, and Holubec (1988) offered five elements of fruitful cooperative learning: positive interdependence, individual accountability, group processing, face-to-face interaction, and collaborative skills. Bellanca and Fogarty (1991) used the acronym BUILD as the basis of creating cooperative learning lessons:

Bring in higher-order thinking
Unite the teams and the class
Insure individual learning and accountability
Look over, step back, and discuss
Develop social skills

Figure 5.4, "BUILD Cooperative Learning Fundamentals," provides an overview of the cooperative learning process.

Bring in Higher-Order Thinking

Each cooperative learning approach needs to embody some higher-order thinking skill or process. A significant higher-order thinking challenge is one way to make the cooperative experience a richer, more profound one than studying alone (see the Higher-Order Thinking Skills section of this chapter for elaboration of that concept).

INSTRUCTION: **127**
THE ART AND
SCIENCE OF
TEACHING IN
EXTENDED TIME
FORMATS

◉ Figure 5.4 BUILD Cooperative Learning Fundamentals

**Key
Questions**

B	**U**	**What Is the Acronym?**	**I**	**L**	**D**
Bring in Higher Order Thinking	**Unify the Teams and the Class**	**What Do the Letters Stand For?**	**Insure Individual Learning and Accountability**	**Look Over, Step Back, and Discuss**	**Develop Social Skills**
To utilize the gifts of the collaborative setting to intensify the cognitive	To create bonding and connections among students in the class and on a team	**What Is Its Function?**	To make sure that rigorous individual learning is taking place	To reflect on the material learned and the experience of learning To help the learning and the experience really belong to the learner	To deepen students' abilities to interact so that the learning can be deeper and richer among the class
Teaching Thinking Skills Directly Graphic Organizers Fat and Skinny Questions	Assigned Roles One Set of Materials Call for One Product From the Team Team Name, Symbol, Slogan	**What Are Some Ways to Do This in the Classroom?**	Random Oral Quizzes Tests Conferences Assigned Section within a Team Project	Reflection Questions P.M.I Chart Team Self-Assessing Checklists	Teaching Social Skills Directly Team Roles of Encourager or Observer "That's a good idea because. . ."

Unify the Teams and the Class

The use of heterogeneous groups actually helps individuals discover that all the gifts of their fellow members are needed to accomplish the assigned work. Cooperative learning groups

- have an assigned role for each person;
- learn explicit social skills;
- are given a challenging task demanding the participation of all;
- are given tasks that weave in higher-order thinking;

- are usually heterogeneous in makeup;
- frequently reflect and process how they are learning and how they are working together as a team.

Ensure Individual Learning and Accountability

The teacher's task is to formulate activities in which individual learning and accountability can be guaranteed. Getting an accurate picture of the individual learning removes one common criticism of cooperative learning structures often voiced by parents and students—that one person is too often burdened with all of the work.

Look Over, Step Back, and Discuss

An integral part of a lesson is the opportunity to step back and talk about what has just occurred. The key to this is questions that the teacher prepares ahead of time. These questions may focus on the content of the lesson, the methods used in the lesson, or the experience of working as a group. Some students may make sense of the lesson only at this point. Even if there are only three or four minutes to do this kind of processing, it is crucial to student learning.

Develop Social Skills

The teacher is called on to teach social skills directly, to provide actual practice time to make the skills automatic and natural, and finally to monitor the ongoing utilization of these skills. It is important to teach social skills in nearly the same way a content discipline is taught throughout the semester. In other words, the teacher cannot assume the students are experienced in the use of social skills on the first day of class. Likewise, the teacher cannot teach all of the necessary skills at once. Deciding which skills are most important, focusing on those, and later phasing others in is part of the role of the teacher. Many middle schools have advisory periods that can help to develop social skills. Some high schools have created advocacy periods that can support social skill development in high school students.

Implications for the Extended Time Format

Cooperative learning approaches are crucial for the extended class format because they

- provide a shift in the intensity of learning activities;
- offer an opportunity for interaction that students appreciate;
- encourage higher-order thinking as content material is worked on and used;
- can help the teacher cover large amounts of material by dividing it among several groups to study and then present to the larger group.

INSTRUCTION: **129**
THE ART AND
SCIENCE OF
TEACHING IN
EXTENDED TIME
FORMATS

Multiple Intelligences

Multiple intelligence (MI) theory, as pioneered by Howard Gardner (1983), emphasizes the importance of personal meaning making and problem solving. In the traditional classroom, out of either habit or convention, most of the activities are based on lecture and computation, which play to only two (verbal/linguistic and logical/mathematical) of the eight intelligences. Conversely, as has been suggested here, brain-compatible instructional strategies such as cooperative learning help develop interpersonal skills (interpersonal intelligence) and at the same time include as many of the other intelligences as possible (see Figure 5.5 for a list of the types of activities that exercise each intelligence). Such activities promote cognitive development through intrinsic motivation, which leads to student desire for lifelong learning and inquiry. Perhaps MI theory benefits education the most in that it necessitates the expansion of teaching repertoire, which in turn has positive implications for teaching in extended time blocks.

In addition, Table 5.1 expands on these activities by placing them within the framework of the four phases of the lesson/unit plan design.

Sensory Activators

One of the ways to do this is through sensory activators. Effective learning and long-term memory are linked together through the interplay of physical movement, emotion, cognition, group interaction, and contextualization. Effective teachers have always included a variety of best practices to promote this interplay. These teachers provide students with the opportunity to develop skills and increase knowledge through active participation in learning processes such as role-plays, field trips, laboratories, performances, projects, and mentoring.

For example, in his Zone of Proximal Development, Vygotsky (1978) theorized that when students interact with others they move from their level of competence to a higher level of skill and understanding through collaboration with more highly skilled and intellectually capable peers (Slavin, 2003). Knowledge, values, beliefs, and skills become socially or communally constructed and shared. Knowledge and learning, therefore, are socially embedded. Because learning requires cognition, social interaction, and behaviors, mental processes are inextricably linked with behaviors and their social context.

Lave and Wenger (1991) believed that learning will occur normally because of the interaction among three key elements; the learning experience or activity, the context, and the cultural influence in which the activity occurs. They called this interplay "situated learning." Like Vygotsky, Lave and Wenger confirmed that social interaction is essential for learning. When students become involved with other learners in a learning community, a cooperative learning group, or with a mentor, they are greatly influenced by the knowledge, beliefs, values, skills, and behaviors specific to the group.

● **Figure 5.5** Gardner's Eight Intelligences

Gardner's Eight Intelligences

Visual/Spatial

Images, graphics, drawings, sketches, maps, charts, doodles, pictures, spatial orientation, puzzles, designs, looks, appeal, mind's eye, imagination, visualization, dreams, nightmares, films, and videos

Logical/Mathematical

Reasoning, deductive and inductive logic, facts, data, information, spreadsheets, databases, sequencing, ranking, organizing, analyzing, proofs, conclusions, judging, evaluations, and assessments

Verbal/Linguistic

Words, wordsmiths, speaking, writing, listening, reading, papers, essays, poems, plays, narratives, lyrics, spelling, grammar, foreign languages, memos, bulletins, newsletters, newspapers, fax, e-mail, speeches, talks, dialogues, and debates

Musical/Rhythmic

Music, rhythm, beat, melody, tunes, allegro, pacing, timbre, tenor, soprano, opera, baritone, symphony, choir, chorus, madrigals, rap, rock, rhythm and blues, jazz, classical, folk, ads and jingles

Bodily/Kinesthetic

Art, activity, action, experiential, hands-on, experiments, try, do, perform, play, drama, sports, throw, toss, catch, jump, twist, twirl, assemble, disassemble, form, re-form, manipulate, touch, feel, immerse, and participate

Interpersonal/Social

Interact, communicate, converse, share understand, empathize, sympathize, reach out, care, talk, whisper, laugh, cry, shudder, socialize, meet, greet, lead, follow, gangs, clubs, charisma, crowds, gatherings, and twosomes

Interpersonal/Introspective

Self, solitude, meditate, think, create, brood, reflect, envision, journal, self-assess, set goals, plot, plan, dream, write, fiction, nonfiction, poetry, affirmations, lyrics, songs, screenplays, commentaries, introspection, and inspection

Naturalist

Nature, natural, environment, listen, watch, observe, classify, categorize, discern patterns, appreciate, hike, climb, fish, hunt, snorkel, dive, photograph, trees, leaves, animals, living things, flora, fauna, ecosystem, sky, grass, mountains, lakes, and rivers

INSTRUCTION: **131**
THE ART AND
SCIENCE OF
TEACHING IN
EXTENDED TIME
FORMATS

 Table 5.1 Multiple Intelligences With Four-Phase Lesson Design

	Inquire	*Gather*	*Process*	*Apply*
Verbal/ Linguistic	Quiz, Test, Recall, Reflect, Review	Document, List, Tell, Find, Write, Listen, Question, Read	Essay, Label, Organize, Paraphrase, Report	Use Analogies, Metaphors, Puns, Similes, Play on Words
Visual/ Spatial	Draw, Embody, Epitomize, Portray, Represent	Describe, Examine, Observe, Monitor, Show, View	Cartoon, Construct Design, Diagram, Illustrate, Map	Dream, Signify Visualize Envision, Imagine, Imply, Symbolize
Logical/ Mathematical	Number, Recap, Summarize, Sum Up, Synthesize	Accumulate, Assemble, Collect, Document, Log, Record	Analyze, Classify, Code, Rank, Reason Compare, Graph,	Create Analogy, Metaphor, and Simile, Assess, Critique, Evaluate, Refine
Musical/ Rhythmical	Duplicate, Repeat, Reiterate	Attend Performances, Audiotape, Collect, Listen	Move, Play, React, Respond, Select, Sing	Compose, Critique, Improvise, Perform
Bodily Kinesthetic	Demonstrate, Reproduce, Run Through	Explore, Interview, Investigate, Prepare	Experiment, Investigate, Rehearse, Study	Construct, Dramatize, Experiment, Perform, Sculpt
Interpersonal	Describe, Explain, Portray, Depict	Affirm, Verify Interact, Interview	Argue, Retell, Tell, Discuss, Express	Arbitrate, Compromise, Debate, Mediate
Intrapersonal	Perceive, Express, Tell, Sense	Express, Journal, React, Reflect	Interpret, Process, Self-Assess, Study	Create, Meditate, Innovate, Judge, Invent, Intuitive
Naturalist	Group, Order, Organize, Recognize	Catch, Observe, Document, Identify	Catalog, Sort, Classify, Relate Photograph	Categorize, Forecast, Predict, Interrelate

As less competent or knowledgeable students move from the fringes or edges of the group to its core, they become more active and more involved within the culture of the group and, as a result, they will take on an expert or the experienced veteran role. These roles learners naturally assume become critical to the learning process. Usually, situated learning happens unintentionally instead of deliberately. Lave and Wenger (1991) called this process "legitimate peripheral participation."

Situated learning is seen naturally in several groups within school programs: members of sports teams, debate teams, bands, orchestras, choirs, drama, student government, dance teams, school to work programs, extracurricular clubs, JROTC, and so forth. Usually, students involved in these groups achieve high levels of skills and knowledge because of their involvement. Social relations and the roles students play within their social structures integrate both cognitive and physical processes in the brain. Practicing for sports, music, art, debate, and other performances requires students to use the same equipment, instruments, skills, and knowledge they will use in a real-life performance.

Exercisers, kinesthetic connectors, can also be helpful tools for bringing small groups of students together by providing them with stimulating and motivating learning activities that can simulate elements of key lesson concepts. These simulation activities turn a passive classroom into an active classroom and provide students with opportunities to interact dynamically with key lesson ideas and concepts. Students are able to interact with their peers, share their knowledge and skills, and assume roles and responsibilities within their small groups as they engage in exercisers.

Teachers can help students make connections between the energizer activity and the key lesson concepts through reflection questions and metacognitive reflections. Because of the nature of exercisers, students will be able to experience an "aha!" moment (Soraci et al., 1994) as they realize the connection between the activity and the lesson concepts.

"Don't worry how practical or logical you are. What's important is where each random thing leads you."

Most will trigger an immediate response. Sometimes, however, you will look at one and think, "This doesn't have anything to do with my problem," and be tempted to reject it and reach for a new one. Don't do it. Force yourself to make a connection. Believe that one way or another everything—whether it's cow's milk or anti-war riots, church services or dried flowers, soap bubbles or knight's armor—is connected to everything else" (Von Oech, 1990, p. 126). Figures 5.6, 5.7, and 5.8 offer examples of sensory activities.

Differentiated Instruction

Differentiated instruction, at its root, is learner centered. Teachers that differentiate their instruction rely on several factors: their knowledge of

INSTRUCTION: **133**
THE ART AND
SCIENCE OF
TEACHING IN
EXTENDED TIME
FORMATS

⦿ **Figure 5.6** Mind Reader

The teacher

- forms groups with three students in each group;

- models for the students three different poses or actions they can perform:

  — (1) *The Thinker*, (2) *Discus Thrower*, or (3) *The Kiss**

  — the three different actions can be anything appropriate for students and ties to a lesson concept, for example, (1) runner, (2) swimmer, and (3) cyclist; (1) painter, (2) photographer, and (3) sculptor; (1) pianist, (2) drummer, and (3) violinist; and (1) Dracula, (2) Frankenstein, and (3) Werewolf;

- informs the groups that the purpose of this energizer is to see if students can read the minds of the other two group members in order to simultaneously without communication strike the same pose or same action at the same time;

- instructs groups to turn their backs to each other and decide silently which action each group member will do without talking to anyone else in the group;

- gives a command so that all three group members quickly turn to face each other and immediately strike the pose each had privately selected;

- allows the students to turn their backs to each other again and select their next pose;

- repeats the same process until the groups are able to read each other's minds and perform the same action or pose.

(* *The Thinker* is Auguste Rodin's classic sculpture from around 1900; *Discus Thrower* is Myron's classic sculpture "Discobolos" from around 460 BCE.; and *The Kiss* is Auguste Rodin's classic sculpture from around 1900 and represents the passionate love of Francesca da Rimini and Paolo Malatesta.)

Curricular Connections

- math—probability and graphing

- science—interpreting physiological cues and brain connection between emotion and thought

- language arts—beliefs about personal relationships

- social studies—art reflects culture, history of art, and impact of sculpture on nationalism

Social-Emotional Skills

- observation, communication, empathy, and problem solving

● **Figure 5.7** Group Knots

The teacher

- forms students into groups of six to eight and tells each group to stand in a circle;
- asks students to take grab the right or left hand of two different students until everyone in the circle is connected to two other people;
- instructs the students to "untie" their knot.

Untying Knots Rules

- Students may not grab both the hands of just one other student.
- Students may not grab hands of the students standing immediately to their right or left but must reach across the circle.
- Students may not let go of hands but may twist their hands for safety reasons.
- Students may step over or go under each other's arms.

Outcome

- Groups may untie the knot and end up in one circle (some students may be facing inward or outward but the circle is complete).
- Groups may untie the knot and end up with either two distinct circles or two interlocked circles.
- Groups may not be able to untie the knot but may make a more complex knot.

Curricular Connections

- math—business investment models and problem solving
- science—the relative nature of time, claustrophobia or other phobias, and impulse control
- language arts—Donne's "No Man Is an Island"
- social studies—situational roles, leadership, motivation, and group dynamics

Social-Emotional Skills

- Group roles, caring for others, equality and social justice, and negotiation

how each of their students learn, their knowledge of each student's skill level and knowledge base, the in-depth knowledge of their discipline, their understanding and commitment to helping each student achieve content standards, their commitment to authentic assessments, and the breadth and competency of their instructional strategies from which they can design authentic learning activities.

Tomlinson (1999) recommended teachers can differentiate in the following three components of the curriculum: (1) content, (2) process, and (3) products and performances.

Content. The first step is for teachers to identify what is truly important for students to learn. That means that teachers need to pay attention to

INSTRUCTION: **135**
THE ART AND
SCIENCE OF
TEACHING IN
EXTENDED TIME
FORMATS

⊙ **Figure 5.8** Machines

The teacher

- writes down the names of machines on uniform slips of paper, one machine per piece of paper;

- forms students into groups of four or five and tells each group to select a leader;

- offers leaders of each group the opportunity to select a slip of paper;

- instructs the groups to work together for five to ten minutes to create their machine:

  - every member of the team must become some part of the machine;

  - groups may be as creative as they want and incorporate props in the creation of their machines;

  - the "machine" can make sounds specific to the machine but may not tell the other groups the name or type of machine they pantomime;

  - other groups will guess which machine each group portrays.

Note: The machines can be *anything* appropriate for students to do in the classroom, for example,

- washing machine, vacuum, chain saw, computer printer, blender, electric can opener, vending machine, coffee maker, lawn mower, leaf blower, snow blower;

- others.

Note: The groups could take a long time in preparation; to avoid problems, allow limited time for groups to prepare their machines.

Curricular Connections

- math—ratios of input energy to output force and comparing the efficiencies of various machines

- science—levers, torque, Newton's laws, sound waves, force, and momentum

- language arts—industrialization and work dynamics

- social studies—evolution of machinery, impact of technology on jobs, and economics of small businesses

Social-Emotional Skills

- responsibility, reliability, active involvement with others, and positive models

---

content and to their curriculum. When planning for content development, Tomlinson and McTighe (2006) suggested following the backward planning approach inspired by Covey (1989). The teacher should keep the end in mind. That is, teachers can identify what reasonable and appropriate knowledge and skills students need to have at the end of each unit. Getting through the textbook and corresponding worksheets is not a reasonable goal because teachers and students are not clear about the truly essential concepts and skills students should be able to demonstrate. Teachers can also consider state and district standards as they prioritize the content of their courses. Once teachers are clear about where they are headed in their units, they can plan backward, scaffolding their lesson plans so that each lesson builds toward the ultimate objective(s) of each unit.

The second step is for teachers to decide what acceptable evidence would indicate their students have achieved the "end" or desired results. Assessment tools, like rubrics, that are clear, specific, realistic, and personalized demonstrate the quality and depth with which students have met course objectives. Assessment pieces can help teachers plan their curriculum because teachers need to identify the knowledge and skills students will acquire and how teachers and students will know that have achieved competence. Each lesson throughout a unit can include assessment activities that help give feedback to both students and teacher what students are achieving. Teachers and students alike can then make appropriate adjustments based on each student's level of achievement and need (see Chapter 6 for further material on assessment).

In the third and final step of content differentiation, teachers select the appropriate learning activities that will help students gain the necessary knowledge and skills. Teachers can choose from a variety of learning activities and assignments that will be most useful for helping students achieve competency. These learning activities can be based in multiple intelligences (Gardner, 1983, 1994, 1995) , P-A-C (Sternberg, 1985), and problem-based learning. In addition, teachers can select from a myriad of best practices the instructional strategies that will be most effective in helping students learn. The instructional choices of teachers include some modification of the following: direct instruction, constructivism, whole class, small group, or individual.

Process. When teachers differentiate the teaching strategies they use to guide students through meaningful learning experiences, they have two considerations. First, what instructional strategies will be most effective in helping students learn? Teachers then incorporate strategies based on learning theories and the different learning styles of their students. Second, what are the individual learning needs of the students? Teachers can adjust individual student expectations based on the level of understanding and competency of each student.

The following matrix in Table 5.2 contains examples of best instructional practices that teachers can use to differentiate instruction during each of the four-phase lesson design. Each of the four phases addresses a different element of the learning process. Students learn best when the instructional strategies their teachers use reinforce learning processes and allow students to develop skills and achieve understanding in a brain-compatible environment. Teachers can also differentiate as they include both critical and creative thinking questions and activities. The instructional strategies should require students to achieve both understanding and apply meaning.

INSTRUCTION: **137**
THE ART AND
SCIENCE OF
TEACHING IN
EXTENDED TIME
FORMATS

⊙ **Table 5.2** Instructional Strategies—Best Practices

Inquire	Gather	Process	Apply
(1) **written evaluation:** agree/disagree statements; true/false quiz	(1) **shared group work:** jigsaw; jigsaw with expert groups; jigsaw and expert groups	(1) **interactive games:** What's My Line?; Jeopardy; Treasure Hunt; Immunity	(1) **projects:** action research; problem-based learning
(2) **individual and group assessment:** human graphs; 4 corners; continuums; clusters; either-ors; performance demonstrations	(2) **experts:** carousel or round robin; learning centers; expert panels; guest experts	(2) **peer teaching:** reciprocal teaching; peer or cross-aged tutoring; student(s) do whole class instruction	(2) **outside the classroom:** field trips; interviews; service learning
(3) **visual representations:** K-W-L; K-D-L; P-M-I; Look-Sound-Feel; graphs	(3) **information search:** internet; library; resource materials; experts	(3) **performances:** skits; role-plays; demonstrations	(3) **multiple intelligences:** displays; individual or group presentations
(4) **content review:** homework; fill-in-the-blanks worksheet; analogy or simile; metaphors	(4) **observations:** demonstrations; examples; research logs	(4) **practice time:** rehearsals; simulations; practice	(4) **portfolios:** portfolios; unit projects; work or internship applications
(5) **discussions:** small group debates; whole class or small group discussions; shared journal writing	(5) **visual organizers:** graphic organizers; charts; storyboards	(5) **individual and/or small group experiences:** laboratories; models; reproductions	(5) **transfer:** curriculum connections; real-world applications

Teachers that use differentiated instruction successfully will be able to engage all learners. And student engagement is essential if they are to learn. That is why it is so important for teachers to vary learning activities within the instructional format as well as across students. In other words, and entire session for students should not consist of all drill and practice, or any single structure or activity.

Products and performances. Third, students typically ask about the performance requirements for the class and for each individual student. Teachers that differentiate provide several ways that their students can achieve the course requirements. Of course, students can demonstrate their knowledge of course content based on written tests and quizzes.

They can also exhibit their knowledge and proficiency of course standards through the products they create, the skills they demonstrate, and/or the performances they prepare. When students demonstrate their competence through the products they generate, they are manifesting their level of cognitive understanding, skill proficiency, and real-life application.

Instructional strategies the teachers select are typically mirrored in the student learning activities that they design and in the formal and informal assessments that they use to evaluate students. Products that students can construct range from a pirate's map to find the treasures of a particular Caribbean island in a sixth-grade social studies class to the egg-drop case designed to protect eggs when it is dropped from significant heights during a high school physics class. Performances that students can prepare include debates about best writers in an eighth-grade language arts class to role-plays about resisting peer pressure to engage in negative behaviors in an elementary health class.

What is important for both teachers and students to remember about designing and creating classroom products is that students are required to be actively engaged in researching, designing, and carrying out the project or performance. In addition, teachers can vary student expectations based on student interest and competency. When student products are well designed they allow students an opportunity to express their unique selves, they challenge without overwhelming students, they offer students a choice in selecting and designing appropriate products, they place the responsibility for learning with students, and they vary the types of evaluations and scoring used.

Higher-Order Thinking Skills

Benjamin S. Bloom's (1956) *Taxonomy of Educational Objectives* proposes a hierarchy of thinking processes that move from the most basic, knowledge, through comprehension, application, analysis, and synthesis, culminating in evaluation. The more advanced and intricate thinking processes are therefore referred to as higher-order thinking skills. Teachers have been challenged for years to ask students to think in a variety of ways. The highly specialized and technology-driven world in which educators and students alike live demands critical thinking and reasoning as never before. The following approaches can be used to elicit higher-order thinking from students.

The Socratic Method

Socrates applied reasoning to arrive at truth by asking questions. He did not lecture or provide answers. He used inductive reasoning instead of relying on traditional thinking ("Everybody thinks this way" or "We've always done it like that") or prescribed doctrine ("We think only what we've been told to think" or "I read it somewhere so it must be true").

INSTRUCTION: **139**
THE ART AND
SCIENCE OF
TEACHING IN
EXTENDED TIME
FORMATS

Socratic irony was his search for truth by assuming he knew nothing about the topic and that he must question everything to arrive finally at truth.

Socrates is famous for creating conceptual conflicts with his questioning techniques. Persons engaged in dialogue with Socrates would then have to revisit what they thought they knew and rethink their position. Teachers can use a similar technique when asking students to actively process new information or learning activities.

By asking questions instead of providing information or lectures, teachers are helping students to think, to discover truth, and to make sense of the topic of the lesson. Socrates was so successful in his approach to learning and discovery that his technique has survived for more than two thousand years.

The key to questioning in the Socratic Method is to create questions that are in a logical progression and that are incremental in moving toward the kinds of insights and concepts that the teacher wants to get across. The questions need to be very concrete and specific. According to Rick Garlikov (The Socratic Method), four critical points are guidelines to creating the questions:

- "they must be interesting or intriguing to the students
- they must lead by incremental
- and logical steps (from the students' prior knowledge or understanding) in order to be readily answered...
- they must be designed to get the students to see particular points" (p. 13).

The purpose of this method is to help students figure out a complicated topic or concern with their own thinking, with their own insights. In this way, the teacher calls forth the students' curiosity and sparks their own motivation to think deeply.

P-A-C

Teachers who have been in the classroom for any length of time have most likely encountered a similar situation, like Teacher Ann. Teacher Ann has just finished assigning homework to her class. The assignment requirements are the same for all students. In this scenario, Teacher Ann finishes her instruction to the students and checks for their understanding:

Teacher Ann: Students, you have just three days to complete this assignment covering the last three chapters. It's worth 25 percent of your final grade. So what are your questions about what I'm asking you to do?

Student A: I don't get this assignment. When are we ever going to use this stuff we've been studying anyway? Why can't I just take a test? I don't want to waste my time on something I won't use.

Student B: I don't mind doing the assignment but may I make a suggestion? I think it would be a lot better if I could change the assignment a little bit. If you'll let Stan and me work together, I promise we'll do a lot more than what you've assigned. I've already got some ideas of how I could make it better.

Student C: Have you prepared a rubric to go along with the assignment? I want to make sure I do everything you want me to do and it really helps me when I know exactly what you're looking for.

All three students are thinking about the course content but in very different ways. Each approaches the assignments with distinct interests and diverse needs. From the feedback provided by the three student examples, the teacher can reflect on not only the quality of the assignment she prepared but also, on the way, she taught the information to the class. She can evaluate how well she included the relevance, context, usefulness, and applications of the information. She can also gain insight into the various ways students think about the information presented during her lessons.

Traditionally, there are three approaches to in-class instruction. These three strategies continue to serve as the basis for much of what goes on in classrooms today. First are didactic presentations where the teacher's role is lecturer or presenter. In this role, teachers do all the preclass work to prepare presentations via lecture, PowerPoint, or some other note-taking format. The second strategy centers on fact-based recall questions where the teacher's role is to manage or direct the classroom thinking and learning activities. Teachers ask students questions to elicit from them their knowledge of facts based on homework assignments, readings, projects, or individual study. Teachers often provide rewards or feedback when students share correct answers. Finally are dialogical or higher-order thinking questions based on in-class experiences where the teacher's role is to facilitate student comprehension and guide students to construct their own meaning and understanding. Following a classroom learning activity like an experiment, a debate, a group discussion, a student presentation, a lab, an energizer, and so forth, teachers might ask metacognitive questions that encourage diversity in student thought and responses.

All three approaches have a place in teachers' repertoire of skills. But it is through the third approach that teachers can have the most meaningful impact on student learning and truly challenge student thinking.

Teachers are familiar with using Bloom's (1956) *Taxonomy of Educational Objectives* as the basis of their higher-order thinking questions. During the past two decades, however, there has been an explosion of techniques teachers can use to elicit higher-order thinking from their students. One of the most interesting and compelling contributions to the field of thinking comes from the work of Robert J. Sternberg (1997). His research on what he called successful intelligence has demonstrated the benefits of

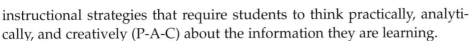

INSTRUCTION: **141**
THE ART AND
SCIENCE OF
TEACHING IN
EXTENDED TIME
FORMATS

instructional strategies that require students to think practically, analytically, and creatively (P-A-C) about the information they are learning.

Sternberg's (1997) triarchic theory of intelligence incorporates three thoughtful and intelligent approaches to learning whereby students can interact with the lesson content. The three legs of his triarchic theory are componential, experiential, and contextual. These three broad categories of thinking are the foundation of how he defined successful intelligence:

> Successful intelligence involves using one's intelligence to achieve the goals one sets for oneself in life, within a specific sociocultural context. Why should teaching for successful intelligence—which involves kinds of analytical, creative, and practical abilities that go beyond those typically emphasized in the schools—raise performance even on tests of memory for learned material? There are two reasons.
>
> First, when material is taught in a variety of pedagogically sound ways—in this case, for memory as well as analytically, creatively, and practically—students have more opportunities to learn and understand the material being taught. If they do not comprehend the material when it is taught in one way, they might comprehend it when it is taught in another. Thus their achievement is likely to improve.
>
> Second, teaching material in a variety of ways enables students to make the most of their intellectual strengths and even to work toward correcting or at least compensating for their weaknesses. Students can learn the material in a way that fits their individual profile of abilities while simultaneously seeing how the material can be learned in a way that is not ideally suited to them. It is important to teach in a way that helps students both capitalize on strengths and correct their weaknesses. (p. 668)

Sternberg's (1997) triarchic theory of intelligence, P-A-C, is defined in the following.

Practical. Contextual or practical intelligence can be defined as intelligent behavior that is developed and defined through interaction within one's environment. When students use practical intelligence, they think pragmatically and apply what they are learning to their lives, to their real world and their life experiences. As students apply their new knowledge, they can use their practical intelligence to shape their environment as well as select appropriate environments.

Analytical. Componential or analytical intelligence can be defined as intelligent behavior that is developed and defined using logic, abstract reasoning, and verbal and mathematical skills. When students use their analytical intelligence, they are thinking scientifically. Traditionally, analytic thinking is considered what makes one truly intelligent and incorporates such critical skills as evaluation, judgment, logical conclusions, and metacognition.

Creative. Experiential or creative intelligence can be defined as intelligent behavior that is developed and defined using original thinking, using divergent thinking, or dealing with novel situations. When students use their creative intelligence they can use their imaginations to innovate, invent, create, and wonder. As original or creative thinkers, students are able to gain new perspectives, make unique or novel connections, generate numerous new ideas, and adapt to unfamiliar situations.

Teachers can incorporate P-A-C in their classrooms by doing the following:

- provide examples that help students identify ways they can link lesson content to the students' real-world behavior;
- ensure that essential skills and knowledge from each lesson are socioculturally relevant to students;
- engage students in strategies that encourage them to cope with the lesson content through new and different situations or in novel and unique ways;
- challenge students to use metacognition as they process and analyze new information and skills and interact with the lesson content;
- encourage students to understand their P-A-C strengths and weakness and incorporate different thinking strategies to help them connect more powerfully with the lesson content.

P-A-C is a helpful model for teachers to ensure that they differentiate their instructional techniques, that they encourage student choice for diverse learning experiences, and that they provide appropriate authentic assessments tied to unique learning experiences. Table 5.3 is a list of specific thinking skills for each of the three types of thinking in P-A-C as well as a practical example of how to translate P-A-C thinking into classroom learning and assessment activities.

Table 5.4 includes several subject areas and examples of questions that can challenge students to think about lesson concepts from the three perspectives included in P-A-C instruction and assessment activities.

Table 5.5 includes examples of P-A-C thinking at the elementary, middle, and high school levels. In the elementary example, a teacher is teaching a unit on state government; in the middle school level, a teacher is teaching an English unit on the writings of J. R. R. Tolkien; and in the high school level, a teacher is teaching a unit on human physiology.

Sternberg's (1997) P-A-C model can be applied easily into the four-phase lesson format. The lesson structure demands that teachers incorporate variety into their lessons by selecting a minimum of four instructional best practices that correlate with the purpose and learning process

⊙ Table 5.3 P-A-C Thinking Skills and Learning and Assessment

Types of Thinking Skills	Examples of Assessment and Learning Activities
Practical Thinking Skills (P) Require students to *apply, implement,* and *use* the new information, knowledge, or skills and to think in practical ways about the new information. Practical thinking includes the following: 1. adapt or adopt 2. connect or relate to real life 3. consider reasonableness 4. demonstrate practicality 5. establish usefulness 6. identify personal applications 7. implement 8. incorporate or integrate 9. judge against experiences 10. make decisions 11. observe/recognize appropriate examples 12. place in context 13. plan 14. rehearse procedures and skills **Question Stems** ● "How will you use . . .?" ● "What kinds of applications . . .?" ● "When might you implement . . .?" ● "Where have you observed . . .?"	**Language Arts (*Hamlet*)** High school students write a report and prepare a class presentation to address the following: ● How are the basic themes of *Hamlet* relevant to your life and your life experiences? ● Cite personal examples that show how you are like Hamlet. ● Who else do you know that is like Hamlet? His uncle? Ophelia? How are they similar? Dissimilar? ● How is your relationship with your parent(s) like Hamlet's relationship with his mother? **Journal Entry** ● What has Hamlet's play taught or reminded you about yourself? ● What insights has *Hamlet* provided you about universal "truths" of human nature, politics, and personal relationships?
Analytical/Critical Thinking Skills (A) Require students to *analyze, compare,* and *evaluate* the new information, knowledge, or skills. Related analytical thinking skills include 1. appraise or assess 2. associate or connect 3. analyze for assumptions and bias 4. classify or categorize 5. compare/contrast 6. critique or explain 7. describe analogies 8. establish cause and effect 9. evaluate 10. explore attributes 11. prioritize or sort 12. reach conclusions 13. reflect or consider 14. sequence **Question Stems** ● "Analyze . . ." ● "Compare and contrast . . ." ● "Categorize . . ." ● "Evaluate . . ." ● "Prioritize . . ."	**Language Arts (*Hamlet*)** High school students write an essay to address the following: ● What are Hamlet's major character flaws? ● What are Hamlet's strengths and weaknesses as a son? As a leader? ● Compare and contrast Hamlet with his murderous uncle. ● Describe how Hamlet relates to men and to women in his life. ● How are twenty-first-century men like the seventeenth-century men portrayed in *Hamlet*? **Journal Entry** ● What qualities recommend Hamlet as a close friend, confidant, or spouse? Which of your qualities recommend you as a friend, son, or daughter? ● How does Hamlet's flaw(s) sabotage his life? In what ways do you sabotage your life? *Continued on next page*

Table 5.3 *Continued*

Types of Thinking Skills	*Examples of Assessment and Learning Activities*
Creative Thinking Skills (C) Require students to imagine, explore, and generalize the new information, knowledge, or skills. Related practical thinking skills include 1. brainstorm 2. construct analogies 3. cope with ambiguities 4. deal with paradox or irony 5. generalize 6. hypothesize 7. imagine/wonder 8. infer 9. invent 10. personify 11. predict or suppose 12. relate 13. satirize 14. synthesize **Question Stems** • "Explore or discover . . ." • "Imagine . . ." • "Pretend . . ." • "Suppose . . ." • "What if . . .?"	**Language Arts (Hamlet)** High school students consider the following to create an outline for a Broadway musical based on Hamlet: • The musical and film of *West Side Story* is a remake of Shakespeare's famous tragic love story *Romeo and Juliet.* If you were to remake Shakespeare's tragedy *Hamlet* into a Broadway musical, how might you adapt the play? • Identify the setting, context, characters, story line, and so forth. • How might you develop the relationships among the main characters? • Explain the conflicts of the story: the conflict among the characters, the social conflict(s), the internal conflicts, and so forth. **Journal Entry** • Why are the human tragedies of the seventeenth century similar to human tragedies today? Are you doomed to repeat the same mistakes your parents made? • Why are the classics in literature and music considered classics? What events or situations in your life would be labeled classic?

addressed in each phase of the lesson. The goals of each phase can be seamlessly correlated with the goals of P-A-C as illustrated in Table 5.6.

Metacognition

Metacognition, simply, is thinking about thinking. It is the process by which a person thinks about how a problem is solved and how that person thought something through to its conclusion. The more aware a person is about the actual thinking process used the more that thinking process can be used to work through other problems. Furthermore, the more one becomes aware of the thinking processes other people use, the more one can apply different thinking processes to work through problems. It is as if

INSTRUCTION: **145**
THE ART AND
SCIENCE OF
TEACHING IN
EXTENDED TIME
FORMATS

◉ **Table 5.4** P-A-C Thinking Skills and Content Disciplines

Subject	Practical	Analytical	Creative
Health	What are your "sex-education" insights from talking to, listening to, or observing your family and friends?	Examine the key issues related to teaching students about an abstinence-only curriculum, a protection/condom-use only, and a combination.	If you had children, what do you think you would say in your first "sex-education" talks? What would you share in your ongoing chats?
History	What lessons from its role in Poland can Russia apply to their ongoing war with Chechnya?	What events and policies of communist Russia gave rise to the Solidarity movement in Poland?	What would have to happen for Russia to resolve its conflict with Chechnya without further bloodshed?
Math	In what ways have you applied Pythagorean Theorum to one of the following: (a) home construction or (b) athletic performance?	Explain the key components of a right triangle using the Pythagorean Theorum.	Demonstrate how you might use Pythagorean Theorum principles to (a) arrange flowers, (b) landscape, (c) paint a picture, and (d) decorate a home.
Music	How will your understanding of arias help you better appreciate the genre of Broadway musicals?	Compare/contrast arias with current pop music, rap, Broadway musical, country western ballad, and so forth.	Imitating the aria genre, compose your own aria, or adapt a song or tune to that style.
Physics	How is "chaos" theory of random events within a system evident in your personal relationships?	What are the essential elements in the complexity of chaos theory in physics?	Design an experiment to demonstrate chaos theory in athletics, leadership, learning, and so forth.
Psychology	What might you say to a friend about the benefits of psychotherapy and cognitive therapy with regards to depression?	Appraise both psychotherapy and cognitive therapy in treating depression using a Venn diagram.	Write a case study to demonstrate the appropriate uses of psychotherapy and cognitive therapy.

by helping students see the variety of thought processes possible, the teacher is giving out more tools for the student to use.

Students can also learn to ask themselves metacognitive questions as they engage in various learning activities. In this way, they become aware of their own learning and thinking processes.

The key to engaging students in the metacognitive is the questions formulated by the teacher. Very often, a teacher asks only what the right

Table 5.5 P-A-C Thinking Skills Applied to Elementary, Middle, and High School

Grade Level Content	Practical Instruction and Assessment	Analytical Instruction and Assessment	Creative Instruction and Assessment
Social Studies Elementary school	Describe, as a campaign manager, how you would organize a classmate's campaign for class president. Identify the classmate whom you think would be a good candidate and describe the reasons this person would make a good president. Explain how you would encourage classmates to vote for your candidate.	Discuss why countries need presidents or rulers. Explain how much responsibility the president/ruler of a country has. Identify the qualifications for the job of president/ruler.	Write a short story about visiting a country that does not elect officials. What kind of people would become the leaders? Imagine what life would be like for everyone if the leaders were not responsible to anyone, if nobody would run for political offices, and if no one is an involved citizen.
Language Arts Middle School	Describe whom you are most like from *Lord of the Rings:* Frodo or Samwise. Identify what you do that makes you a loyal friend, teammate, and family member.	Compare the "power of the ring" to the power of the seven deadly sins: envy, gluttony, greed, lust, pride, sloth, and wrath. Explain how Gollum manifests each of the seven.	Imagine what could be the ring in your life. Write a poem or song about the "ring" and the influence it has on their lives. Explore the journey they are on to rid themselves of or overcome their ring.
Physiology High School	Explain how your body will change from both aerobic and anaerobic exercises. Describe which energy system you will emphasize and detail your training regimen to incorporate both adequately. Explore how will you deal with injury and motivation issues related to both.	Describe the energy pathways and cardiovascular responses to both aerobic and anaerobic exercises. Explain which muscle fiber types respond to the intensity and duration of both aerobic and anaerobic conditioning programs. Compare the nutritional requirements of both types of exercises.	Design your ideal exercise equipment that could easily train both aerobic and anaerobic energy systems. Construct the perfect anaerobic and aerobic conditioning programs for the athlete of choice using your new piece of equipment.

INSTRUCTION: **147**
THE ART AND
SCIENCE OF
TEACHING IN
EXTENDED TIME
FORMATS

◉ **Table 5.6**   P-A-C Thinking Skills and Four Phases

Inquire	*Gather*	*Process*	*Apply*
The purpose of this phase is for students to inquire about the purpose of the lesson and for teachers to inquire about the knowledge and experience base of the students.	The purpose of this phase is for students to gather new information, observe new skills, evaluate the value of the information, and analyze its appropriateness.	The purpose of this phase is for students to utilize the new information and skills to produce a product or prepare a performance to demonstrate their understanding.	The purpose of this phase is for students to adapt the new information and skills into their real lives; students look for connections and practical uses.
The inquire phase relates to both the **analytical** and **practical thinking** that require students to recall personal experiences and knowledge so they can evaluate their current level of understanding.	The gather phase relates to Sternberg's **analytical thinking** that requires students to evaluate, analyze, and compare-contrast information.	The process phase relates to Sternberg's **creative thinking** and requires students to design, invent, produce, imagine, and discover.	The apply phase relates to Sternberg's **practical thinking** and requires students to use, implement, utilize, and find connections.

answer to something is. Additional questions could be the following: How did you arrive at that answer? What clues in the reading led you to arrive at the conclusion you have arrived at? What steps did you go through to figure this out? Many students already are clear about how they think things through. Other students may not be so clear. These questions bring consciousness to thinking skills. In an age that requires more and more employees to be able to think clearly and even think quickly, metacognitive questions are crucial.

The Three-Story Intellect Model

James Bellanca and Robin Fogarty (1991) constructed the concept of the three-story intellect based on a quote by Oliver Wendell Holmes. The three stories (floors in a building) refer to levels of understanding and the sequence of the steps in achieving the highest level that would allow one to apply all that has been gathered and processed. The gathering level is concerned with getting facts and material before the student. Note the key words that call forth this level: name, describe, recite, count, and so forth. This is an important step but does not guarantee that the student has really learned the material. The processing level calls for working with the material in such a way that understanding and meaning occurs. Note some key words that assist this level of thinking: explain why, compare and contrast, categorize, sequence, and so forth. The applying level engages the student in actually using the information in some creative way. Note some key words that move a student into applying: predict, imagine, evaluate, create, construct, and so forth. The four-phase lesson design examples throughout this book are built upon the three-story intellect but add the inquire phase before Bellanca and Fogarty's "first story" of gathering (see Figure 5.9, "The Three-Story Intellect").

Experience/Identify/Apply/Generalize

The acronym EIAG is an active processing model developed by H. Stephen Glenn (Glenn & Nelson, 1988). This circular model shows that the thinking process is continuous and reflective and that the questions remain linked to the learning activity.

E (experience) refers to questions that ask students to reflect on the experience they have had. Even though teachers design learning activities to be consistent for each student—the same lab experiment, same chapter to study, same novel to read, and same homework assignments—the reaction of each student to the learning activity may vary widely. What one student observes, attends to, feels, and thinks about might be something completely different from other students because of the difference in their previous experiences, skill levels, and understanding. Each learning activity, therefore, can be quite different for each student. Questions asking students to reflect on what their experiences were provide all students with diverse insights into what others encountered. They can appreciate diverse perspectives because of their shared differences.

The following are examples of E questions:

- What just happened?
- What was your experience in the class?
- What did you observe during the activity?
- What was the sequence of events?

I (identify) questions direct students to contemplate four different thinking tasks. This category of questions asks students to describe what their thoughts were; what subsequent feelings, attitudes, or moods they experienced; what changes in their behaviors occurred; and what new discoveries, insights, or perceptions resulted from the experience.

The following are examples of I questions:

- What were you thinking about during the activity?
- How did you feel about the successes and failures of the experience?
- What did you do differently from what you thought you were going to do?
- What new insights did you gain from the activity?
- What changes in perception occurred because of the experience?

A (analyze) questions require the students to examine the "whys" of their thoughts, feelings, behaviors, and understandings. Why do they feel

INSTRUCTION: **149**
THE ART AND
SCIENCE OF
TEACHING IN
EXTENDED TIME
FORMATS

◉ **Figure 5.9**   The Three-Story Intellect

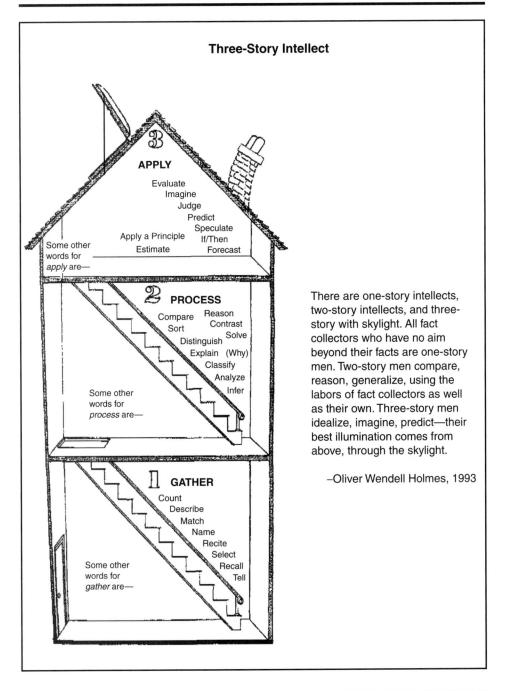

Three-Story Intellect

There are one-story intellects, two-story intellects, and three-story with skylight. All fact collectors who have no aim beyond their facts are one-story men. Two-story men compare, reason, generalize, using the labors of fact collectors as well as their own. Three-story men idealize, imagine, predict—their best illumination comes from above, through the skylight.

–Oliver Wendell Holmes, 1993

SOURCE: Bellanca and Fogarty (2003)

the way they do? Why do they think what they are thinking? Why did they act the way they did? Where did their insights come from? What connections did they make?

The following are examples of A questions:

- What influenced your thoughts during the activity?
- How did your thoughts change your feelings during the experience?
- Which thoughts and feelings had the greatest impact on your behaviors?
- What connections did you make that helped you understand the concepts and make sense of the activity?
- How did your perceptions change because of the experience?

G (generalize) questions encourage students to consider ways to apply the skills and information to other circumstances. These questions can help students make the transfer from learning the concepts and skills in the classroom to applying these skills and concepts in real-life situations. These questions provide relevancy and demonstrate various contexts of alternative ways to use the classroom skills and concepts.

The following are examples of G questions:

- Where might you be able to apply what you have learned outside this classroom?
- Describe some real-life situations where you have seen these skills used.
- What response would you give to someone who asks, "Why do I have to learn this stuff? Will I ever use it again?"
- What connections did you make with this lesson and some of your past experiences?
- If you were to write a prescription of when and how to use what you have learned from this lesson, what would it be?

Graphic Organizers

As discussed in the previous chapter, graphic organizers are tools that students can use to aid in such thought and organizational processes as synthesizing information, constructing relationships, identifying associations, making connections, organizing data, analyzing and generating ideas, and exploring shared attributes of concepts. Students can further use graphic organizers to order, sort, classify, and arrange their thinking. Implicit in the name "graphic organizers" is the visual component of this tool. Students not only are able to practice numerous thinking skills with graphic organizers but also are able to organize their thoughts and to capture their thinking visually.

Figure 5.10 "Graphic Organizers" makes the connection between the use of graphic organizers and the higher-order thinking skills they exercise. In addition, the figure provides a visual illustration of each of the seventeen types discussed.

INSTRUCTION: **151**
THE ART AND
SCIENCE OF
TEACHING IN
EXTENDED TIME
FORMATS

Figure 5.10 Graphic Organizers

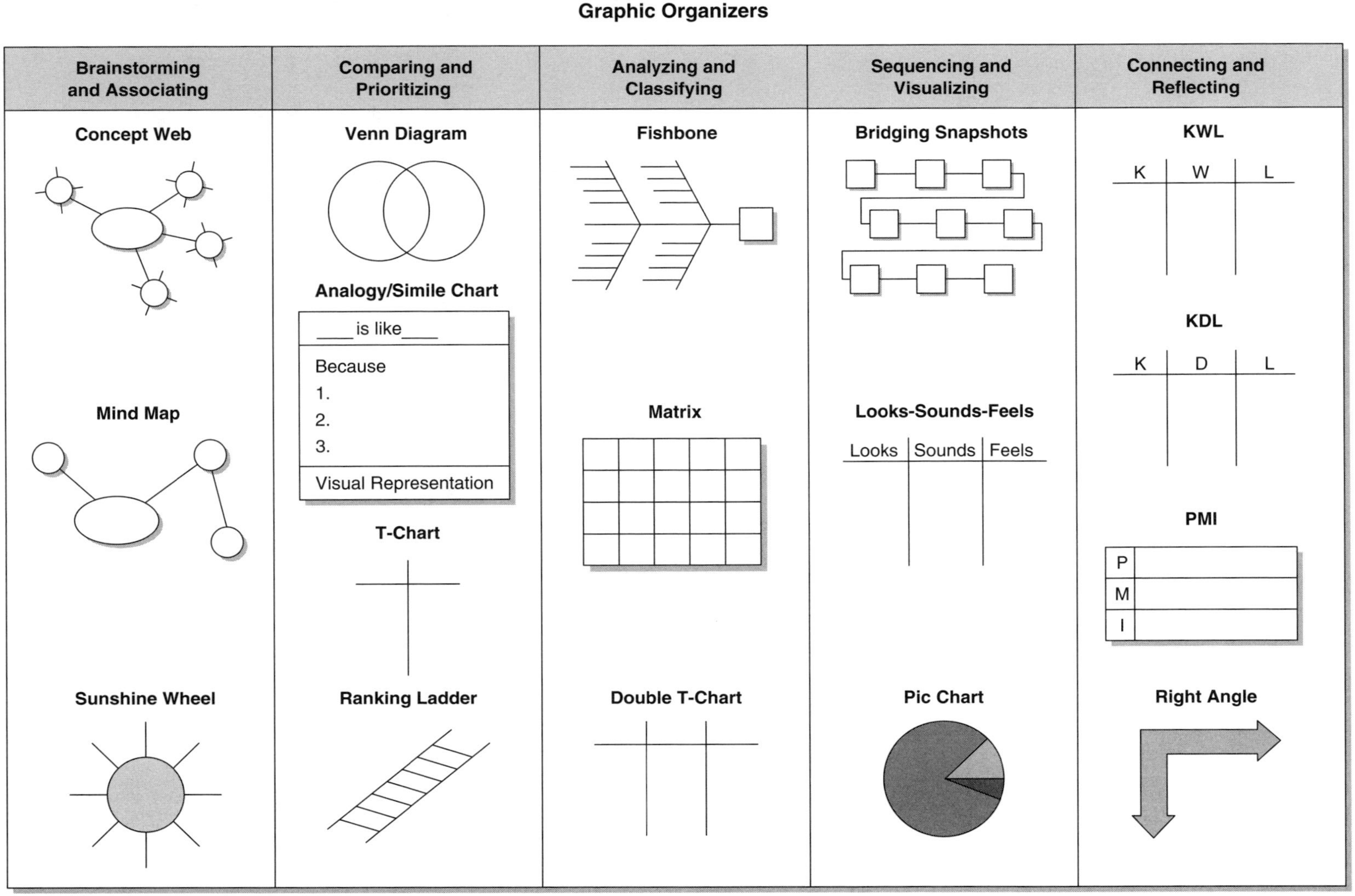

Graphic Organizers

Brainstorming and Associating	Comparing and Prioritizing	Analyzing and Classifying	Sequencing and Visualizing	Connecting and Reflecting
Concept Web	Venn Diagram	Fishbone	Bridging Snapshots	KWL
Mind Map	Analogy/Simile Chart — is like — Because 1. 2. 3. Visual Representation / T-Chart	Matrix	Looks-Sounds-Feels (Looks | Sounds | Feels)	KDL
		Double T-Chart	Pic Chart	PMI (P M I)
Sunshine Wheel	Ranking Ladder			Right Angle

Concept Web

The inner circle represents the major concept or topic, key theme, or main idea to explore. The lines that extend away from the circle and end in smaller circles are subtopics or minor themes of the main idea. Lines and bubbles that emanate from the subtopic circles are sub-subtopic points. Students can use this graphic organizer to explore shared attributes of a topic or concept and to construct the relationship of subtopics, sub-subtopics, and so forth, with the topic. For example, in a science class, students explore the details of invertebrates (topic), locomotion (subtopic), and various types of locomotion (sub-subtopic).

Mind Map

This is similar to a concept web and sunshine wheel in structure. The primary difference is that instead of words captured in circles or bubbles, ideas are represented by pictures or visuals. Students can use this graphic organizer to illustrate ideas visually instead of using words. For example, in an algebra class, students can explore uses of quadratic equations through pictures that represent appropriate applications. In a foreign language class, it could be used to represent various definitions and appropriate use of specific words or phrases.

Sunshine Wheel

The circle is the topic, issue, cue, or suggestion and the lines extending out from the inner circle like rays of sunshine indicate insights and ideas generated because of thinking about the topic. Students can use this graphic organizer to generate ideas or brainstorm suggestions. For example, in an English class, students can brainstorm ideas for a short story they are to write as well as possible plot lines, characters, and setting among other things.

Venn Diagram

In its most frequent use, two overlapping circles are used to show the unique characteristics and shared characteristics of two topics. However, other shapes can be used. In the area where the shapes overlap, elements that are shared or held in common are identified. In the nonoverlapping space, elements unique to each are listed. Students can use this graphic organizer to construct relationships and show differences. For example, in a biology class, sea lions and walruses can be compared/contrasted. In a music class, spirituals and country/western music can be compared/contrasted. In the four-phase lesson plan in Chapter 3, Can Prejudice Kill a Mockingbird?, students are asked to construct a Venn diagram comparing/contrasting characters in the novel *To Kill a Mockingbird.*

Analogy/Simile Chart

Unfamiliar concepts are compared to something that is familiar and known or understood. Students can use analogies as a graphic organizer

INSTRUCTION: **153**
THE ART AND
SCIENCE OF
TEACHING IN
EXTENDED TIME
FORMATS

to represent the relationship between divergent or disparate entities visually, one of which is clearly understood, the other which is not. The comparison assists the students' understanding of the difficult concept. For example, in a high school science class an analogy can be made for the function of an enzyme. An enzyme is like a (blank) because (blank).

T-Chart

Information is organized in two columns with headings such as (1) pre- and post-, (2) before and after, (3) pros and cons, (4) either/or, (5) better and worse, and (6) benefits and detriments. Students can use this graphic organizer to synthesize information and record it. For example, in a geography class, students can compare Poland's political and socioeconomic situation before and after the Solidarity movement. And in a psychology class they can identify the pros and cons of Freud's psychotherapy process.

Ranking Ladder

What is the rank order of the data? How is the information prioritized? What is most important and what is least important? Students can use this graphic organizer to prioritize, order, or rank data and information. For example, in a business class, students rank the following budget items in terms of most important to least important: research and development, personnel training, advertising, facility and building upkeep, and technology.

Fishbone

The head of the fishbone, or box, represents a problem to solve, an issue to address, or an event to plan. The bones along the body represent the causes of the problem and solutions for each cause, major components of an issue with accompanying details, or essential elements of an event and specifics of each. Students can use this graphic organizer to identify associations, solve problems, address issues, or analyze details. For example, in a sociology class, students can address the glass-ceiling problem in America and suggest ways to resolve the issue.

Matrix/Grid

Any number of intersecting horizontal and vertical lines is used to classify, compare, and categorize. Elements are listed on the left column and characteristics for comparison or analysis are used to label the subsequent columns of the grid. Students can use this graphic organizer to analyze details and classify data. The matrix can be helpful in making decisions, drawing conclusions, or making inferences. For example, in a language arts class, students can identify characters in a novel or play and evaluate each character for strengths, weaknesses, roles, contribution to the story, and relationship to other characters.

Double T-Chart

This is similar to a T-Chart in function, but instead of two columns, there are three. Students can use this graphic organizer to synthesize information or data and arrange it into three categories. For example, in a physics class, students can list the effects of gravity on three things: mass and weight, fluid dynamics, and motion. And in a theatre class, students can reflect on the impact of a play they have performed by identifying, what they learned, so what did the play mean to them, now what will they do with the information. KWL, KDL, and Looks-Sounds-Feels are types of Double T-Charts.

Bridging Snapshots

Sequence charts, flowcharts, storyboards, or timetables are used to show succession of information in which students can make connections sequentially. For example, in a physiology class, students can sequence the steps an impulse follows from the brain to the motor unit, to a muscle fiber, to the return, and to homeostasis. In a technology class, students can design a storyboard of the sequence of camera shots they will take to create a public service advertisement.

Looks-Sounds-Feels

What does it look like (relative to its behaviors, physical characteristics, or visual qualities)? What does it sound like (its message or meaning, its auditory or acoustic characteristics, or its tonal qualities)? What does it feel like (its emotions, its sensations or sensitivity, its tangible or material characteristics, or its tactile qualities)? Students can use this graphic organizer to explore shared attributes. For example, in a biology class, what does a whale look like, sound like, or feel like? And in a psychology class, what does a bipolar condition look like, sound like, or feel like?

Pie Chart

The pie represents the whole, the big picture, or the entire set of data or information. The segments or slices of the pie represent parts, fractions, or percentages of the whole. Students can use this graphic organizer to construct relationships among parts of a whole, to show divisions, or to show relative size of the pieces of the pie. For example, in a physical education class, students can determine the percentage of time a football team spends on offense and defense compared with their opponents. They can also identify how much of the offensive time is spent executing passing plays and how much in running plays.

KWL

This graphic organizer was originated by Donna Ogle in 1986. (What do you know about the topic? What do you want to know? What have

INSTRUCTION: **155**
THE ART AND
SCIENCE OF
TEACHING IN
EXTENDED TIME
FORMATS

you learned about the topic from the lesson or unit?) Students can use this graphic organizer to reflect on their knowledge, to identify deficiencies, and to assess what they have learned. For example, in a chemistry class,

- what do students know about the periodic table;
- what do they want to know that will help them understand the table;
- what have they learned after a lesson or unit on the periodic table.

KDL

What do you know? What do you do? What have you learned about the relationship between knowledge and behavior, or what do you want to learn that will help you align behavior with knowledge? Students can use this graphic organizer to reflect on knowledge, identify behaviors, and evaluate incongruencies and/or connections between knowledge and behavior. For example, in a health class, what do students know about the importance and benefits of a personal fitness program? Do they exercise regularly? What do they want to learn that can help them get started exercising or exercise more consistently?

PMI

What are the pluses (positives)? What are the minuses (negatives)? What else is interesting or intriguing? Students can use a PMI chart to evaluate content, data, or results. For example, in a health class, what is positive about managed health care? What is negative about managed health care? What are some interesting points about managed health care?

Right Angle

What are the facts? What are your thoughts, opinions, feelings, expectations, and predictions about those facts? Students can use this graphic organizer to identify facts beside the horizontal line and to associate their own thoughts and feelings about the facts below the vertical line. Students are asked to distinguish fact from hearsay or conjecture, to link facts with their thoughts about the facts and the resulting feelings and reactions to the facts, to change the direction of their thinking about the facts, and to use facts to predict. For example, in a history class, students can list facts about land mine use around the world, identify how they feel about land mine use, and predict what they think will eventually happen with the use of land mines. And in a technology class, students can describe the current state of technology and privacy, how they feel about individual privacy rights, and how they think technology and privacy rights will be resolved.

PROFESSIONAL LEARNING COMMUNITIES: PATHWAY TO A NEW PARADIGM

Bringing about a community of learners necessitates a school culture of professional development. The successful transition to extended time formats is dependent upon a shift in teachers' perceptual orientation, or understanding of the world around them. Those whose worldview is relatively rigid and inflexible tend to gravitate to a lecture-style approach. Consequently, such teachers may need more intensive training than do those who hold more fluid, dynamic, and flexible views and who are more easily adapted to brain-compatible teaching approaches suited to extended time formats (R. N. Caine & G. Caine, 1997). An approach to teacher development that supports substantive professional growth will help bring about a paradigm shift by the entire school community. Professional development that focuses on brain-compatible instructional strategies is an important component of best practice within an extended time frame.

A RAND study recently concluded that "new teaching strategies can require as much as fifty hours of instruction, practice, and coaching before teachers become comfortable with them," while another study concluded that fifty days were needed (U.S. Department of Education, 1994). Canady and Rettig (1995) suggested a minimum of five (optimally ten) full-day workshops where teachers transitioning into extended time formats can learn teaching and classroom management techniques. In addition, they need to interact with and model teachers experienced in teaching in these extended time frames. At any rate, such "sustained periods of professional development" (Cushman, 1995) are nowhere more imperative than when teaching in the block. Happily, another study of education reform efforts conducted in 1994 found that "allowing schools and districts to reconfigure schedules to provide time for collaboration and learning is possibly the most cost-efficient means of providing at least some of the time required" (O'Day, Goertz, & Floden, 1995, p. 57) for teachers to learn how to improve student achievement.

It is important to remember that instructional time need not be sacrificed on the altar of professional learning communities. "Ironically, the change to block scheduling that has generated a need for new teaching strategies can also provide extended time during the school day for staff development" (Canady & Rettig, 1995, p. 14). Two- to fifteen-day "mini-terms" can be built into a school year in which teachers alternate staff development and instruction assignments as discussed in Chapter 3. In addition, see Figures 5.11, "Staff Development in a Semester System," and Figure 5.12, "Staff Development in a Trimester System."

Staff development is one factor in becoming a professional learning community.

The various brain-compatible techniques and strategies discussed in this chapter come together in Sample Four-Phase Lesson Plan. It is

INSTRUCTION: **157**
THE ART AND
SCIENCE OF
TEACHING IN
EXTENDED TIME
FORMATS

◉ Figure 5.11 Staff Development in a Semester System

First Half of the First Semester	Break	Second Half of the First Semester	Break	First Half of the Second Semester	Break
	Group 1—Staff Development		Group 2—Staff Development		Group 3—Staff Development
	Group 2 & 3—Enrichment Courses		Group 1 & 3—Enrichment Courses		Group 1 & 2—Enrichment Courses

◉ Figure 5.12 Staff Development in a Trimester System

First Trimester	Break	Second Trimester	Break	Third Trimester
	Group 1—Staff Development		Group 2—Staff Development	
	Group 2 & 3—Enrichment Courses		Group 1 & 3—Enrichment Courses	

designed as a culminating lesson of a unit on population trends and changes. The curriculum connection includes foreign language, mathematics (statistics), technology, and health. If teachers work in teams that include both a foreign language and health teacher, they can team teach this lesson. The foreign language selected can be one that students take in school or one that is spoken by students in school. The foreign language focus is to strengthen vocabulary and to understand foreign cultures better. The health focus for this lesson is nutrition; however, any health issue could be addressed such as diseases, accidents, lifestyle choices (e.g., alcohol consumption and smoking), or health care availability. Just about any content area can be taught in a foreign language, allowing students to increase their language fluency while working on a different content area.

Sample Four-Phase Lesson Plan

GENDER, AGE, AND PYRAMIDS— ONLY YOUR SARCOPHAGUS KNOWS FOR SURE!

Level: Middle

Curriculum Integration: Social science, mathematics, foreign language (Spanish), technology, and health

Multiple Intelligences

- ☑ Bodily/Kinesthetic
- ☐ Interpersonal
- ☐ Intrapersonal
- ☑ Logical/Mathematical

- ☐ Musical
- ☐ Naturalist
- ☑ Verbal/Linguistic
- ☑ Visual/Spatial

Content Standards

SOCIAL STUDIES

Understands that culture and experience influence people's perceptions of places and regions

Understands global development and environmental issues

Understands the forces of cooperation and conflict that shape the divisions of Earth's surface

Understands the patterns and networks of economic interdependence on Earth's surface

Understands the changes that occur in the meaning, use, distribution, and importance of resources

HEALTH

Knows the availability and effective use of health services, products, and information

Knows environmental and external factors that affect individual and community health

Understands essential concepts about nutrition and diet

Understands how eating properly can help reduce health risks

FOREIGN LANGUAGE

Uses the target language to engage in conversations, express feelings and emotions, and exchange opinions and information

TECHNOLOGY

Evaluates electronic sources of information

INSTRUCTION: **159**
THE ART AND
SCIENCE OF
TEACHING IN
EXTENDED TIME
FORMATS

MATHEMATICS

Understands and applies basic and advanced concepts of statistics and data analysis

GRAPHIC ORGANIZERS

Inquire Phase: None
Gather Phase: Students choose from several graphic organizers
Process Phase: Students create chart of visual and labels
Apply Phase: Matrix

TECHNOLOGY

Internet research of additional information on approved and recommended Web sites

ESSENTIAL QUESTION

How can statistics influence an understanding of critical historical health issues among different countries?

Gender, Age, and Pyramids—Only Your Sarcophagus Knows for Sure!

Mr. McCullogh is a third-year social studies teacher in a bilingual magnet middle school. He is currently teaching American history, and in this unit, he is teaching his students about United States population growth, population distribution by age and gender, and population changes over time because of food availability, health care, diseases, wars, and so forth. His students speak Spanish as their primary language or speak English as their primary language, and they are learning to speak in both Spanish and English. He teaches the course in both languages. In addition to the social studies content, he is cooperating with both the math and health teachers and has integrated graphs and statistics taught by the math teacher as well as the history of health care addressed by the health teacher. This lesson is the third of six lessons on American history and the westward expansion, especially the Mexican-American War and the influence of Latin immigrants from Central and South America. He wants to challenge the students to create their own population pyramids based on research on various Spanish-speaking countries in the Americas and to compare them with the same period in the United States. Students will explore the reasons for differences/similarities in their population pyramids, particularly the impact of wars and disease like the yellow fever epidemics in the United States.

INQUIRE PHASE

TWENTY-FIVE MINUTES

Inquire Activity

Objective: Students discuss their population pyramid homework assignment in Spanish and synthesize the information they gathered.

ATTEND

A population pyramid is a graph that shows patterns of population change by using four values:

- total country population by decade or five-year interval;
- percent of population that is male for each decade or five-year interval;
- percent of population that is female for each decade or five-year interval;
- year of birth of each decade or five-year interval (see Figure 5.13, "Population Pyramid").

Picking up on the lesson presented the previous day from which students completed a population pyramid for homework, the teacher

Figure 5.13 Population Pyramid

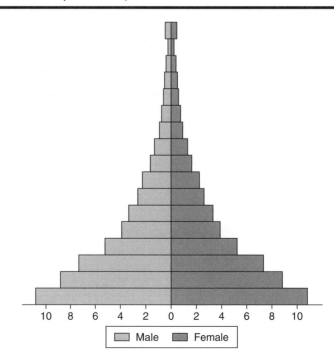

INSTRUCTION: **161**
THE ART AND
SCIENCE OF
TEACHING IN
EXTENDED TIME
FORMATS

- pairs students and directs their attention by beginning the following dialogue in Spanish: "Think about all the information you collected for your population pyramid assignment. What are some key words that relate in some way to your pyramids? Please share them with the class using Spanish."

Experience: Today, Population Pyramids; Tomorrow the World!

The teacher

- writes student responds in Spanish and in English on the chalk board or pyramid chart paper; words students suggest may include the following:

hombre: man	familia: family
mujer: woman	generación: generation
gente: people	piramide: pyramid
decenio: decade	por ciento: percent
abuelos: grandparents	joven: young
ancianidad: old age	muerte: death
vecino: neighbor	cuarenta: forties

- corrects or clarifies any mispronunciations.

Student pairs

- create a statement regarding population pyramids using the previous words;
- volunteer to share their statements in both English and Spanish;
- repeat the process two or three times using different words from the list each time;
- review their homework projects with each other and share the results of their population pyramids with the class.

REFLECT

Students

- place their completed population pyramid homework assignment in their working portfolio;
- add this latest entry on their portfolio's contents sheet;
- look through portfolio entries to see if something needs to be removed or reworked;
- use a portfolio assessment rubric to evaluate their portfolios (see Figure 5.14 "Portfolio Evaluation Rubric").

◉ Figure 5.14 Portfolio Evaluation Rubric

Qualities Evaluated	Level of Work			
	Excellent	**Accomplished**	**Developing**	**Beginning**
Organization	Deliberate and effective Includes up-to-date contents page	Organized Has contents page	Organizational structure not readily apparent Contents page is outdated and/or missing entries	Disorganized No contents page
Presentation	Dynamic and unique	Effort evident	Some effort evident	Little effort evident
Entries Included	Evidence growth and superior work	A variety of entries demon-strate growth	Lack of apparent rationale for inclusion	Few entries or shows little or no growth

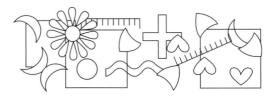

② GATHER PHASE

TWENTY-FIVE MINUTES

Gather Activity

Objective: Students evaluate a new population pyramid.

ATTEND

The teacher asks

- based on what you have learned about creating population pyramids, what do you think you can determine by merely looking at the pyramid?

Students

- are assigned to one of five small, expert groups, with the direction to evaluate the same population pyramid but with each group focusing on one of the following:
  —demographic transition stage (first, second, or third)
  —health issues

INSTRUCTION: **163**
THE ART AND
SCIENCE OF
TEACHING IN
EXTENDED TIME
FORMATS

—economics

—historical trends and events

—type(s) of government

- identify details of the population pyramid based on patterns and implied statistics;
- prepare a pyramid chart of their expert assessment in their expert groups;
- stay in their expert groups, rotate from pyramid chart to pyramid chart, evaluating each pyramid chart, adding insights or raising questions about interpretations;
- after three or four rotations, groups return to their original expert pyramid charts to reflect on the additions or questions and refine their pyramid charts. Groups share their expert pyramid charts with the rest of the class.

EXPERIENCE: "GRAPHIC DEMOGRAPHICS"

Students

- prepare a graphic organizer (concept map, matrix, fishbone, etc.) of key points from all five topics for use in evaluating population pyramids;
- share their graphic organizers with other groups and the class;
- place completed organizers in their working portfolio.

REFLECT

The teacher asks the following questions:

- What information can be determined from evaluating a population pyramid?
- What new insights have you gained about the formal process of evaluating population pyramids?
- What will you remember to do the next time you are asked to interpret population pyramids or other graphs and tables?

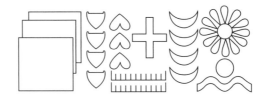

PROCESS PHASE

TWENTY-FIVE MINUTES

Process Activity

Objective: Students select a Spanish-speaking country and create a population pyramid based on information they gather about the country.

ATTEND

The teacher calls student attention to the next task by asking the following questions:

- In what part(s) of the world do people speak Spanish?
- Why have those places adopted that language?
- Does the language commonly spoken in a place have an effect on the culture or vice versa?

EXPERIENCE: "SPANNING THE GLOBE"

Students in small groups

- choose a specific Spanish-speaking country (Bolivia, Cuba, Mexico, Puerto Rico, Spain, etc.) and determine what kind of information they want to gather about that country;
- jigsaw resources to search for specific information on the Internet they can use to create a population pyramid;
- share their pyramids with two or three other groups;
- submit their pyramids to the teacher, who selects a few pyramids to facilitate a class discussion on the information presented in the pyramids.

REFLECT

The teacher asks the following questions:

- What interesting facts did you learn about the country you researched?
- Which sources were most helpful in finding the information you needed?
- How did you find those sources?
- How could you help other students who are having difficulty finding information they need, regardless of the topic?

INSTRUCTION: **165**
THE ART AND
SCIENCE OF
TEACHING IN
EXTENDED TIME
FORMATS

APPLY PHASE

FIFTEEN MINUTES

Apply Activity

Objective: Students consider nutritional factors that can influence population density.

ATTEND

The teacher asks

- What kind of food do you typically eat for breakfast?
- How healthy do you think your breakfast is? Tell a partner.

Students

- list all the breakfast foods they eat and/or that are typical for persons in their community;
- evaluate the foods, using a nutrition resource guide, for (1) calories of fat, carbohydrate, and protein; (2) vitamins and minerals; and (3) nutrient density.

EXPERIENCE: "BREAKFAST OF CHAMPIONS"

The teacher

- leads a discussion on the role of nutrition in longevity, diseases, health problems, growth and development, and so forth;
- assigns a homework project in which students select two persons from the following list to interview to ask what breakfast foods they ate when they were thirteen or fourteen years old:
  —their parents or another adult the age of their parents,
  —their grandparents or someone the age of their grandparents,
  —someone who grew up in a Spanish-speaking country and is the age of their parents or older.

Students will

- Analyze the nutritional content of the foods and compare/contrast the differences among the three generations and record the findings in a matrix: (1) their own breakfast analysis, (2) their parents, and (3) their grandparents.

Figure 5.15 Four-Level Homework Evaluation Rubric

Qualities Evaluated	Level of Work			
	A (4)	**B (3)**	**C (2)**	**Not Yet (1)**
Analysis of Nutritional Content	A wide variety of foods were appropriately analyzed, taking into account several factors	Derived from only two nutritional factors	Derived from one nutritional factor	Foods listed but not evaluated for nutritional content
Data Collection	Surveyed two or more persons from each of three generations	Surveyed one person from each of three generations	Surveyed two generations	Surveyed only self
Organization and Presentation of Data	Used appropriate words in Spanish Supplied a carefully drawn and accurate graph that accounts for all variables in the foods and the persons interviewed	Supplied an accurate and neatly drawn graph	Graph supplied was insufficient to represent all the variables	Raw data only, no graph
Comments:				

The teacher, in conjunction with the class,

- creates a four-level rubric that further defines the assignment and is used later to evaluate their homework assignment. An example of such a rubric is Figure 5.15 "Four-Level Homework Evaluation Rubric."

REFLECT

The teacher asks the following questions:

- What are five things you learned about the many factors and circumstances that can influence a population both positively and negatively?

INSTRUCTION: **167**
THE ART AND
SCIENCE OF
TEACHING IN
EXTENDED TIME
FORMATS

- What are some reasons governments and health organizations monitor a population by organizing details in graphs like a population pyramid?
- If you were the president of a Third World country, what would be the first thing(s) you would do to improve the quality of life for your people?

REFLECTIVE QUESTIONS

1. What are some of the instructional strategies you currently use?

2. Looking at Chapter 5, what are some additional strategies you would like to try?

3. How would you decide which classes to try these in?

4. How would you know these strategies worked?

Assessment: Measuring Achievement and Growth in Extended Time Formats 6

Authentic classroom assessments provide teachers with a repertoire of tools to measure student growth.... [T]eachers need to create vivid, colorful, and true moving pictures of a student as he or she develops and grows over the course of a year.

—Burke, 1994, p. xxi

THE RIGHT STUFF

One of the assessment tools that teachers will continue to be use is objective testing. Practical alternatives and sound arguments exist, however, for a new brain-compatible and authentic means of measuring student achievement. Grant Wiggins (1989) suggested that educators should actually teach to the test, but the tests to which they teach need to be very different from what they are now. The *right* kind of assessment is central to the learning process and engages students in real-life situations and applications. Kay Burke (1994) defined assessment as the "process of gathering evidence" (p. xvi). If this is so, then clearly, the more diverse the sources of evidence, the more accurate the picture one can create of student strengths, abilities, and learning differences. In addition, by addressing assessment *during* the instructional-design stage—what Ferrarra and McTighe (1996) and Wiggins (1989) call "backward planning"—the entire curricular process is shaped for the better. More brain-compatible assessments actually promote the instructional process like those in the *process phase* of a four-phase lesson plan. Conversely, the practice of teaching to the rigidity

◉ Figure 6.1 Standardized Tests Versus Brain-Compatible Assessment

Standardized Testing	*Brain-Compatible Assessment*
• results based on a mythical standard or norm, which requires that a certain percentage of children fail	• establishes an environment where each child has the opportunity to succeed
• pressures teachers to narrow their curriculum so that they can specifically concentrate on the test material	• allows teachers to develop meaningful curricula and assess within the content of that program
• emphasizes a single-instance assessment, which has no relation to the learning taking place in the classroom	• assessment is ongoing throughout the unit of study and provides an accurate picture of student achievement
• focuses on errors and mistakes rather than on what has been accomplished	• puts the emphasis on student strengths rather than weaknesses
• focuses too much importance on single sets of data (i.e. test scores) in making educational decisions	• provides multiple sources of evaluation that give an in-depth view of student progress
• treats all students in a uniform way	• treats each student as a unique human being
• discriminates against some students because of cultural background and learning style	• provides the opportunity to eliminate cultural bias and gives everyone an equal chance to succeed
• regards instruction and assessment as separate activities	• regards instruction and assessment as a single, integrated activity
• answers are final, there is no opportunity for reflection or revision	• engages the student in a continual process of self-evaluation, learning, and feedback, as well as revision
• focuses on the "right" answer without regard for understanding	• deals with comprehension and the learning process as much as the final product
• inexpensive and easy to administer and grade	• more difficult to achieve consistent, objective scoring results
• often provides results that can be simplified to a single numerical score	• data cannot easily be simplified as a single number
• easy to compare and contrast different populations of students	• difficult to compare different students populations

Adapted from *Brain-Compatible Assessments* by Diane Ronis. ©1999 by Corwin Press. Reprinted with permission.

ASSESSMENT: **171**
MEASURING
ACHIEVEMENT AND
GROWTH IN
EXTENDED TIME
FORMATS

of the conventional standardized test with its set of mysterious "correct" answers is outdated and counterproductive. Figure 6.1 illustrates the differences between standardized test formats and their brain-compatible counterparts.

Surface knowledge, fact-based rather than context-based learning (the type most often measured by standardized tests), "does not prepare students to solve complex problems and apply the knowledge to unexpected and complex real-life situations" (G. Caine, R. N. Caine, & Crowell, 1994, p. 47). What is called for is the development within students of dynamic thinking that can adapt to changing circumstances and conditions. Complex thinking is a journey into ambiguous, messy arenas of facts and opinions, which calls for very different kinds of assessment tools. Fogarty and Stoehr (1995) offer the "triassessment model," which suggests a combination of three approaches to assessment:

- traditional test and quiz assessment;
- gathering samples of actual ongoing work into a portfolio;
- observations of students actually carrying out processes, demonstrations, and performances.

The key to the triassessment model is varying the types of assessment a teacher uses, much the same way a teacher needs to vary instructional strategies. (See Chapters 4 and 5.) Evidence from various assessment approaches provides a multidimensional view—a "moving" picture, so to speak—that more accurately depicts a student's knowledge, understanding, and capability than can any one type alone. In addition, higher levels of thinking are best measured by authentic, less traditional forms of assessment. Figure 6.2, "Forms of Assessment," suggests the benefits and characteristics of three forms of assessment.

CAUGHT IN THE ACT OF LEARNING: AUTHENTIC ASSESSMENT

As discussed in previous chapters, there is a necessity for students to perceive a connection between the curriculum and their real lives. Without some kind of relationship, there is little motivation to become involved with course content. The same can be said of the form of assessment used to determine what a student has learned. It is not that quizzes, multiple-choice tests, and standardized tests are ineffective; rather, it is that these forms are not enough to give witness to what students "know" or can "do." Alternative, authentic forms of assessments can be utilized to gain a clear understanding of student learning.

Authentic assessments are those evaluative tools that are relevant and connected to real-life situations. In addition, they recognize the myriad of different student learning styles and provide repeated and various opportunities for students to demonstrate what they have learned. The important connection between "authentic" classroom learning tasks and

	Traditional Assessment	*Portfolio Assessment*	*Performance Assessment*
Definition	Written summaries of learnings	A collection of work samples from a unit or a semester or a year	Direct observation of a student's perform-ance
Time Component	Periodically	Continually add evidence	Toward the end of a lesson or unit
Benefits	• Easy to grade • Answers are often right or wrong • Displays knowl-edge of details	• Shows growth and development	• Focuses on what a student does, or on skills a student can demonstrate
Intelligences	• Verbal/Linguistic • Logical/ Mathematical • Visual/Spatial	• Visual/Spatial • Intrapersonal • Verbal/Linguistic • Logical/ Mathematical • Interpersonal	• Visual/Spatial • Bodily/Kinesthetic • Verbal/Linguistic • Logical/ Mathematical • Interpersonal
Assessment Tool	**Answer sheet** • Graphic Organizers • Journals	**Rubric** • Standards • Criteria • Indicators • Checklist • Graphic Organizers • Reflections on Portfolio Contents	• Musical/Rhythmic • Naturalist **Rubric** • Standards • Criteria • Indicators • Checklist

Adapted from *Best Practices for the Learner-Centered Classroom* by Robin Fogarty. ©1995 SkyLight Training and Publishing, Inc. Reprinted with permission of SkyLight Professional Development, Arlington Heights, IL.

"authentic" assessment techniques needs to exist; using the first without the second runs counter to common sense. In the same vein, if educators are facilitating the acquisition of higher level thinking skills, then the assessment itself needs to be rigorous enough to measure the depth of understanding such an approach brings about (Burke, 1999).

Authentic assessments are an excellent system for providing students with a natural and immediate feedback loop. Students using an authentic assessment tool are aware of the performance requirements as they

ASSESSMENT: **173**
MEASURING
ACHIEVEMENT AND
GROWTH IN
EXTENDED TIME
FORMATS

rehearse; they are assessed according to the very requirements they have been rehearsing, and then they are provided feedback regarding how closely they have met the requirements. With the feedback that is part of every assessment tool, students can make immediate alterations in their performance or emerging understanding. Feedback that is specific and immediate is essential to ensure that knowledge or skills are integrated into an appropriate schema and successfully stored in long-term memory. Without consistent and effective feedback, mistakes or "bugs" may be rehearsed again and again, creating an inappropriate schema stored in long-term memory. Students who have created a malformed schema may never realize their mistake. If and when a misunderstanding or mispatterning is realized, students may have to exert an exhaustive effort to modify their schema. In addition, the timing of feedback needs to be consistent and immediate. Delays in feedback are not harmful as long as teachers provide students with feedback at a time when they can clearly and accurately recall their performance. Authentic assessment tools are ideal for providing students with immediate, consistent, and accurate feedback.

A pleasant by-product of authentic assessment is the emotional context in which the assessment takes place. Emotion plays a central role not only in learning and memory, but also in the conditions under which a person is best able to recall and apply information. Because authentic assessment is ongoing and is an integral part of the instructional process, the test anxiety often associated with more traditional forms of assessment, most notably the standardized test, is not present. Students are relatively free from stress and are better able to demonstrate what they know.

Longer class times permit authentic assessment in ways that shorter class periods cannot. A traditional fifty-minute class period barely provides enough time for teachers to impart the *who*, *what*, and *when* of the curricular material. Larger blocks of time allow teachers to guide students to the *why* and *how* elements of the learning equation. Students have time to internalize the material and demonstrate that they know how to apply the material to real-life tasks and situations. Remembering Burke's (1999) definition of assessment as the process of gathering evidence, the question for teaching in extended time formats becomes, "What other methods can teachers use to obtain evidence of student understanding?" Skillful teachers expand the variety of assessment forms they use whenever possible. Employing conferences, graphic organizers, journals, logs, observation checklists, portfolios, and rubrics provides teachers *and* the students themselves with evidence that learning is occurring. Each is now discussed.

Conferences allow opportunities for the teacher to meet one-on-one with a student or a student team. While other class teams are working on projects or other tasks, the teacher can meet with students and verbally check on what learning is going on. Block scheduling offers the kind of multitask lesson flow that permits teacher-student conferencing.

Graphic organizers are visual tools to help students organize and process a great deal of information. (For a more detailed discussion, see Chapter 5.)

Journals and *logs* are ongoing writing opportunities that allow students to write and reflect upon ongoing learning. Journals are open ended and contain more personal reflections than logs, which are used for more content-specific reflections, such as thoughts or observations about a science experiment, Internet search, field trip, or service-learning experience. In addition, journals and logs offer the type of low-intensity activity essential to pulsed learning.

Observation checklists are lists of specific criteria a teacher uses to determine a student's level of mastery of an activity or concept. Such checklists can include performance criteria related to the following.

General Observations	Specific Criteria
• Social skills	• Disagrees with ideas not the person
• Group dynamics	• Encourages fellow students on his or her team
• Presentation skills	• Speaks clearly and at a moderate rate
• Laboratory procedures	• Uses appropriate visual tools while presenting
• Steps in the writing and/or researching process	• Gathers all the lab material before beginning the lab procedure
	• Documents each research source

Performance criteria are usually derived from the broader content standards by the teacher, by a teacher team, or by a department.

Portfolios are collections and samples of student work chosen by the teacher and the student to represent the student's growth and achievement. Portfolios are not just snapshots but moving pictures that illuminate achievement and growth over time. Like journals and logs, portfolio collection and reflection time are low-intensity activities that, in addition to their use in the assessment process, also serve as counterpoints to higher intensity activities. In its simplest form, the portfolio process has three stages: collection, selection, and reflection (Fogarty, 1997a).

- *Collection.* Choosing the work that may be appropriately placed in the portfolio or gathering artifacts or exhibits that add dimension to an entry or to the overall presentation of the portfolio.
- *Selection.* Determining what materials to include in the portfolio. It is important to note that not only "perfect" work is included. Work that reflects progress and illuminates the process of learning is not only appropriate but also necessary to draw a full picture of achievement.
- *Reflection.* Thinking about a specific entry's meaning and purpose.

Rubrics use specific performance criteria and standards to be achieved to evaluate the level of student performance on a task or activity. Rubrics give clear guidelines to the student of what "good" and "good enough"

ASSESSMENT: **175**
MEASURING
ACHIEVEMENT AND
GROWTH IN
EXTENDED TIME
FORMATS

look like before they undertake a task. The teacher then uses the rubric to ascertain student achievement. The student isn't left guessing what the teacher is looking for.

Figure 6.3 shows an open "rubric template" that teachers may use themselves or with students when constructing such an assessment tool. The column on the far left side of the template is where performance elements such as communication, organization, teamwork, accuracy, originality, and presentation can be listed. Whoever constructs the rubric generally selects one or two labels for each performance level ("accomplished" and "B," for example). Students may want to use more trendy or informal language to label the levels. Teachers need to make sure the terms are positive ones such as (from lowest to highest level):

First Base—Second Base—Third Base—Home Run!
Apprentice—Expert—Master
Needs more thought—Awesome!

The template shows four levels, but rubrics can have as few as two levels—"acceptable" and "unacceptable," for example. Two-level rubrics are often constructed to evaluate journal entries. The specific performance criteria fill in the rest of the grid. It is perhaps easiest to begin with what the best possible work would look like. At the highest level, the criteria are challenging and akin to what may have been formerly considered "extra

◉ Figure 6.3 Rubric Template

Essential Elements of Perormance		Performance Levels			
		Proficient Excellent/ Advanced "A" "4"	Accomplished Good "B" "3"	Basic Acceptable "C" "2"	Novice Not Yet "D" "1"
		Specific Performance Criteria ———————————————→			

⊙ Figure 6.4 Evaluation Tools Modeled

Tool	As Illustrated in Figures
Four-Level Rubric	3.8, 6.3 (template), 6.5
Group Presentation Rubric	1.11
Teacher Observation	4.7
Portfolio Evaluation Rubric	5.14
Student Self-Assessment	4.9

credit." It is only by going the extra mile, so to speak, that students can attain the highest level.

Figure 6.4 directs the reader to other figures in this book that illustrate the various assessment tools just discussed as part of the four-phase lesson plans at the end of the chapters.

Students who underperform on traditional tests can communicate their mastery of material through projects, performances, or demonstrations. Further, authentic assessment is perhaps the best chance for students to show "how they are smart" in terms of their own unique development of the intelligences. This presents a real challenge to teachers accustomed to working within the confines of the traditional time and assessment structure. Therefore, ongoing staff development is a necessary ingredient of successful extended time formats.

ASSESSMENT FOR LEARNING

Some assessments are used to hold schools accountable for their educational task.

Other assessments are used to help rank students, or to decide whether students are prepared for the next grade level. The primary aim of the movement toward assessment for learning is "on any assessment for which the first priority is to serve the purpose of promoting students' learning" (Black, Harrison, Lee, Marshall, & Wiliam, 2003, p. 2). A primary characteristic of this assessment is how strongly it is linked on an ongoing basis with the entire process of learning. Assessment for learning enables the teacher to clearly see what needs to be taught and retaught, perhaps in a different way. Assessment for learning offers the student feedback to delineate exactly where the student needs to focus the next steps of learning. In this way, the downbeat of assessment for learning is in formative assessment. "Evidence of surveys of teacher practice shows that formative assessment is not at present a strong feature of classroom work" (Black et al., 2003, p. 2). This suggests that many teachers are good at summative assessments—that is, an end-of-chapter quiz, an end-of-unit test, or an

ASSESSMENT: **177**
MEASURING
ACHIEVEMENT AND
GROWTH IN
EXTENDED TIME
FORMATS

end-of-unit paper or project. What teachers need help on is the ongoing kind of assessment that could be very informative for the teacher and the teaching as well as for the student and the learning. The promise of this movement is "that the changes involved will raise the scores of their students on normal conventional tests" (Black et al., 2003, p. 2).

The strategies involved in formative assessment included questioning, feedback, sharing criteria with learners, and self-assessment (Black et al., 2003, p. 22). To target just a few suggestions from extensive research in the area of assessment for learning, implementing wisdom from the past has included the use of "wait time." Research from decades ago established how effective just waiting ten to fifteen seconds for a student to think through the answer to a question promoted both learning and thinking.

In the area of feedback, studies have shown that feedback without a grade encouraged the student "to take action on the feedback" (Black et al., 2003, p. 43). Many students began to discover that the comments made a big difference in their subsequent work.

One method of sharing criteria with students has been the use of rubrics. The elements of the rubric are shared right from the beginning of the assigned task. In this way, students discover that their own effort decides their grade. The clearer the rubric and criteria, the less wondering there is about why a student received a certain grade. Finally, "one of the most powerful instructional tools to help students internalize the criteria and recognize quality work is to have students develop the criteria . . . with the teacher" (Burke, 1999, p. 89).

Lastly, in the area of self-assessment and its importance, "it is very difficult for students to achieve a learning goal unless they understand that goal and can assess what they need to do to reach it" (Black et al., 2003, p. 49). When this occurs regularly, more and more of the responsibility for learning is placed upon the student, where it belongs. Related to this is the value of peer assessment. When the criteria are crystal clear, then it is possible for peers to assess others' work. Sometimes the evaluation of a peer can go farther than that of the teacher!

One study reports real changes in how teachers thought about their own teaching: "They now think of their teaching in terms of facilitation students' learning, rather than feeling that they have to 'get through' the curriculum at all costs" (Black et al., 2003, p. 91.)

NO CHILD LEFT BEHIND (NCLB)

Thomas Armstrong (2006) made a strong argument regarding the impact of NCLB on the conversations and the decisions about what happens inside public schools. He wrote, "Aside from any specific problems inherent in the law itself, however, what seems most troubling about NCLB is that it represents the culmination of a movement that has been gathering steam in American education for over eighty years. The most destructive legacy of NCLB may turn out to be that it hijacks the dialogue in education away from talking about the education of human beings...and toward a focus on tests, standards, and accountability" (p. 8).

While tests, standards, and accountability themselves are not destructive, if educators lose sight of the humanity of their students because they focus on how students perform on a standardized test instead of what students are becoming, then tests, standards and accountability can become destructive. And students aren't the only ones who can be damaged by a system that values test scores over individual students; teachers can also be harmed. Some educators are reduced to teaching their students just so they achieve higher test scores, and in the process, they lose their love of truly educating, inspiring, and supporting their students to become the best of themselves.

It is fortunate that teachers can benefit from NCLB. Teachers who are motivated to help students achieve often find themselves self-evaluating and discussing with groups of teachers what they are doing in the classroom that works to encourage students to love learning. Teachers can see the benefits of forming professional learning communities. All of these are positive steps to improve learning.

According to Brandi, one of my graduate students and a current teacher, "Teachers are really talking to each other in my school. They look at the data and try to find ways to improve what they are doing for kids in the classroom. There is more energy and commitment to work together instead of staying isolated." When educators work together, they can become a powerful voice for what is best for students, not what is best for the system or the politician. And teachers talking together help schools become exciting places for student learning and growth.

When educators use the four-phase lesson design, including brain-compatible learning practices, they are doing what is best for students. Incorporating the four-phase lesson format naturally encourages the classroom to become student centered. The focus is on how students learn best, how students support each other in the learning process, how students can be more responsible learners, and how what students are learning informs their lives. As a result of the lesson design, teachers identify and value what each student can contribute to the learning process, and they explore ways to make rich and in-depth learning experiences for their students. Teachers can become the mentors and models they intended to become when they chose a career in education.

TESTING MATTERS

A Fact of Life

For better or worse, schools and their programs are often judged by the outcomes of standardized tests. Testing is a fact of life. While standardized tests will no doubt remain an educational constant, how schools and teachers relate to the tests will have a huge impact on their students. In an alternative scheduling context, the question of standardized testing is all the

ASSESSMENT: **179**
MEASURING
ACHIEVEMENT AND
GROWTH IN
EXTENDED TIME
FORMATS

more pronounced. The success of alternative scheduling is often judged by the performance of students in the block relative to their peers learning under a traditional schedule (Benton-Kupper, 1999). Perhaps the two biggest perceived challenges to the efficacy of a block schedule are scope and recency of materials covered. "If the focus remains on surface learning and low-level recall, then the recency of exposure is critical!" (Rettig & Canady, 1996, p. 10). But if the material is covered in depth, greater retention for longer periods can be achieved. Teachers experienced in the block report that they can discern little educational significance between the differences in retention of students who recently completed a class over retention of those students with greater time lapses between courses. So once again, the question appears not so much to be one of the assessment or testing process, but one of curricular material and instructional approaches.

The greatest predictor of student performance is what actually takes place in the classroom, whether it takes place in the block or within a conventional schedule. Students taught with strategies that tap into their long-term memory have a better chance to recall material on standardized tests than they would if their short-term memory were the focus. (See Chapter 1 for a discussion of memory.) In addition to teaching to long-term memory, teachers need to employ the best practices in structuring extended class time. If teachers fail to use the time in the block efficiently, a decrease in standardized test scores can result.

By postponing higher order thinking goals, skills remediation classes have a deleterious effect on the standardized test scores of students placed in these classes. Low-achieving students suffer most from a proficiency-driven curriculum (measured by standardized tests) because they are consigned indefinitely to dull and repetitive skills instruction that does not enable them to grasp underlying concepts (Levin, Glass, & Meister, 1987). It is lucky that brain-compatible learning approaches can have a dramatic impact even on students who have previously been labeled "low achieving." When instructional approaches are varied, when the curriculum content is made relevant and applicable to real-life situations, learning moves from mere rote memorization to deeply internalized, usable information. When this occurs, the material can be retained far longer than was previously thought possible. Longer class times allow teachers more occasions to discern how well the material is being absorbed and to decide whether any reteaching strategies are needed to enable students to better grasp the material (Fitzgerald, 1996).

Iron Out the "Forgetting Curve"

Some schools teaching in the block prepare their students for standardized tests by scheduling *structured review sessions*. Such sessions are scheduled three or four weeks before the tests are given. Their purpose is to help students recall the significant details needed for the test. If the original class work has emphasized the frameworks and the concepts, then the review sessions need only remind the students of these frameworks and concepts and then help the students get on top of the details again. On the other hand, if the original class work neglected sense-making frameworks and concepts, then it is as if the students are just beginning to absorb the details needed for the tests. This will make preparing for the standardized tests doubly difficult (College Boards Online, 1999).

Extended time formats permit the teacher to spend time teaching the concepts and the overall frameworks of the material being presented. Probing questions that help students make connections to other material can be just the connections needed to push the material into long-term memory.

While student performance on standardized tests isn't the purpose of teaching, brain-compatible teaching methodologies that lay out frameworks and concepts as containers for crucial facts and information greatly enable peak student performance on such tests (Burke, 1992). The more brain-compatible the structured review sessions are, the more powerful and long-lasting their effect will be. Students working within a system that harnesses the power of cooperative learning, recognizes multiple intelligences, facilitates the expansion of higher-order thinking skills, and provides adequate time for learning and metacognition retain information for use on standardized tests and beyond.

Tests Are Changing

Today, some standardized tests are very different from the simple multiple-choice tests of years ago (Burke, 1992). The ability to think and to transfer and connect information is increasingly becoming part of standardized tests. Because the tests are changing, it is even more important than ever that teaching in the block emphasize concepts, frameworks, higher order thinking skills, and applications to real life. Details are important. Discrete pieces of information will continue to be tested; however, much more is demanded of students in the real world than recollection of isolated bits of information. The brain-compatible pedagogy that alternative scheduling facilitates and encourages is well suited to meet the rigorous demands society and the economy place on the educational system.

Measure Up

The ultimate reason—and perhaps the only valid reason for implementing a program such as alternative block scheduling—is because it has a positive impact on student achievement. Possibly the easiest way (or at least, the most frequently used way) to "judge" student success and program success is through testing. So naturally, the first trial block scheduling must undergo is how it fares under the glare of standardized testing. Studies have shown that students in the block have fared as well on such tests as their counterparts in traditionally scheduled classes (Baylis, 1983). Several studies have found that both student conduct (attendance,

ASSESSMENT: **181**
MEASURING
ACHIEVEMENT AND
GROWTH IN
EXTENDED TIME
FORMATS

attention, and morale) and academic performance (content mastery, posttest versus pretest gains, and standardized test scores) are improved when block scheduling is instituted (Baylis, 1983; Benton-Kupper, 1999; Carroll, 1994a).

ASSESSMENT IN FOUR-PHASE LESSON AND UNIT DESIGN

When teachers use the four-phase lesson design with its repeated attend-experience-reflect cycle, they have an automatic, built-in format for providing students with thoughtful feedback in the form of authentic assessment. The design provides teachers with a structure for helping students process their learning, evaluate their respective levels of performance, and use authentic assessment as a natural part of the learning process.

The assessment process is integral to the learning process. Students need to engage in defining the performance criteria and working toward attaining high standards. Authentic assessment helps students achieve "excellence" because they know in advance what it looks like from the rubric or other format for the criteria.

The Sample Four-Phase Lesson Plan is a structured review lesson in preparation for students taking a college advanced-placement (AP) test and, as already stated, is a method for "ironing out," or recalling information previously stored in long-term memory. "Science Schmience or Who Framed Sir Isaac Newton?" is offered here as a sample of what could be included in a unit taught in a minisession (see the discussion of yearly schedules in Chapter 3). The purposes of the lesson are to assist students in remembering important information, identifying ways to associate the information, and familiarizing themselves with the AP test-question format. The curriculum connection is science. The AP European history teacher may want to invite one or more of the science teachers (physics, psychology, chemistry, biology, physiology) to act as a resource person during this lesson. While science was selected as the focus of this lesson, the focus could be any of the broad topics covered in AP European history such as art, music, literature, economics, government, war, or any other applicable topic.

Notice how students manipulate the course content in a variety of ways. Students do all of the talking and discussing during this lesson. Since students are reviewing in preparation for a major test, it is critical that they share their knowledge and insights with each other, practice saying things they might actually write, and hear how others have connected the information to clarify their own understanding and to remember details and concepts.

Sample Four-Phase Lesson Plan

SCIENCE SCHMIENCE OR WHO FRAMED SIR ISAAC NEWTON?

Level: Secondary

Curriculum Integration: European history and science

Multiple Intelligences

- ☑ Bodily/Kinesthetic
- ☑ Interpersonal
- ❏ Intrapersonal
- ☑ Logical/Mathematical

- ❏ Musical
- ❏ Naturalist
- ☑ Verbal/Linguistic
- ☑ Visual/Spatial

Content Standards

WORLD HISTORY (EUROPEAN)

Understands major trends, technological advances, cultural innovations, and political, social, and cultural redefinitions in Europe from 4000 BCE to the twentieth century

Understands the impact of scientific and technological innovations on twentieth-century society

Understands major reasons for the great disparities between scientifically advanced industrialized nations and developing nations

SCIENCE

Understands the nature of scientific knowledge

Understands the scientific enterprise

GRAPHIC ORGANIZERS

Inquire Phase: Double T-Chart

Gather Phase: T-Chart

Apply Phase: Student choose from several graphic organizers

TECHNOLOGY

Internet research of additional information approved and recommended Web sites

ESSENTIAL QUESTION

How can connecting historical events with scientific discoveries reinforce a deeper understanding of those events?

Science Schmience or Who Framed Sir Isaac Newton?

Ms. Howell is an experienced and highly respected high school AP European history teacher. Throughout the course, she connects advancement in scientific discoveries with critical events in European history. She works with the science teachers in order to identify the important advances in science that also relate to the course content of the science teachers. This lesson is a culminating lesson for her AP course. Ms. Howell

ASSESSMENT: **183**
MEASURING
ACHIEVEMENT AND
GROWTH IN
EXTENDED TIME
FORMATS

has two objectives. First, she wants students to recall and discuss with each other important historical events and science discoveries; and second, she wants students to review different kinds of AP questions. She asks students to practice writing their own European history AP questions, to share their questions with other students, and for all students to practice answering the student-generated questions, to prepare themselves for the upcoming AP exam.

INQUIRE PHASE

TWENTY MINUTES

Inquire Activity Option A
Objective: To recall events from European history and arrange them in chronological order.

ATTEND
The teacher begins a dialogue in the following way:
- Today is a review of European history from the scientists' point of view.
- Think about all the scientific advances and issues that have had an impact on the political, economic, social, religious, intellectual, and artistic development of Europe.
- Discuss some of your thoughts with a classmate next to you.

EXPERIENCE: "HUMAN TIMELINE"
Each student does the following:
- Independently chooses an event from European history
- Draws a picture or other visual representation of the event on a five-by-seven-inch card or blank sheet of paper
- Secures their completed card or paper to the front of their shirt with tape
- Moves about the room to find one or more other students who have depicted the same event or an event that influenced or was influenced by their event
- Lines up in chronological order with those they have identified as being somehow related to their topic
- Discusses their event within their small group and then shares the events they depicted with the rest of the class

REFLECT

Students write in their metacognitive journals about their perceptions of how recent scientific discoveries have impacted today's culture, society, and government.

Inquire Activity Option B

Objective: Students recall and relate historical events having to do with science and the course of European history.

ATTEND

Teachers ask the following questions to start a class discussion:

- Do you think you have a good memory? Why or why not?
- Is a good memory important in an age when computers contain trillions of bits of information? Why or why not?

EXPERIENCE: "WHERE SCIENCE AND HISTORY COLLIDE"

Students do the following:

- Working alone, list every issue or event that comes to mind related to European history and science
- Compare their lists in pairs or triads

The teacher then does the following:

- Leads a whole-class discussion following each brainstorm and small-group sharing and records the information on chart paper using a Double T-Chart labeled "Date," "European Historical Event," and "Scientific Advancement"
- Repeats the process two or three times

REFLECT

The teacher asks the class the following questions:

- What reminders were there for you during the human timeline activities?
- What did you hear that became clearer, made more sense, or introduced new connections to you?
- What can you do to remember this information?

ASSESSMENT: **185**
MEASURING
ACHIEVEMENT AND
GROWTH IN
EXTENDED TIME
FORMATS

 **GATHER PHASE**

TWENTY-FIVE MINUTES

Gather Activity Option A

Objective: Students "gather"—from other students and their own memory—specific elements of European history that were affected by scientific discoveries.

ATTEND

The teacher begins a class discussion that will introduce the students to the experience:

- In our next experience, you will have to think like a detective.
- Does anybody know what *deductive reasoning* means?
- When would it be used? And by whom?
- If I told you that inductive reasoning uses the opposite method of determining information of deductive reasoning, what do you think the term means?

EXPERIENCE: "ROVING INVESTIGATORS"

The teacher does the following:

- Writes one person, place, event, or issue on a three-by-five-inch card, filling out as many cards as there are ideas generated in the inquire phase (at least one for every student).
- Randomly places one card on the back of each student without the student knowing what item is on his or her back.

Students then do the following:

- Meander around the room asking "yes or no" or "true or false" questions of each other to determine the entry on their backs.
- May not give hints and must answer truthfully.
- Determine who or what is on their backs, then turn in their cards to the teacher and receive a different card.
- Continue investigating until every card is identified or until time is up.

Gather Activity Option B

Objective: Students design memory aids.

ATTEND

The teacher asks the following questions to begin a class discussion:

- When you were younger, how did you memorize spelling words?
- Do you or did you go about studying for a test on the plot and meaning of a novel differently than you would have studied for a spelling test?

EXPERIENCE: "LEFT TO THEIR OWN DEVICES"

In groups of three or four, students design mnemonics and visuals, write lyrics to familiar tunes, or invent other ways to help them remember details about the names, places, and events on the cards.

REFLECT—"TALKING CIRCLES"

Students do the following:

- Stand in two concentric circles, with half of the students on the inside circle and the other half on the outside circle.
- Face each other to talk with another student. One circle moves clockwise, while the other moves counterclockwise, moving ahead by one person each time the teacher asks one of the questions below. Each new pair exchanges their answer with the person they encountered on the circle.

The teacher asks and records students' responses on a T-Chart labeled "Important Events" and "Why Important":

- Of all the information you talked about today, what do you think are the most critical points for you to remember? Why?
- Why is it important to remember this information, beyond taking the AP exam?
- How is your world different today because of what happened in Europe?
- Enough other pertinent questions to complete the circle's cycle once.

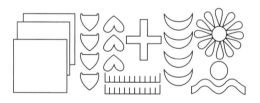

 **PROCESS PHASE**

THIRTY MINUTES

Process Activity

Objective: Students create mock AP test questions.

ATTEND

The teacher focuses student attention on the next experience by beginning a discussion:

- You are going to create some questions that are AP test quality. What do you think makes an excellent AP question? Share with a partner.

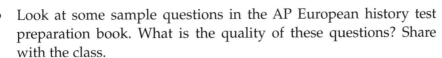

ASSESSMENT: **187**
MEASURING
ACHIEVEMENT AND
GROWTH IN
EXTENDED TIME
FORMATS

- Look at some sample questions in the AP European history test preparation book. What is the quality of these questions? Share with the class.
- Let's decide what makes a good AP question.

Students and teachers create a checklist for writing test questions.

Students do the following:

- Working in groups of three, look through the AP test preparation manual to become familiar with the types of questions posed on the test.
- Determine characteristics of the test questions and the accompanying multiple-choice options.
- Share their findings with the class in order to develop a master set of criteria for use in evaluating the questions the student triads create. The rubric can be used for student self-evaluation, as refined directions for the activity, and as the instrument with which the students are evaluated on the experience.)

EXPERIENCE: "MOCK QUESTIONS"

Students do the following:

- Working in the same groups and using the established criteria (see Figure 6.5), generate mock questions with a focus on science (three multiple-choice questions that include answer options and one essay question).
- Join another group and answer each other's test questions. Answers are discussed and groups give feedback to each other on the quality of the questions they created.
- Move to a different group and repeat the process one or two more times.
- Submit their test questions to the teacher.

The teacher then does the following:

- Randomly selects questions to ask the whole class.
- Facilitates a discussion on each question, reinforcing appropriate responses and eliciting multiple answers.
- Evaluates each group's questions using the rubric.

REFLECT

The teacher asks the following questions, prompting student discussion:

- What do you think makes a good test question?
- How will knowing how good test questions are written help you be a better test taker?
- What procedure should you follow when answering multiple-choice and essay questions to improve the quality of your answers?

◉ Figure 6.5 Mock Question Criteria

	Performance Levels			
	Novice	**Adequate**	**Accomplished**	**Advanced**
Directions				
Clarity	Difficult to understand	Not entirely clear	Clearly stated	Very clearly and concisely stated
Questions				
Precision	Murky and unfocused	Too narrow or too broad	Appropriate for the material	Highly focused and appropriate
Accuracy	Unrelated to the material	Several inaccurate references with a few accurate ones	Mostly accurate	Totally accurate and challenging
Coverage	Only covered a small part of assignment	Covered one-half of the material	Covered three-quarters of the material	Covered all the material and pushed higher level thinking skills
Options				
Number Provided	None provided	2 provided	4 provided	5 challenging options provided
Length	Options not described well	Length of options revealed the answer	All but one option of similar length	Equal length for each option, pushing real thinking to choose
Mechanics				
Spelling	4 or more errors	2-3 errors	1 error	No errors
Grammar	4 or more errors	2-3 errors	1 error	No errors
Punctuation	4 or more errors	2-3 errors	1 error	No errors

ASSESSMENT: **189**
MEASURING
ACHIEVEMENT AND
GROWTH IN
EXTENDED TIME
FORMATS

APPLY PHASE

FIFTEEN MINUTES

Apply Activity

Objective: Students make meaning from the material by making connections between its various elements.

ATTEND

Students do the following:

- Identify practical reasons for understanding and remembering information taught in AP European history.
- Write in their personal reflection journal their thoughts on the following questions:
  —What are some legitimate reasons for U.S. high school students to study European history?
  —In what ways are you a different person from the person who began this structured review class?
  —What long-term impact will what you learned about European history and test taking have on your life?

EXPERIENCE: "CROSS-CONTENT CONNECTIONS"

Students do the following:

- In small groups, create a graphic organizer, chart, graph, or other visual that demonstrates the relationship between science and any one of the following as it pertains to European history: visual arts, music, literature, economics, social systems, religion, war, government, or agriculture.
- Prepare to share their visual during the next class.

REFLECT

The teacher poses the following questions:

- What is one thing that worries you most about taking the AP exam?
- What would you like to review before you take the exam?
- Who is in the best position to help you prepare for the exam?

Homework Assignment

Students individually review their notes, books, or other sources to add information to their copy of the group visual they have started.

REFLECTIVE QUESTIONS

1. What assessment strategies do you currently use?

2. What is helpful about them? What is unhelpful about them?

3. What formative assessment strategies might work in your classes?

4. What summative assessment strategies might work in your classes?

5. In an upcoming unit, add some different assessment strategies.

6. How might these differing strategies affect your students?

References

Armstrong, T. (2006). *The best schools.* Alexandria, VA: Association for Supervision and Curriculum Development.

Baylis, C. A. (1983). *Summary of an investigation into the relative effects on student performance on a "block" vs. "non-block" scheduled developmental semester* (ED244711). Paper presented to the Developmental Education Committee at Allegheny County College, Monroeville, PA.

Bellanca, J., & Fogarty, R. (2001). *Blueprints for achievement in the cooperative classroom* (3rd ed.). Thousand Oaks, CA: Corwin Press.

Benton-Kupper, J. (1999). Can less be more? The quantity versus quality issue of curriculum in a block schedule. *Journal of Research and Development in Education, 32*(3), 168–177.

Black, P., Harrison, C., Lee, C., Marshall, B., & Wiliam, D. (2003). *Assessment for learning.* New York: Open University Press.

Bloom, B. S., et al. (1956). *Taxonomy of educational objectives. Handbook 1: Cognitive domain.* New York: David McKay.

Boyett, J. H. (with Boyett, J. T.). (1995). *Beyond workplace 2000: Essential strategies of the corporation.* New York: Plume Penguin.

Brett, M. (1996). Teaching block-scheduled class periods. *The Education Digest, 62*(1), 34–37.

Brozo, W. G. (2006, September). Bridges to literacy for boys. *Educational Leadership, 64*(1), 71–74.

Bruer, J. T. (1998). Brain science, brain fiction. *Educational Leadership, 56*(3), 14–18.

Bruer, J. T. (1999). In search of . . . Brain-based education. *Phi Delta Kappan, 80*(9), 649–755.

Burke, K. (Ed.). (1992). *Authentic assessment: A collection.* Thousand Oaks, CA: Corwin Press.

Burke, K. (2005). *How to assess authentic learning* (4th ed.). Thousand Oaks, CA: Corwin Press.

Caine, G., Caine, R. N., & Crowell, S. (1994). *MindShifts: A brain-based process for restructuring schools and renewing education.* Tucson, AZ: Zephyr Press.

Caine, R. N., & Caine, G. (1991). *Making connections: Teaching and the human brain.* Alexandria, VA: Association for Supervision and Curriculum Development.

Caine, R. N., & Caine, G. (1997). *Education on the edge of possibility.* Alexandria, VA: Association for Supervision and Curriculum Development.

Caine, R. N., Caine, G., McClintic, C., & Klimek, K. (2005). *12 brain/mind learning principles in action.* Thousand Oaks, CA: Corwin Press.

Canady, R. L., & Rettig, M. D. (1993). The power of innovative scheduling. *Educational Leadership, 53*(3), 4–10.

Canady, R. L., & Rettig, M. D. 1995. *Block scheduling: A catalyst for change in high schools.* Princeton, NJ: Eye on Education.

Carroll, J. M. (1994a). Organizing time to support learning. *The School Administrator 51*(30), 26–28, 30–33.

Chapman, C. (1993). *If the shoe fits . . . : How to develop multiple intelligences in the classroom.* Thousand Oaks, CA: Corwin Press.

Chapman, C., & Freeman, L. (1996). *Multiple intelligences centers and projects.* Thousand Oaks, CA: Corwin Press.

College Boards Online. (1999). *SAT: Tips. New York: Educational Testing Service.* Retrieved from http://www.collegeboard.org/sat/html/students/prep006.html

Costa, A. L. (2008). *The school as a home for the mind* (2nd ed.). Thousand Oaks, CA: Corwin Press.

Covey, S. (1989). *Seven habits of highly effective people: Restoring the character ethic.* New York: Simon & Schuster.

Csikszentmihalyi, M. (1990). *Flow: The psychology of optimal experience.* New York: Harper & Row.

Cushman, K. (Ed.). (1995). Using time well: Schedules in essential schools. *Horace, 12*(2). Retrieved February 12, 1999, from http://www.essentialschools.org/pubs/horace/12/v12n02.html

D'Arcangelo, M. (1998). The brains behind the brain. *Educational Leadership, 56*(3), 20–25.

Emig, V. B. (1997). *A multiple intelligences inventor, 39*(7), 47–50.

Fitzgerald, R. (2002). *How to integrate the curricula* (2nd ed.). Thousand Oaks, CA: Corwin Press.

Fogarty, R. (1991). *The mindful school: How to integrate the curricula.* Thousand Oaks, CA: Corwin Press.

Fogarty, R. (Ed.). (1996). *Block scheduling: A collection of articles.* Thousand Oaks, CA: Corwin Press.

Fogarty, R. (2001). *Brain-compatible classrooms* (2nd. ed.). Thousand Oaks, CA: Corwin Press.

Fogarty, R. (1997b). *Problem-based learning and other curriculum models for the multiple intelligences classroom.* Thousand Oaks, CA: Corwin Press.

Fogarty, R., & Stoehr, J. (2008). *Integrating curricula with multiple intelligences* (2nd ed.). Thousand Oaks, CA: Corwin Press.

Gardner, H. (1983). *Frames of mind: The theory of multiple intelligences.* New York: Basic Books.

Gardner, H. (1994). Educating for understanding. *Phi Delta Kappan, 75*(7), 563–565.

Gardner, H. (1995). Reflections on multiple intelligences. *Phi Delta Kappan, 77*(10), 200–209.

Gardner, H. (1999). *Intelligence reframed.* New York: Basic Books.

Gardner, H. (2000). *The disciplined mind.* New York: Penguin Books.

Gardner, H. (2006). *Multiple intelligences: New horizons.* New York: Basic Books.

Garlikov, R. (n.d.). The Socratic method: Teaching by asking instead of by telling. Retrieved December 12, 2006, from http://www.garlikov.com/Soc_Meth.html

Garlikov, R. (n.d.). Using the Socratic method. Retrieved December 12, 2006, from http://www.garlikov.com/teaching/smmore.htm

Gaubatz, N. (2003). Course scheduling formats and their impact on student learning. *The National Teaching and Learning Forum, 12*(1). Retrieved January 2, 2007, from http://www.ntlf.com/html/lib/suppmat/1201course.htm

Glasser, W. (1990). *The quality school.* New York: HarperPerennial.

Glenn, H. S., & Nelsen, J. (1988). *Raising self-reliant children in a self-indulgent world.* Rocklin, CA: Prima Publishing & Communications.

Goleman, D. (1995). *Emotional intelligence.* New York: Bantam Books.

Hayes Jacobs, H. (1997). *Mapping the big picture.* Alexandria, VA: Association for Supervision and Curriculum Development.

Heiberger, D. W., & Heiniger-White, M. C. (2000). *S'cool moves for learning.* Shasta, CA: Integrated Learner Press.

Jensen, E. (1998). How Julie's brain learns. *Educational Leadership, 56*(3), 45.

Jensen, E. (2000). Moving with the brain in mind. *Educational Leadership, 58*(3), 34–37.

Johnson, D. W., & Johnson, R. (1986). *Circles of learning: Cooperation in the classroom.* Alexandria, VA: Association for Supervision and Curriculum Development.

Johnson, D. W., Johnson, R., & Holubec, E. J. (1988). *Cooperation in the classroom.* Edina, MN: Interaction Book Company.

Kendall, J. S., & Marzano, R. J. (1997). *Content knowledge: A compendium of standards and benchmarks for K–12 education* (2nd ed.). Alexandria, VA: Association for Supervision and Curriculum Development.

King, K., & Gurian, M. (2006, September). Teaching to the minds of boys. *Educational Leadership, 64*(1), 56–61.

King, M. L., Jr. (1964). *Letter from Birmingham jail.* Philadelphia: American Friends Service Committee.

Kovalik, S. (1997). *Integrated thematic instruction: The model* (3rd ed.). Kent, WA: Books for Educators.

Lave, J., & Wenger, E. (1991, September). *Situated learning: Legitimate peripheral participation.* Boston: Cambridge University Press.

Lazear, D. (1999). *Eight ways of knowing* (3rd ed.). Thousand Oaks, CA: Corwin Press.

LeDoux, J. (1996). *The emotional brain: The mysterious underpinnings of emotional life.* New York: Simon & Schuster.

Lee, H. (1960). *To kill a mockingbird.* New York: Harper Collins.

Levin, H., Glass, G., & Meister, G. (1987). Cost effectiveness of computer assisted instruction. *Education Review, 11,* 50–72.

Lewis, C. W., Dugan, J. J., Winokur, M. A., & Cobb, R. B. (2005). The effects of block scheduling on high school academic achievement. *NASSP Bulletin, 89*(645), 72–87.

McTighe, J., & Ferrarra, S. (1996). *Assessing learning in the classroom.* Washington, DC: National Education Association.

Moran, S., Kornhaber, M., & Gardner, H. (2006). Orchestrating multiple intelligences. *Educational Leadership, 64*(1), 22–27.

National Education Commission on Time and Learning. (1994). *Prisoners of time.* Washington, DC: Author. Retrieved March 3, 1999, from http://www.ed.gov/pubs/PrisonersOfTime/Dimensions.html

O'Day, J., Goertz, M. & Floden, R. (1995). *Building capacity for education reform (CPRE Policy Briefs, RB-18).* New Brunswick, NJ: Consortium for Policy Research in Education.

Ogle, D. (1986). K-W-L group instruction strategy. In A. Palincsar, D. Ogle, B. Jones, & E. Carr (Eds.), *Teaching techniques as thinking* (Teleconference resource guide). Alexandria, VA: Association for Supervision and Curriculum Development.

Price, L. F. (2005). The biology of risk taking. *Educational Leadership, 62*(7), 22–26.

Rettig, M. D., & Canady, R. L. (1996). All around the block: The benefits and challenges of a non-traditional school schedule. *The School Administrator, 53*(8), 8–12.

Ripley, A. (2005). Who says a woman can't be Einstein? *Time, 165*(10), 51–57.

Rosenfield, I. (1988). *The invention of memory.* New York: Basic Books.

Sadowski, M. (1996). Just like starting over: The promises and pitfalls of block scheduling. *The Harvard Education Letter, 12*(6), 1–3.

Shore, R. (1995). How one high school improved school climate. *Educational Leadership, 52*(5), 76–78.

Slavin, R. (2003). *Educational psychology: Theory and practice.* (7th ed.). Boston: Allyn and Bacon.

Soraci, S. A., Franks J., Bransford J., Chechile R., Belli R., Carr M., et al. (1994). Incongruous item generation effects: A multiple-cue perspective, *Journal of Experimental Psychology: Learning, Memory, and Cognition, 20,* 1, 67–78.

Sousa, D. A. (2006). *How the brain learns* (3rd ed.). Thousand Oaks, CA: Corwin Press.

Sprenger, M. (1988). Memory lane is a two-way street. *Educational Leadership, 56*(3), 65–67.

Sprenger, M. (1999). *Learning and memory: The brain in action.* Thousand Oaks, CA: Corwin Press.

Sprenger, M. (2003). *Differentiation through learning styles and memory.* Thousand Oaks, CA: Corwin Press.

Sternberg, R. (1985). *Beyond IQ: A triarchic theory of human intelligence.* New York: Cambridge University Press.

Sternberg, R. J. (1997). *Thinking styles.* New York: Cambridge University Press.

Sternberg, R. (1997). What does it mean to be smart? *Educational Leadership, 55*(7), 20–24.

Sternberg, R., Torff, B., & Grigorenko, E. (1998). Teaching triarchically improves student achievement. *Journal of Educational Psychology, 90,* 374–385.

Sternberg, R. J., & Grigorenko, E. L. (2008). *Teaching for successful intelligence* (2nd ed.). Thousand Oaks, CA: Corwin Press.

Sylwester, R. (1995). *A celebration of neurons: An educator's guide to the human brain.* Alexandria, VA: Association for Supervision and Curriculum Development.

Tapscott, D. (1999). Educating the net generation. *Educational Leadership, 56*(5), 7–11.

Tomlinson, C. A. (1999). *The differentiated classroom.* Alexandria, VA: Association for Supervision and Curriculum Development.

Tomlinson, C. A. (2001). *How to differentiate instruction in mixed-ability classrooms.* (2nd ed.). Alexandria, VA: Association for Supervision and Curriculum Development.

Tomlinson, C. A., & McTighe, J. (2006). *Integrating differentiated instruction and understanding by design.* Alexandria, VA: Association for Supervision and Curriculum Development.

Von Oech, R. (1990). *A whack on the side of the head.* New York: Warner Books.

Vygotsky, L. S. (1978). *Mind in society.* (M. Cole, V. John-Steiner, S. Scribner, & E. Souberman, Eds.). Cambridge, MA: Harvard University Press.

Wallis, C. (2006a). Blame it on Teletubbies. *Time, 168*(18), 65.

Wallis, C. (2006b). Inside the autistic mind. *Time, 167*(20), 42–48.

Wassermann, S. (1991). Shazam! You're a teacher. *Phi Delta Kappan, 80*(6), 464–468.

Wiggins, G. (1989). Teaching to the (authentic) test. *Educational Leadership, 46*(7), 41–47.

Wolfe, P. (2001). *Brain matters: Translating research into classroom practice.* Alexandria, VA: Association for Supervision and Curriculum Development.

Wyatt, L. D. (1996). More time, more training. *The School Administrator, 53*(8), 16–18.

Index

Activities
in brain-compatible learning, 24 (figure), 28–30
in content differentiation, 136
in experience component, 58
for multiple intelligences, 129–132, 130 (figure), 131 (table)
Adolescents, brain development in, 21–22
Amygdala
in autistic brains, 23
in brain structure, 7 (figure), 7 (table)
Analogy/simile chart, 151 (figure), 152–153
Analytical intelligence, 141–142, 143 (table), 145 (table), 146 (table), 147 (table)
Analyze, in EIAG, 148–150
Application, of curriculum, xii
Applying level, 148, 149 (figure)
Apply phase
for biology lesson, 41–42
brain compatibility in, 52
guidelines for using, 54 (table)
instructional strategies for, 137 (table)
for integrated elementary lesson, 117–119
for integrated middle school lesson, 165–167
for language arts lesson, 92–93
in lesson design, 44 (figure), 45, 50–52
multiple intelligences in, 131 (table)
P-A-C used in, 147 (table)
of processing model, 44 (figure)
questions during, 57 (table)
schemata in, 53 (table)
for science lesson, 189
teacher role in, 51
in unit design, 63 (figure), 64 (figure), 67, 69–70
Armstrong, Thomas, 177–178
Assessment
authentic, 171–176, 176 (figure)
brain-compatible, 169–181
in content differentiation, 136
differentiated instruction and, 137–138
emotional context of, 173
formative, 177

forms of, 172 (figure)
in four-phase lesson design, 181
in four phases, 60
for learning, 176–177
performance, 171, 172 (figure)
portfolio, 171, 172 (figure)
student self-assessment, 119 (figure), 177
tools for, 173–176, 176 (figure)
traditional, 171, 172 (figure)
triassessment model of, 171
uses of, 176–177
See also Rubrics; Standardized tests
Attend component, 58
Authentic assessment, 171–176, 176 (figure)
Autism, brain development and, 22–23
Autonomy, adolescent need for, 22
Axon, 3 (figure), 3 (table), 5

Backward planning, 135
Beginning-end-middle (BEM) principle, 124–125
Being oneself, adolescent need for, 22
Bellanca, James, 126, 147
Belonging, adolescent need for, 22
Biology lesson plan, 31–42
Block 8 plan, 81–82, 82 (figure)
Block scheduling
content, skills, and processes in, 77–78
directed choices in, 75–77
emotion and, 74–75
engagement in, 76–77
explanation of, 71–72
formats of, 81–84
meaning-filled content in, 79–81
personalization in, 73–74
school climate and, 78–79
trust and belonging in, 72–75
See also Extended time formats
Bloom, Benjamin S., 138, 140
Bodily/kinesthetic intelligence, 18
Brain
adolescent, 21–22
autistic, 22–23
child, 19–20
functions of, 8–23

Brain *(continued)*
  hemispheres of, 2, 2 (figure)
  learning in, 15–16
  male *vs.* female, 20–21, 20 (table), 21 (table)
  nerve cells of, 2–4, 3 (figure)
  schemata in, 12–15
  sections of, 4–8, 4 (table)
  structure of, 1–8
Brain cells, 2–4
Brain compatibility
  in apply phase, 52
  in four-phase lesson design, 47 (figure)
  in gather phase, 49
  in inquire phase, 48
  in process phase, 50
Brain-compatible assessment, 169–181
  vs. standardized tests, 170 (figure)
  See also Assessment
Brain-compatible curriculum, 107–109
Brain-compatible instruction, educational principles for, 122–125, 123 (figure)
Brain-compatible instructional strategies, 126–155
  cooperative learning approaches, 126–128
  differentiated instruction, 132–138
  for higher-order thinking skills, 138–150
  multiple intelligences, 129–132
  professional development for, 156, 157 (figure)
Brain-compatible learning
  activity in, 24 (figure), 28–30
  chunking in, 27
  content in, 24 (figure), 26–28, 79–81
  directed choices in, 75–77
  elements of, 72 (figure), 73 (figure)
  energy in, 30
  environment for, 30–31, 77–79
  hands-on experience in, 26
  learner in, 24–26, 24 (figure)
  in low-achieving students, 179
  motivation in, 25
  multiple intelligences in, 29–30
  nine facets of, 23–30
  personal context in, 25
  reflection in, 27–28
  sample lesson plan for, 31–42
  standardized tests and, 179–181
  time in, 71–72
  trust and belonging in, 72–75
Brain stem, 4 (table), 7 (figure), 8
Bridging snapshots, 151 (figure), 154
BUILD cooperative learning, 126–128, 127 (figure)
Burke, Kay, 169

Caine, Geoffrey, 43, 76
Caine, Renate, 43, 76
Canady, Robert Lynn, 78, 81, 97

"Can Prejudice Kill a Mockingbird?" lesson, 55, 84–93
Carroll, Joseph, 72, 83
Case studies, 104–105
Cells, of brain, 2–4, 3 (figure)
Cerebellum, 6–8, 7 (figure)
Chapman, Carolyn, 71
Children, brain development in, 19–20
Chunking, in brain-compatible learning, 27
Circles of Learning (Johnson and Johnson), 99
"Circles That Cycle" lesson plan, 103 (figure), 109–119
Civil rights content, curricular framework for, 101
Cognitive environment, 17 (table)
Cognitive process
  in adolescents, 22
  emotion in, 29
Community, in selective abandonment, 97
Concentration, in pulsed learning, 122
Concept web, 151 (figure), 152
Conferences, 173
Connections
  in extended time formats, 80–81
  with prior knowledge, 26–27
Consider, in learning progression, 44 (figure)
Consultant role, in inquire phase, 48
Content
  in brain-compatible learning, 24 (figure), 26–28, 79–81
  brain-compatible presentation of, 124, 125 (figure)
  curricular frameworks for, 100–105
  depth of understanding of, 79
  differentiation in, 134–136
  in extended time formats, 77–78
  graphic organizers for, 100
  increasing amount of, 95–97
  jigsawing of, 99–100
  meaning from, 79–81
  in P-A-C, 139–144
  prioritizing, 135–136
  relevancy and application of, xii
  selective abandonment of, 97–99
Context
  in brain-compatible learning, 25
  in gather phase, 65
Cooperative learning approaches, 126–128, 127 (figure)
Copernican plan, 83, 83 (figure)
Copernicus, Nicolaus, 83
Corpus callosum, 2, 2 (figure), 7 (figure), 23
Costa, Arthur, 97
Covey, Stephen, 135
Creative intelligence, 142, 144 (table), 145 (table), 146 (table), 147 (table)

Criteria, sharing, 177
Curricular frameworks, 100–105
    case studies, 104–105
    EIAG, 148–150
    performance-based learning, 104
    problem-based learning, 104
    project-oriented curricula, 102
    service learning, 104
    thematic units, 102–103, 103 (figure)
Curriculum
    brain-compatibility of, 107–109
    content requirements for, 95–97
    essential, 98, 98 (figure)
    extraneous, 98 (figure), 99
    frameworks for, 100–105
    graphic organizers for, 100
    integration of, 107, 108 (figure)
    jigsawing of, 99–100
    mapping, 105–107, 106 (figure)
    prioritizing in extended time formats,
        96 (figure), 97–107
    selective abandonment of, 97–99
    supportive, 98 (figure), 99

Data. *See* Information
Declarative knowledge, in schemata, 12
Declarative memory storage, 10–11, 10
    (table)
Dendrites, 3–4, 3 (figure), 3 (table), 16
Differentiated instruction, 132–138
Directed choices, in brain-compatible
    learning, 75–77
Disruptions, in traditional schedules, 78
Double t-chart, 151 (figure), 154

Education
    brain research applied to, 1
    personal connection in, 73–74
Educational principles, 122–125
EIAG (Experience/Identify/Apply/
    Generalize), 148–150
Electronic media, in dynamic classroom,
    109
Elementary lesson plan, 109–119
Emotion
    in authentic assessment, 173
    in brain-compatible learning, 28–29,
        72–75
    in child brain development, 20
    in cognition, 29
    in learning, 16, 25
    in traditional teaching, 28
Emotional memory, 10 (table), 11 (table)
Energy, in brain-compatible learning, 30
Engage, in learning progression, 44 (fig-
    ure)
Engagement, in extended time formats,
    76–77
Environment
    autism and, 23

    for brain-compatible learning, 30–31,
        77–79
    elements of, 17 (table)
    in learning, 17–18
Episodic memory, 10 (table), 11 (table)
Essential curriculum, 98, 98 (figure)
Existential intelligence, 19
Experience
    in EIAG, 148
    hands-on, 26
Experience component, 58
Experience/Identify/Apply/Generalize.
    See EIAG
Extended time formats
    alternative models of, 81–84
    authentic assessment in, 173
    connections in, 80–81
    content in, 77–78
    cooperative learning in, 128
    curriculum priorities in, 96 (figure),
        97–107
    directed choices in, 75–77
    educational principles for, 122–125
    emotion and, 74–75
    engagement in, 76–77
    evaluating success of, 179, 180–181
    explanation of, 71–72
    focus in, 75–76
    in learning climate, 31
    meaning-filled content in, 79–81
    old lesson plans in, xi
    pedagogy for, 121–122
    personalization in, 73–74
    processes in, 77–78
    professional development for, 156, 157
        (figure)
    school climate and, 78–79
    skills in, 77–78
    trust and belonging in, 72–75
    See also Block scheduling
Exterior brain, 4 (table), 5, 5 (figure), 6
    (table)
Extraneous curriculum, 98 (figure), 99

Facilitator role, in process phase, 50
Facts, in long-term memory, 123–124
Feedback
    in authentic assessment, 173
    in formative assessment, 177
Female brain, *vs.* male brain, 20–21, 20
    (table), 21 (table)
Fishbone, 151 (figure), 153
Fitzgerald, Ron, 122
Focus, in extended time formats, 76
Fogarty, Robin, 76, 126, 147
Football, schema of, 13
4 × 4 plan, 82–83, 82 (figure)
Four-phase lesson design, 43–70, 46 (figure),
    47 (figure)
    assessment in, 181

Four-phase lesson design *(continued)*
  benefits of, 60–62
  differentiated instruction in, 136, 137
    (table)
  instructional strategies for, 136, 137
    (table)
  internal structure, 59–60
  multiple intelligences in, 45, 46 (figure),
    131 (table)
  P-A-C used in, 142–144, 147 (table)
  questions in, 55
  vs. traditional lesson design, 60, 61
    (table)
  unit design and, 62–67
Four-phase lesson sample, 31–42
Four phases
  activities of, 59–60
  BEM principle and, 125
  components of, 58–59
  guidelines for using, 54 (table)
  integrated assessment in, 60
  in schemata development, 52, 53 (table)
  See also Apply phase; Gather phase;
    Inquire phase; Process phase
Four-phase unit design, 46 (figure), 47
    (figure), 62–67, 63 (figure), 66 (figure)
  assessment in, 181
  example, 67–70
  helpfulness of, 67
  phases in, 62–67, 64 (figure)
Frames of Mind (Gardner), 18
Frontal lobes, 5 (figure), 6 (table)

Gardner, Howard, 18, 29–30, 79, 129
Garlikov, Rick, 139
Gathering level, 147, 149 (figure)
Gather phase
  for biology lesson, 37–38
  brain compatibility in, 49
  guidelines for using, 54 (table)
  instructional strategies for, 137 (table)
  for integrated elementary lesson, 114–115
  for integrated middle school lesson,
    162–163
  for language arts lesson, 89–91
  in lesson design, 44 (figure), 45, 49
  multiple intelligences in, 131 (table)
  P-A-C used in, 147 (table)
  of processing model, 44 (figure)
  questions during, 56 (table)
  schemata in, 53 (table)
  for science lesson, 185–186
  teacher role in, 49
  in unit design, 63 (figure), 64 (figure),
    65, 69
"Gender, Age, and Pyramids" lesson, 55,
    156–167
Generalize, in EIAG, 150
Glasser, William, 74
Glenn, H. Stephen, 148

Glial cells, 4
Graphic organizers, 100, 150–155, 151
    (figure), 173
Group knots activity, 134 (figure)
Group presentation rubric, 40 (table)

Hands-on experience, in brain-compatible
    learning, 26
Hemispheres of brain, 2, 2 (figure)
Higher-order thinking skills
  approaches for, 138–150
  in cooperative learning, 126
  graphic organizers for, 150–155, 151
    (figure)
  in P-A-C, 143–144 (table)
Hippocampus, 7 (figure), 7 (table), 9
History unit, example, 67–70
Holmes, Oliver Wendell, 147
Holubec, E. J., 126
Homework, rubric for, 166 (figure)
Hypothalamus, 7 (figure), 7 (table)

Identify
  in EIAG, 148
  in learning progression, 44 (figure)
Images, in schemata, 12
Immediate memory, 8–9
Individual, in cooperative learning, 128
Information
  chunking, 27
  energy and, 30
  in immediate memory, 8–9
  in long-term memory, 9, 123–124
  relating to prior knowledge, 26–27
  in working memory, 9
Inner brain, 4 (table), 6–8, 7 (figure), 7 (table)
Inquire phase
  for biology lesson, 34–37
  brain compatibility in, 48
  guidelines for using, 54 (table)
  instructional strategies for, 137 (table)
  for integrated elementary lesson, 111–113
  for integrated middle school lesson,
    160–162
  for language arts lesson, 86–88
  in lesson design, 44 (figure), 45, 48
  multiple intelligences in, 131 (table)
  P-A-C used in, 147 (table)
  of processing model, 44 (figure)
  questions during, 56 (table)
  schemata in, 53 (table)
  for science lesson, 183–184
  teacher role in, 48
  in unit design, 63 (figure), 64 (figure),
    65, 68–69
Instructional strategies
  brain-compatible, 126–155
  cooperative learning approaches,
    126–128
  differentiated instruction, 132–138

in four-phase lesson design, 136, 137
  (table)
for higher-order thinking skills,
  138–150
with memory paths, 11 (table)
multiple intelligences, 129–132, 130
  (figure), 131 (table)
professional development on, 156, 157
  (figure)
sensory activators, 129–132, 133
  (figure), 134 (figure), 135 (figure)
traditional, 140
varying, 125
Intelligence, in P-A-C, 141–142
Intelligences, multiple, 18–19
Intensity, in working memory, 9
Interpersonal/social intelligence, 19
Intrapersonal/introspective intelligence,
  19

Jacobs, Heidi Hayes, 105
Jigsawing, 99–100
Johnson, David, 99, 126
Johnson, Roger, 99, 126
Journals, 174

KDL, 151 (figure), 155
Kendall, John S., 96, 97
Kovalik, Susan, 95, 107
KWL, 151 (figure), 154–155

Laboratories, for hands-on experience, 26
Language arts lesson plan, 84–93
Lave, J., 129
Learner, in brain-compatible learning,
  24–26, 24 (figure)
Learning
  assessment for, 176–177
  dendrites in, 15
  emotion in, 16
  environment in, 17–18
  movement in, 16–17
  multiple intelligences in, 18–19
  natural progression of, 44 (figure)
  process of, 15–16
  schemata in, 15
  social interaction in, 129–132
  See also Brain-compatible learning
Left hemisphere of brain, 2
Lesson plans. See Four-phase lesson
  design; Traditional lesson plans
Limbic system, 6, 7 (figure)
Linear orderings, in schemata, 12
Logical/mathematical intelligence, 18
Logs, 174
Long-term memory, 9–12
  in extended time formats, 79
  in inquire phase, 48
  vs. long-term storage, 9
  metacognition in, 27–28

motivation and, 25
in teaching, 8
teaching to, 123–124
Long-term storage, 9
Looks-sounds-feels, 151 (figure), 154
Low-achieving students, 179

Machines activity, 135 (figure)
Male brain, vs. female brain, 20–21, 20
  (table), 21 (table)
Marzano, Robert J., 96, 97
Matrix/grid, 151 (figure), 153
McTighe, J., 135
Meaning
  in attend component, 58
  from content, 79–81
  emotion in, 29
  environment in, 31
  in long-term memory, 9
  from patterns, 27
  personal. See Personal meaning
  in reflect component, 59
Mediator role, in apply phase, 51
Memorization, xii, 123
Memory, 8–12
  immediate, 8–9
  limbic system in, 6
  long-term. See Long-term memory
  prior knowledge in, 26–27
  short-term, 8–9
  working, 9
Memory paths, with instructional strategies, 11 (table)
Memory storage
  declarative, 10–11, 10 (table)
  nondeclarative, 10–11, 10 (table)
Mental model. See Schemata
Metacognition, 27–28, 144–147
Mid-brain. See Inner brain
Middle school lesson plan, 109–119
Mind map, 151 (figure), 152
Mind reader activity, 133 (figure)
Motivation, in brain-compatible learning,
  25–26
Motor cortex, 5 (figure), 6 (table)
Motor skill memory, 7–8, 10 (table), 11
  (table)
Motor skills, in child brain development, 20
Movement
  cerebellum in, 6–8
  in learning, 16–17
  in working memory, 9
Multiple intelligences
  in brain-compatible learning, 29–30
  in four-phase lesson design, 45, 46 (fig-
    ure), 131 (table)
  as instructional strategy, 129–132, 130
    (figure), 131 (table)
  in learning, 18–19
  sensory activators for, 129–132

Muscle memory. *See* Motor skill memory
Musical/rhythmic Intelligence, 18
Myelination, 5, 22

Naturalist intelligence, 19
Nerve cells, in brain, 2–4, 3 (figure)
Neural connections, in child brain devel-
    opment, 20
Neurons, 2–4, 3 (figure)
Neurotransmitters, 3 (figure), 3 (table), 4
No Child Left Behind (NCLB), 177–178
Nondeclarative memory storage, 10–11, 10
    (table)
Novelty, in working memory, 9

Observation checklists, 174
Occipital lobes, 5, 5 (figure), 6 (table)
Ogle, Donna, 154
Outer brain. *See* Exterior brain

P-A-C (practical-analytical-creative),
    139–144, 143–144 (table), 145 (table),
    146 (table), 147 (table)
Parietal lobes, 5 (figure), 6 (table)
Patterns, chunking information and, 27
Pedagogy, brain-compatible, 121–122
Performance, differentiated instruction
    and, 137–138
Performance assessment, 171, 172 (figure)
Performance-based learning, 104
Personal connection, in education, 73–74
Personal context, in brain-compatible
    learning, 25
Personal meaning, adolescent need for, 22
Physical environment, 17 (table)
Pie chart, 151 (figure), 154
Plasticity, 4
PMI, 151 (figure), 155
Portfolio assessment, 171, 172 (figure)
Portfolios, 174
Practical intelligence, 141, 143 (table), 145
    (table), 146 (table), 147 (table)
Prefrontal cortex, 5, 22
Presenter role, in gather phase, 49
Prior knowledge, in brain-compatible
    learning, 26–27
Problem-based learning, 104
Procedural knowledge, in schemata, 12
Procedural memory, 10 (table), 11 (table)
Processes
    in differentiated instruction, 136–137
    in extended time formats, 77–78
Processing level, 147–148, 149 (figure)
Processing model, in four-phase lesson
    design, 43, 44 (figure)
Process phase
    for biology lesson, 39–41
    brain compatibility in, 50
    guidelines for using, 54 (table)
    instructional strategies for, 137 (table)

    for integrated elementary lesson, 116
    for integrated middle school lesson, 164
    for language arts lesson, 91–92
    in lesson design, 44 (figure), 45, 50
    multiple intelligences in, 131 (table)
    P-A-C used in, 147 (table)
    of processing model, 44 (figure)
    questions during, 57 (table)
    schemata in, 53 (table)
    for science lesson, 186–188
    teacher role in, 50
    in unit design, 63 (figure), 64 (figure),
        67, 69
Products, differentiated instruction and,
    137–138
Professional development, 156, 157 (fig-
    ure)
Project-oriented curricula, 102
Propositions, in declarative knowledge, 12
Provide, in learning progression, 44 (figure)
Pulsed learning, 122, 124 (figure)

Questions
    during apply phase, 57 (table)
    in cooperative learning, 128
    in EIAG, 148–150
    in four-phase lesson design, 55
    during gather phase, 56 (table)
    during inquire phase, 56 (table)
    metacognitive, 145–147
    during process phase, 57 (table)
    in Socratic method, 139

Ranking ladder, 151 (figure), 153
Real life, as learning context, 25
Recitation, in curriculum, xii
Reflect component, 58
Reflection
    in brain-compatible learning, 27–28
    connections and, 80–81
Relevancy
    in brain-compatible learning, 25
    of curriculum, xii
Rettig, Michael, 78, 81, 97
Right angle, 151 (figure), 155
Right hemisphere of brain, 2
Rubrics
    authentic assessment with, 174–176,
        175 (figure)
    formative assessment with, 177
    for group presentation, 40 (table)
    for homework evaluation, 166 (figure)
    for Venn diagram, 90 (figure)

Schemata, 12–15
    accuracy of, 14
    components of, 12
    development of, 13–14
    feedback and, 173
    four phases in development of, 52

function of, 14
 guidelines for development of, 53 (table)
 implications for teaching, 14–15
 modifications to, 14–15
School calendar, alternatives for, 84
School climate, extended time formats and, 78–79
Science lesson plan, 181–190
"Science Schmience" lesson, 55, 181–190
Selective abandonment, 97–99
Self-assessment, 119 (figure), 177
Semantic memory, 10 (table), 11 (table)
Senses, in brain-compatible learning, 28–29, 129–132
Sensory activators, 129–132, 133 (figure), 134 (figure), 135 (figure)
Service learning, 104
Short-term memory, 8–9
Situated learning, 129–132
Skills, in extended time formats, 77–78
Skills remediation classes, 179
Social/emotional environment, 17 (table)
Social interaction, 129–132
Social skills, in cooperative learning, 128
Socrates, 138–139
Socratic irony, 139
Socratic method, 138–139
Space, for working memory, 9
Standardized tests
 vs. brain-compatible assessment, 170 (figure)
 content coverage for, 95
 in No Child Left Behind, 177–178
 reality of, 178–179
 structured review sessions for, 179–180
Sternberg, Robert J., 140–141
Storage, *vs.* long-term memory, 9
Strategies, in engagement, 77
Structured review sessions, 179–180
Student benefit, in four-phase lesson design, 47 (figure)
Students
 emotional support for, 73–74
 low-achieving, 179
Student self-assessment, 119 (figure), 177
"Student Tic-Tac-Toe," 34–35, 35 (figure)
Sunshine wheel, 151 (figure), 152
Supportive curriculum, 98 (figure), 99
Sylwester, Robert, 1, 126
Synapses, 3–4, 3 (figure), 3 (table)

Tasks, with movement, 17
Taxonomy of Educational Objectives (Bloom), 138, 140
T-chart, 151 (figure), 153

Teacher
 in apply phase, 51
 in four-phase lesson design, 47 (figure)
 in gather phase, 49
 in inquire phase, 48
 personal connection with, 73–74
 in process phase, 50
 in selective abandonment, 97–98
Teacher collaboration
 with curriculum integration, 107
 with curriculum maps, 105–107, 106 (figure)
 No Child Left Behind and, 178
Teaching
 implications of schemata for, 14–15
 to long-term memory, 123–124
 multiple intelligences in, 19
Temporal lobes, 5 (figure), 6 (table)
Textbooks, *vs.* electronic media, 109
Thalamus, 7 (figure), 7 (table)
Thematic units, 102–103, 103 (figure)
Threat, autistic perception of, 23
Three-story intellect model, 147–148, 149 (figure)
Time
 adequate amount of, 71–72
 in brain-compatible learning, 71–81
 for working memory, 9
Tomlinson, C. A., 134, 135
Traditional assessment, 171, 172 (figure)
Traditional lesson plans
 design of, 43–44
 in extended time blocks, xi
 vs. four-phase, 60, 61 (table)
Trust and belonging, in brain-compatible learning, 72–75

Unifying, in cooperative learning, 127–128
Unit
 lessons in, 62–67
 See also Four-phase unit design

Venn diagram, 90 (figure), 151 (figure), 152
Verbal/linguistic intelligence, 18
Visual/spatial intelligence, 18
Vygotsky, L. S., 129

Wenger, E., 129
"What's On Your Mind?" lesson plan, 31–42, 55
Wiggins, Grant, 169
Working memory, 9
Wyatt, L. D., 121

Zone of Proximal Development, 129

**CORWIN
PRESS**

The Corwin Press logo—a raven striding across an open book—represents the union of courage and learning. Corwin Press is committed to improving education for all learners by publishing books and other professional development resources for those serving the field of PreK–12 education. By providing practical, hands-on materials, Corwin Press continues to carry out the promise of its motto: **"Helping Educators Do Their Work Better."**